Microsoft®
Excel®
Dashboards &
Reports

for
dummies®
A Wiley Brand

Microsoft® Excel®
Dashboards & Reports

4th Edition

by Michael Alexander

A Wiley Brand

Microsoft® Excel® Dashboards & Reports For Dummies®, 4th Edition

Published by: **John Wiley & Sons, Inc.,** 111 River Street, Hoboken, NJ 07030-5774, www.wiley.com

Copyright © 2022 by John Wiley & Sons, Inc., Hoboken, New Jersey

Published simultaneously in Canada

For general information on our other products and services, please contact our Customer Care Department within the U.S. at 877-762-2974, outside the U.S. at 317-572-3993, or fax 317-572-4002. For technical support, please visit https://hub.wiley.com/community/support/dummies.

Wiley publishes in a variety of print and electronic formats and by print-on-demand. Some material included with standard print versions of this book may not be included in e-books or in print-on-demand. If this book refers to media such as a CD or DVD that is not included in the version you purchased, you may download this material at http://booksupport.wiley.com. For more information about Wiley products, visit www.wiley.com.

Library of Congress Control Number: 2022931501

ISBN 978-1-119-84439-6 (pbk); ISBN 978-1-119-84440-2 (ebk); ISBN 978-1-119-84441-9 (ebk)

SKY10033711_030822

Contents at a Glance

Table of Contents

Introduction

The term *business intelligence* (BI), coined by Howard Dresner of Gartner, Inc., describes the set of concepts and methods to improve business decision-making by using fact-based support systems. Practically speaking, BI is what you get when you analyze raw data and turn that analysis into knowledge. BI can help an organization identify cost-cutting opportunities, uncover new business opportunities, recognize changing business environments, identify data anomalies, and create widely accessible reports.

Over the past few years, the BI concept has overtaken corporate executives who are eager to turn impossible amounts of data into knowledge. As a result of this trend, whole industries have been created. Software vendors that focus on BI and dashboarding are coming out of the woodwork. New consulting firms touting their BI knowledge are popping up virtually every week. And even the traditional enterprise solution providers, like Business Objects and SAP, are offering new BI capabilities.

This need for BI has manifested itself in many forms. Most recently, it has come in the form of dashboard fever. Dashboards are reporting mechanisms that deliver business intelligence in a graphical form.

Maybe *you've* been hit with dashboard fever. Or maybe your manager is hitting you with dashboard fever. Nevertheless, you're probably holding this book because you're being asked to create BI solutions (that is, dashboards) in Excel.

Although many IT managers would scoff at the thought of using Excel as a BI tool, Excel is inherently part of the enterprise BI tool portfolio. Whether or not IT managers are keen to acknowledge it, most of the data analysis and reporting done in business today is done by using a spreadsheet. You have several significant reasons to use Excel as the platform for your dashboards and reports, including

>> **Tool familiarity:** If you work in corporate America, you are conversant in the language of Excel. You can send even the most seasoned of senior vice presidents an Excel-based reporting tool and trust that they will know what to do with it. With an Excel reporting process, your users spend less time figuring out how to use the tool and more time looking at the data.

>> **Built-in flexibility:** In most enterprise dashboarding solutions, the capability to perform analyses outside the predefined views is either disabled or unavailable. How many times have you dumped enterprise-level data into Excel so that you can analyze it yourself? I know I have. You can bet that if you give users an inflexible reporting mechanism, they'll do what it takes to create their own usable reports. In Excel, features such as pivot tables, autofilters, and Form controls let you create mechanisms that don't lock your audience into one view. And because you can have multiple worksheets in one workbook, you can give your audience space to do their own side analysis as needed.

>> **Rapid development:** Building your own reporting capabilities in Excel can liberate you from the IT department's resource and time limitations. With Excel, not only can you develop reporting mechanisms faster, but you also have the flexibility to adapt more quickly to changing requirements.

>> **Powerful data connectivity and automation capabilities:** Excel is not the toy application some IT managers make it out to be. With its own native programming language and its robust object model, Excel can be used to automate processes and can import data from a wide range of external data sources. With a few advanced techniques, you can make Excel a hands-off reporting mechanism that practically runs on its own.

>> **Little to no incremental costs:** Not all of us can work for multibillion-dollar companies that can afford enterprise-level reporting solutions. In most companies, funding for new computers and servers is limited, let alone funding for expensive BI reporting packages. For those companies, leveraging Microsoft Office is frankly the most cost-effective way to deliver key business reporting tools without compromising too deeply on usability and functionality.

All that being said, it's true that Excel has so many reporting functions and tools that it's difficult to know where to start. Enter your humble author, spirited into your hands via this book. Here, I show you how you can turn Excel into your own personal BI tool. Using a few fundamentals and some of the new BI functionality that Microsoft has included in this latest version of Excel, you can go from reporting data with simple tables to creating meaningful reporting components that are sure to wow management.

About This Book

The goal of this book is to show you how to leverage Excel functionality to build and manage better reporting mechanisms. Each chapter in this book provides a comprehensive review of the technical and analytical concepts that help you create better reporting components — components that can be used for both dashboards and reports. It's important to note that this book is not a guide to visualizations or dashboarding best practices — although those subjects are worthy of their own book. This book is focused on the technical aspects of using Excel's various tools and functionality and applying them to reporting.

The chapters in this book are designed to be standalone chapters that you can selectively refer to as needed. As you move through this book, you'll be able to create increasingly sophisticated dashboard and report components. After reading this book, you'll be able to

>> Analyze large amounts of data and report them in a meaningful way.

>> Gain better visibility into data from different perspectives.

>> Quickly slice data into various views on the fly.

>> Automate redundant reporting and analyses.

>> Create interactive reporting processes.

This book covers features released as of the October 2021 update of Office 365. The functionality covered here is available to those on Office 365 subscriptions and those using the standalone (perpetual license) version of Office/Excel 2021 for the desktop. Please note that this book is not applicable to Microsoft Excel for Mac.

Excel is available in several versions, including a web version and a version for tablets and phones. Though this book was written for the desktop version of Excel, much of the information here will also apply to the web and tablet versions.

Over the last few years, Microsoft has adopted an agile release cycle, releasing updates to Office 365 practically on a monthly basis. This is great news for those who love seeing new features added to Excel. It's not so great if you're trying to document the features of these tools in a book.

Microsoft will likely continue to add new bells and whistles to Excel at a rapid pace after this book is published. So you may encounter new functionality not covered in this book. That said, Excel has a broad feature set, much of which is stable and here to stay. So, even though changes will be made to Excel, they won't be so drastic as to turn this book into a doorstop. The core functionality covered in this book will remain relevant — even if the mechanics change a bit.

Foolish Assumptions

I make three assumptions about you as the reader. I assume that you

>> Have already installed Microsoft Excel.

>> Have some familiarity with the basic concepts of data analysis, such as working with tables, aggregating data, and performing calculations.

>> Have a strong grasp of basic Excel concepts such as managing table structures, creating formulas, referencing cells, filtering, and sorting.

Icons Used in This Book

As you read this book, you'll see icons in the margins that indicate material of interest (or not, as the case may be).This section briefly describes each icon in this book.

Tips are nice because they help you save time or perform a task without having to do a lot of extra work. The tips in this book are time-saving techniques or pointers to resources that you should try in order to get the maximum benefit from Excel.

Try to avoid doing anything marked with a Warning icon, which (as you might expect) represents a danger of one sort or another.

Whenever you see this icon, think *advanced* tip or technique. You might find these tidbits of useful information too boring for words, or they could contain the solution you need to get a program running. Skip these bits of information whenever you like.

If you don't get anything else out of a particular chapter or section, remember the material marked by this icon. This text usually contains an essential process or a bit of information you ought to remember.

Beyond the Book

In addition to the book you have in your hands, you can access some extra content online. Check out the free Cheat Sheet for tips on adding symbol fonts to your Excel dashboards and reports, as well as a list of online resources for even more information on Excel dashboards and reports. Just go to www.dummies.com and type **Microsoft Excel Dashboards & Reports For Dummies Cheat Sheet** in the Search box.

If you want to follow along with the examples in this book, you can download the sample files at www.dummies.com/go/exceldashboardsreportsfd4e. The files are organized by chapter.

Where to Go from Here

It's time to start your Excel dashboarding adventure! If you're a complete dashboard novice, start with Chapter 1 and progress through the book at a pace that allows you to absorb as much of the material as possible. If you've got the basics down and you're interested in advanced charting techniques that help create meaningful visualizations, skip to Part 3. Turn to Part 4 for an in-depth look at turning your basic dashboards into macro-driven interactive reporting.

1

Getting Started with Excel Dashboards and Reports

IN THIS PART . . .

Discover how to think about your data in terms of creating effective dashboards and reports and get a solid understanding of the fundamentals and basic ground rules for creating effective dashboards and reports.

Uncover the best practices for setting up the source data for your dashboards and reports and explore the key Excel functions that help you build effective dashboard models.

Explore how pivot tables can enhance your analytical and reporting capabilities as well as your dashboards.

Dive into Power Query and explore some of the ways to incorporate external data into your reporting mechanisms.

Chapter **1**

Getting in the Dashboard State of Mind

I n his song "New York State of Mind," Billy Joel laments the differences between California and New York. In this homage to the Big Apple, he implies a mood and a feeling that come with thinking about New York. I admit it's a stretch, but I'll extend this analogy to Excel — don't laugh.

In Excel, the differences between building a dashboard and creating standard table-driven analyses are as great as the differences between California and New York. To approach a dashboarding project, you truly have to get into the dashboard state of mind. As you'll come to realize in the next few chapters, dashboarding requires far more preparation than standard Excel analyses. It calls for closer communication with business leaders, stricter data modeling techniques, and the following of certain best practices. It's beneficial to have a base familiarity with fundamental dashboarding concepts before venturing off into the mechanics of building a dashboard.

In this chapter, you get a solid understanding of these basic dashboard concepts and design principles as well as what it takes to prepare for a dashboarding project.

Defining Dashboards and Reports

It isn't difficult to use *report* and *dashboard* interchangeably. In fact, the line between reports and dashboards frequently gets muddied. I've seen countless reports referred to as dashboards just because they included a few charts. Likewise, I've seen many examples of what could be considered dashboards but have been called reports.

Now, this may all seem like semantics to you, but it's helpful to clear the air and understand the core attributes of what are considered to be reports and dashboards.

Defining reports

The report is probably the most common application of business intelligence. A *report* can be described as a document that contains data used for reading or viewing. It can be as simple as a data table or as complex as a subtotaled view with interactive drill-downs, similar to Excel's Subtotal or Pivot Table functionality.

The key attribute of a report is that it doesn't lead a reader to a predefined conclusion. Although reports can include analysis, aggregations, and even charts, reports often allow for the end users to apply their own judgment and analysis to the data.

To clarify this concept, Figure 1-1 shows an example of a report. This report shows the National Park overnight visitor statistics by period. Although this data can be useful, it's clear this report isn't steering the reader toward any predefined judgment or analysis; it's simply presenting the aggregated data.

	A	B	C	D	E	F
4		**Number of Visitors (thousands)**				
5		2009	2010	2011	2012	2013
6	Great Smoky Mountains NP	9,198	9,316	9,367	9,167	9,192
7	Grand Canyon NP	4,105	4,002	4,125	4,326	4,402
8	Yosemite NP	3,369	3,362	3,379	3,281	3,304
9	Olympic NP	3,416	3,691	3,225	3,074	3,143
10	Yellowstone NP	2,759	2,974	3,019	2,868	2,836
11	Rocky Mountain NP	3,140	2,988	3,067	2,782	2,798
12	Cuyahoga Valley NP	3,123	3,218	2,880	3,306	2,534
13	Zion NP	2,218	2,593	2,459	2,677	2,587
14	Grand Teton NP	2,535	2,613	2,356	2,360	2,463
15	Acadia NP	2,517	2,559	2,431	2,208	2,051
16	Glacier NP	1,681	1,906	1,664	2,034	1,925
17	Hot Springs NP	1,297	1,440	1,561	1,419	1,340
18	Hawaii Volcanoes NP	1,343	1,111	992	1,307	1,661

FIGURE 1-1: Reports present data for viewing but don't lead readers to conclusions.

Defining dashboards

A *dashboard* is a visual interface that provides at-a-glance views into key measures relevant to a particular objective or business process. Dashboards have three main attributes:

>> Dashboards are typically graphical in nature, providing visualizations that help focus attention on key trends, comparisons, and exceptions.

>> Dashboards often display only data that are relevant to the goal of the dashboard.

>> Because dashboards are designed with a specific purpose or goal, they inherently contain predefined conclusions that relieve the end user from performing his own analysis.

Figure 1-2 illustrates a dashboard that uses the same data shown in Figure 1-1. This dashboard displays key information about the national park overnight-visitor stats. As you can see, this presentation has all the main attributes that define a dashboard. First, it's a visual display that allows you to quickly recognize the overall trending of the overnight-visitor stats. Second, you can see that not all the detailed data is shown here — you see only the key pieces of information relevant to support the goal of this dashboard, which in this case would be to get some insights on which parks would need some additional resources to increase visitor rates. Finally, by virtue of its objective, this dashboard effectively presents you with analysis and conclusions about the trending of overnight visitors.

FIGURE 1-2:
Dashboards provide at-a-glance views into key measures relevant to a particular objective or business process.

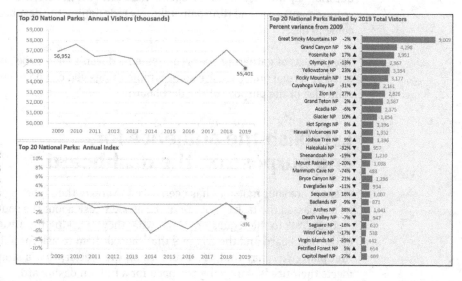

Preparing for Greatness

Imagine that your manager asks you to create a dashboard that tells him everything he should know about monthly service subscriptions. Do you jump to action and slap together whatever comes to mind? Do you take a guess at what he wants to see and hope it's useful? These questions sound ridiculous, but these types of situations happen more than you think. I'm continually called to create the next great reporting tool but am rarely provided the time to gather the true requirements for it. Between limited data and unrealistic deadlines, the end product often ends up being unused or having little value.

This brings me to one of the key steps in preparing for dashboarding: collecting user requirements.

In the non–IT world of the Excel analyst, user requirements are practically useless because of sudden changes in project scope, constantly changing priorities, and shifting deadlines. The gathering of user requirements is viewed to be a lot of work and a waste of valuable time in the ever-changing business environment. But as I mention at the start of this chapter, it's time to get into the dashboard state of mind.

Consider how many times a manager has asked you for an analysis and then said "No, I meant this." Or "Now that I see it, I realize I need this." As frustrating as this can be for a single analysis, imagine running into it again and again during the creation of a complex dashboard with several data integration processes. The question is, would you rather spend your time on the front end gathering user requirements or spend time painstakingly redesigning the dashboard you'll surely come to hate?

The process of gathering user requirements doesn't have to be an overly complicated or formal one. Here are some simple things you can do to ensure you have a solid idea of the purpose of the dashboard.

Establish the audience for, and purpose of, the dashboard

Chances are your manager has been asked to create the reporting mechanism and he has passed the task to you. Don't be afraid to ask about the source of the initial request. Talk to the requesters about what they're asking for. Discuss the purpose of the dashboard and the triggers that caused them to ask for a dashboard in the first place. You may find, after discussing the matter, that a simple Excel report meets their needs, foregoing the need for a full-on dashboard.

If a dashboard is indeed warranted, talk about who the end users are. Take some time to meet with a few of the end users to talk about how they'd use the dashboard. Will the dashboard be used as a performance tool for regional managers? Will the dashboard be used to share data with external customers? Talking through these fundamentals with the right people helps align your thoughts and avoids the creation of a dashboard that doesn't fulfill the necessary requirements.

Delineate the measures for the dashboard

Most dashboards are designed around a set of measures, or *key performance indicators (KPIs)*. A KPI is an indicator of the performance of a task deemed to be essential to daily operations or processes. The idea is that a KPI reveals performance that is outside the normal range for a particular measure, so it therefore often signals the need for attention and intervention. Although the measures you place into your dashboards may not officially be called KPIs, they undoubtedly serve the same purpose — to draw attention to problem areas.

REMEMBER

The topic of creating effective KPIs for your organization is a subject worthy of its own book and is out of the scope of this endeavor. For a detailed guide on KPI development strategies, pick up David Parmenter's *Key Performance Indicators: Developing, Implementing, and Using Winning KPIs* (Wiley Publishing, Inc.). That book provides an excellent step-by-step approach to developing and implementing KPIs.

The measures used on a dashboard should absolutely support the initial purpose of that dashboard. For example, if you're creating a dashboard focused on supply chain processes, it may not make sense to have human resources head-count data incorporated. It's generally good practice to avoid nice-to-know data in your dashboards simply to fill white space or because the data is available. If the data doesn't support the core purpose of the dashboard, leave it out.

TIP

Here's another tip: When gathering the measures required for the dashboard, I find that it often helps to write a sentence to describe the measure needed. For example, rather than simply add the word *Revenue* into my user requirements, I write what I call a *component question,* such as "What is the overall revenue trend for the past two years?" I call it a *component question* because I intend to create a single component, such as a chart or a table, to answer the question. For instance, if the component question is "What is the overall revenue trend for the past two years?" you can imagine a chart component answering this question by showing the two-year revenue trend.

I sometimes take this a step further and actually incorporate the component questions into a mock layout of the dashboard to get a high-level sense of the data the dashboard will require. Figure 1-3 illustrates an example.

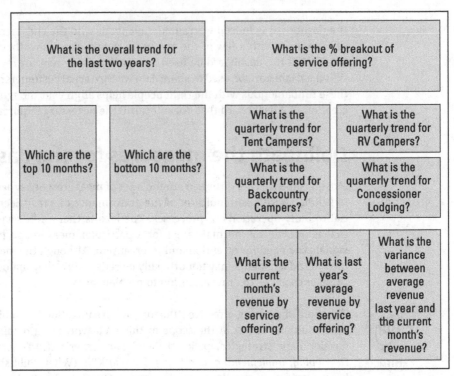

FIGURE 1-3:
Each box in this dashboard layout mockup represents a component and the type of data required to create the measures.

Each box in this dashboard layout mockup represents a component on the dashboard and its approximate position. The questions within each box provide a sense of the types of data required to create the measures for the dashboard.

Catalog the required data sources

When you have the list of measures that need to be included on the dashboard, it's important to take a tally of the available systems to determine whether the data required to produce those measures is available. Ask yourself the following questions:

>> Do you have access to the data sources necessary?

>> How often are those data sources refreshed?

>> Who owns and maintains those data sources?

>> What are the processes to get the data from those resources?

>> Does the data even exist?

These are all questions you need answered when negotiating dashboard development time, data refresh intervals, and change management.

TIP

Conventional wisdom says that the measures on your dashboard shouldn't be governed by the availability of data. Instead, you should let dashboard KPIs and measures govern the data sources in your organization. Although I agree with the spirit of that statement, I've been involved in too many dashboard projects that have fallen apart because of lack of data. Real-world experience has taught me the difference between the *ideal* and the *ordeal*.

If your organizational strategy requires that you collect and measure data that is nonexistent or not available, press Pause on the dashboard project and turn your attention to creating a data collection mechanism that will get the data you need.

Define the dimensions and filters for the dashboard

In the context of reporting, a *dimension* is a data category used to organize business data. Examples of dimensions are Region, Market, Branch, Manager, or Employee. When you define a dimension in the user requirements stage of development, you're determining how the measures should be grouped or distributed. For example, if your dashboard should report data by employee, you need to ensure that your data collection and aggregation processes include employee detail. As you can imagine, adding a new dimension after the dashboard is built can get complicated, especially when your processes require many aggregations across multiple data sources. The bottom line is that locking down the dimensions for a dashboard early in the process definitely saves you headaches.

Along those same lines, you want to get a clear sense of the types of filters that are required. In the context of dashboards, *filters* are mechanisms that allow you to narrow the scope of the data to a single dimension. For example, you can filter on Year, Employee, or Region. Again, if you don't account for a particular filter while building your dashboarding process, you'll likely be forced into an unpleasant redesign of both your data collection processes and your dashboard.

If you're confused by the difference between dimensions and filters, think about a simple Excel table. A dimension is like a column of data (such as a column containing employee names) in an Excel table. A filter, then, is the mechanism that allows you to narrow your table to show only the data for a particular employee. For example, if you apply Excel's AutoFilter to the Employee column, you are building a filter mechanism into your table.

Determine the need for drill-down features

Many dashboards provide *drill-down features* that allow users to "drill" into the details of a specific measure. You want to get a clear understanding of the types of drill-downs your users have in mind.

To most users, *drill-down feature* means the ability to get a raw data table supporting the measures shown on the dashboard. Although getting raw data isn't always practical or possible, discussing these requests will, at minimum, allow you to talk to your users about additional reporting, links to other data sources, and other solutions that may help them get the data they need.

Establish the refresh schedule

A *refresh schedule* refers to the schedule by which a dashboard is updated to show the latest information available. Because you're the one responsible for building and maintaining the dashboard, you should have a say in the refresh schedules — your manager may not know what it takes to refresh the dashboard in question.

While you're determining the refresh schedule, keep in mind the refresh rates of the different data sources whose measures you need to get. You can't refresh your dashboard any faster than your data sources. Also, negotiate enough development time to build macros that aid in automation of redundant and time-consuming refresh tasks.

A Quick Look at Dashboard Design Principles

When collecting user requirements for your dashboarding project, there's a heavy focus on the data aspects of the dashboard: the types of data needed, the dimensions of data required, the data sources to be used, and so on. This is a good thing — without solid data processes, your dashboards won't be effective or maintainable. That being said, here's another aspect to your dashboarding project that calls for the same fervor in preparation: the *design aspect*.

Excel users live in a world of numbers and tables, not visualization and design. Your typical Excel analysts have no background in visual design and are often left to rely on their own visual instincts to design their dashboards. As a result, most Excel-based dashboards have little thought given to effective visual design, often resulting in overly cluttered and ineffective user interfaces.

The good news is that dashboarding has been around for such a long time that there's a vast knowledge base of prescribed visualization and dashboard design principles. Many of these principles seem like common sense; even so, these are concepts that Excel users don't often find themselves thinking about. Because this chapter is about getting into the dashboard state of mind, I break that trend and review a few dashboard design principles that improve the look and feel of your Excel dashboards.

Many of the concepts in this section come from the work of Stephen Few, a visualization expert and the author of several books and articles on dashboard design principles. This book is primarily focused on the technical aspects of building reporting components in Excel, but this section offers a high-level look at dashboard design. If you find that you're captivated by the subject, feel free to visit Stephen Few's website at www.perceptualedge.com.

Rule number 1: Keep it simple

Dashboard design expert Stephen Few has the mantra, "Simplify, simplify, simplify." The basic idea is that dashboards cluttered with too many measures or too much eye candy can dilute the significant information you're trying to present. How many times has someone told you that your reports look "busy"? In essence, this complaint means that too much is going on in the page or screen, making it hard to see the actual data.

Here are a few actions you can take to ensure simpler and more effective dashboard designs.

Don't turn your dashboard into a data repository

Admit it. You include as much information in a report as possible, primarily to avoid being asked for additional information. We all do it. But in the dashboard state of mind, you have to fight the urge to force every piece of data available onto your dashboards.

Overwhelming users with too much data can cause them to lose sight of the primary goal of the dashboard and focus on inconsequential data. The measures used on a dashboard should support the initial purpose of that dashboard. Avoid the urge to fill white space for the sake of symmetry and appearances. Don't include nice-to-know data just because the data is available. If the data doesn't support the core purpose of the dashboard, leave it out.

Avoid the fancy formatting

The key to communicating effectively with your dashboards is to present your data as simply as possible. There's no need to wrap it in eye candy to make it more interesting. It's okay to have a dashboard with little to no color or formatting. You'll find that the lack of fancy formatting only serves to call attention to the actual data. Focus on the data and not the shiny happy graphics. Here are a few guidelines:

>> **Avoid using colors or background fills to partition your dashboards.** Colors, in general, should be used sparingly, reserved for providing information about key data points. For example, assigning the colors red, yellow, and green to measures traditionally indicates performance level. Adding these colors to other sections of your dashboard only serves to distract your audience.

>> **De-emphasize borders, backgrounds, and other elements that define dashboard areas.** Try to use the natural white space between components to partition the dashboard. If borders are necessary, format them to hues lighter than the ones you've used for your data. Light grays are typically ideal for borders. The idea is to indicate sections without distracting from the information displayed.

>> **Avoid applying fancy effects such as gradients, pattern fills, shadows, glows, soft edges, and other formatting.** Excel makes it easy to apply effects that make everything look shiny, glittery, and generally happy. Although these formatting features make for great marketing tools, they don't do your reporting mechanisms any favors.

>> **Don't try to enhance your dashboards with clip art or pictures.** They not only do nothing to further data presentation, but they also often just look tacky.

Limit each dashboard to one printable page

Dashboards, in general, should provide at-a-glance views into key measures relevant to particular objectives or business processes. This implies that all the data is immediately viewable on the one page. Although including all your data on one page isn't always the easiest thing to do, there's much benefit to being able to see everything on one page or screen. You can compare sections more easily, you can process cause-and-effect relationships more effectively, and you rely less on short-term memory. When a user has to scroll left, right, or down, these benefits are diminished. Furthermore, users tend to believe that when information is placed out of normal view (in areas that require scrolling), it's somehow less important.

But what if you can't fit all the data on one sheet? First, review the measures on your dashboard and determine whether they really need to be there. Next, format your dashboard to use less space (format fonts, reduce white space, and adjust column and row widths). Finally, try adding interactivity to your dashboard, allowing users to dynamically change views to show only those measures that are relevant to them.

Use layout and placement to draw focus

As I discuss earlier in this chapter, only measures that support the dashboard's utility and purpose should be included on the dashboard. However, it should be said that just because all measures on your dashboard are significant, they may not always have the same level of importance. In other words, you'll frequently want one component of your dashboard to stand out from the others.

Instead of using bright colors or exaggerated sizing differences, you can leverage location and placement to draw focus to the most important components on your dashboard.

Various studies have shown that readers have a natural tendency to focus on particular regions of a document. For example, researchers at the Poynter Institute's Eyetrack III project have found that readers view various regions on a screen in a certain order, paying particular attention to specific regions onscreen. The researchers use the diagram in Figure 1-4 to illustrate what they call *priority zones*. Regions with the number 1 in the diagram seem to have high prominence, attracting the most attention for longer periods. Meanwhile, number 3 regions seem to have low prominence.

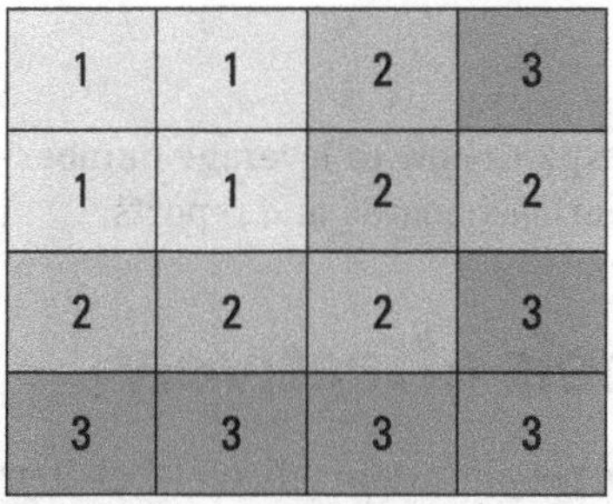

FIGURE 1-4:
Studies show that users pay particular attention to the upper left and middle left of a document.

You can leverage these priority zones to promote or demote certain components based on significance. If one of the charts on your dashboard warrants special focus, you can simply place that chart in a region of prominence.

TIP

Note that surrounding colors, borders, fonts, and other formatting can affect the viewing patterns of your readers, de-emphasizing a previously high-prominence region.

Format numbers effectively

There will undoubtedly be lots of numbers on your dashboards. Some of them will be in charts, and others will be in tables. Remember that every piece of information on your dashboard should have a reason for being there. It's important that you format your numbers effectively to allow your users to understand the information they represent without confusion or hindrance. Here are some guidelines to keep in mind when formatting the numbers on your dashboards and reports:

>> **Always use commas to make numbers easier to read.** For example, instead of 2345, show 2,345.

>> **Use decimal places only if that level of precision is required.** For instance, there's rarely a benefit to showing the decimal places in a dollar amount, such as $123.45. In most cases, the $123 will suffice. Likewise in percentages, use only the minimum number of decimals required to represent the data effectively. For example, instead of 43.21%, you may be able to get away with 43%.

>> **Use the dollar symbol only when you need to clarify that you're referring to monetary values.** If you have a chart or table that contains all revenue values, and there's a label clearly stating this, you can save room and pixels by leaving out the dollar symbol.

>> **Format very large numbers to the thousands or millions place.** For instance, rather than display 16,906,714, you can format the number to read 17M.

TIP

In Chapter 5 of this book, you explore how to leverage number-formatting tricks to enhance the readability of your dashboards and reports.

Use titles and labels effectively

It's common sense, but many people often fail to label items on dashboards effectively. If your manager looks at your dashboard and asks you, "What is this telling me?" you likely have labeling issues. Here are a few guidelines for effective labeling on your dashboards and reports:

» **Always include a timestamp on your reporting mechanisms.** This minimizes confusion when distributing the same dashboard or report in monthly or weekly installments.

» **Always include some text indicating when the data for the measures was retrieved.** In many cases, the timing of the data is a critical piece of information when analyzing a measure.

» **Use descriptive titles for each component on your dashboard.** This allows users to clearly identify what they're looking at. Be sure to avoid cryptic titles with lots of acronyms and symbols.

» **Although it may seem counterintuitive, it's generally good practice to de-emphasize labels by formatting them with hues lighter than the ones used for your data.** Lightly colored labels give your users the information they need without distracting them from the information displayed. Ideal colors for labels are colors commonly found in nature: soft grays, browns, blues, and greens.

Chapter **2**

Building a Super Model

O ne of Excel's most attractive features is its flexibility. You can create an intricate system of interlocking calculations, linked cells, and formatted summaries that work together to create a final analysis. However, years of experience have brought me face to face with an ugly truth: Excel is like the cool gym teacher who lets you do anything you want — the freedom can be fun, but a lack of structure in your data models can lead to some serious headaches in the long run.

What's a data model? A *data model* provides the foundation upon which your reporting mechanism is built. When you build a spreadsheet that imports, aggregates, and shapes data, you're essentially building a data model that feeds your dashboards and reports.

Creating a poorly designed data model can mean hours of manual labor maintaining and refreshing your reporting mechanisms. On the other hand, creating an effective model allows you to easily repeat monthly reporting processes without damaging your reports or your sanity.

The goal of this chapter is to show you the concepts and techniques that help you build effective data models. In this chapter, you discover that creating a successful reporting mechanism requires more than slapping data onto a spreadsheet.

Although you see how to build cool dashboard components in later chapters, those components won't do you any good if you can't effectively manage your data models. On that note, let's get started.

Data Modeling Best Practices

Building an effective model isn't as complicated as you may think. It's primarily a matter of thinking about your reporting processes differently. Most people spend very little time thinking about the supporting data model behind a reporting process. If they think about it at all, they usually start by imagining a mockup of the finished dashboard and work backward from there.

Rather than see only the finished dashboard in your head, try to think of the end-to-end process. Where will you get the data? How should the data be structured? What analysis will need to be performed? How will the data be fed to the dashboard? How will the dashboard be refreshed?

Obviously, the answers to these questions are highly situation-specific. However, some data modeling best practices will guide you to a new way of thinking about your reporting process. These are discussed in the next few sections.

Separating data, analysis, and presentation

One of the most important concepts in a data model is the separation of data, analysis, and presentation. The fundamental idea is that you don't want your data to become too tied into any one particular way of presenting that data.

To wrap your mind around this concept, think about an invoice. When you receive an invoice, you don't assume that the financial data on the invoice is the true source of your data. It's merely a presentation of data that's actually stored in a database. That data can be analyzed and presented to you in many other manners: in charts, in tables, or even on websites. This sounds obvious, but Excel users often fuse data, analysis, and presentation.

For instance, I've seen Excel workbooks that contain 12 tabs, each representing a month. On each tab, data for that month is listed along with formulas, pivot tables, and summaries. Now what happens when you're asked to provide a summary by quarter? Do you add more formulas and tabs to consolidate the data on each of the month tabs? The fundamental problem in this scenario is that the tabs actually represent data values that are fused into the presentation of your analysis.

For an example more in line with reporting, take a look at Figure 2-1. Hard-coded tables like this one are common. This table is an amalgamation of data, analysis, and presentation. Not only does this table tie you to a specific analysis, but there's little to no transparency into what the analysis exactly consists of. Also, what happens when you need to report by quarter or when another dimension of analysis is needed? Do you import a table that consists of more columns and rows? How does that affect your model?

FIGURE 2-1:
Avoid hard-coded tables that fuse data, analysis, and presentation.

	Jan	Feb	Mar	Apr	May	Jun	Jul
Sales	3.69 M	6.99 M	5.77 M	4.96 M	8.48 M	4.71 M	7.48 M
% Distribution	5%	9%	7%	6%	10%	6%	9%

The alternative is to create three layers in your data model: a data layer, an analysis layer, and a presentation layer. You can think of these layers as three different worksheets in an Excel workbook: one sheet to hold the raw data that feeds your report, one sheet to serve as a staging area where the data is analyzed and shaped, and one sheet to serve as the presentation layer. Figure 2-2 illustrates the three layers of an effective data model.

As you can see in Figure 2-2, the raw data set is located on its own sheet. Although the data set has some level of aggregation applied to keep it manageably small, no further analysis is done on the Data sheet.

The analysis layer consists primarily of formulas that analyze and pull data from the data layer into formatted tables commonly referred to as *staging tables*. These staging tables ultimately feed the reporting components in your presentation layer. In short, the sheet that contains the analysis layer becomes the staging area where data is summarized and shaped to feed the reporting components.

There are a couple of benefits to this setup. First, the entire reporting model can be refreshed easily by simply replacing the raw data with an updated data set. The formulas on the Analysis tab continue to work with the latest data. Second, any additional analysis can easily be created by using different combinations of formulas on the Analysis tab. If you need data that doesn't exist in the Data sheet, you can easily append a column to the end of the raw data set without disturbing the Analysis or Presentation sheets.

TIP

You don't necessarily have to place your data, analysis, and presentation layers on different worksheets. In small data models, you may find it easier to place your data in one area of a worksheet while building staging tables in another area of the same worksheet.

DATA

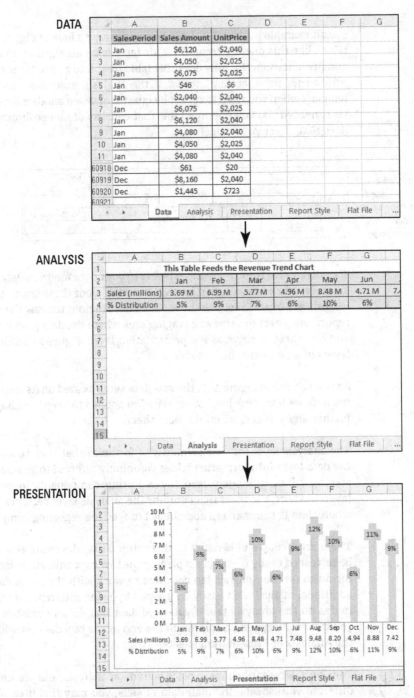

	A	B	C	D	E	F	G
1	SalesPeriod	Sales Amount	UnitPrice				
2	Jan	$6,120	$2,040				
3	Jan	$4,050	$2,025				
4	Jan	$6,075	$2,025				
5	Jan	$46	$6				
6	Jan	$2,040	$2,040				
7	Jan	$6,075	$2,025				
8	Jan	$6,120	$2,040				
9	Jan	$4,080	$2,040				
10	Jan	$4,050	$2,025				
11	Jan	$4,080	$2,040				
60918	Dec	$61	$20				
60919	Dec	$8,160	$2,040				
60920	Dec	$1,445	$723				
60921							

Data   Analysis   Presentation   Report Style   Flat File   ...

ANALYSIS

	A	B	C	D	E	F	G
1		This Table Feeds the Revenue Trend Chart					
2		Jan	Feb	Mar	Apr	May	Jun
3	Sales (millions)	3.69 M	6.99 M	5.77 M	4.96 M	8.48 M	4.71 M	7.
4	% Distribution	5%	9%	7%	6%	10%	6%
5							
6							
7							
8							
9							
10							
11							
12							
13							
14							
15							

Data   Analysis   Presentation   Report Style   Flat File   ...

PRESENTATION

	Jan	Feb	Mar	Apr	May	Jun	Jul	Aug	Sep	Oct	Nov	Dec
Sales (millions)	3.69	6.99	5.77	4.96	8.48	4.71	7.48	9.48	8.20	4.94	8.88	7.42
% Distribution	5%	9%	7%	6%	10%	6%	9%	12%	10%	6%	11%	9%

Data   Analysis   Presentation   Report Style   Flat File   ...

FIGURE 2-2:
An effective data model separates data, analysis, and presentation.

Along those same lines, remember that you're not limited to three worksheets, either. That is to say, you can have several sheets that provide the raw data, several sheets that analyze, and several that serve as the presentation layer.

Wherever you choose to place the different layers, keep in mind that the idea remains the same. The analysis layer should primarily consist of formulas that pull data from the Data sheets into staging tables used to feed your presentation. Later in this chapter, you explore some of the formulas that can be used in your analysis sheets.

Starting with appropriately structured data

Not all data sets are created equal. Although some data sets work in a standard Excel environment, they may not work for data modeling purposes. Before building your data model, ensure that your source data is appropriately structured for dashboarding purposes.

At the risk of oversimplification, I assert that data sets typically used in Excel come in three fundamental forms:

>> The spreadsheet report

>> The flat data file

>> The tabular data set

The punch line is that only flat data files and tabular data sets make for effective data models. I review and discuss each of these different forms in the next few sections.

Spreadsheet reports make for ineffective data models

Spreadsheet reports display highly formatted, summarized data and are often designed as presentation tools for management or executive users. A typical spreadsheet report makes judicious use of empty space for formatting, repeats data for aesthetic purposes, and presents only high-level analysis. Figure 2-3 illustrates a spreadsheet report.

Although a spreadsheet report may look nice, it doesn't make for an effective data model. Why? The primary reason is that these reports offer you no separation of data, analysis, and presentation. You're essentially locked into one analysis.

	Europe			North America		
France				**Canada**		
Segment	Sales Amount	Unit Price		Segment	Sales Amount	Unit Price
Accessories	$48,942	$7,045		Accessories	$119,303	$22,381
Bikes	$3,597,879	$991,098		Bikes	$11,714,700	$3,908,691
Clothing	$129,508	$23,912		Clothing	$383,022	$72,524
Components	$871,125	$293,854		Components	$2,246,255	$865,410
Germany				**Northeast**		
Segment	Sales Amount	Unit Price		Segment	Sales Amount	Unit Price
Accessories	$35,681	$5,798		Accessories	$51,246	$9,666
Bikes	$1,602,487	$545,175		Bikes	$5,690,285	$1,992,517
Clothing	$75,593	$12,474		Clothing	$163,442	$30,969
Components	$337,787	$138,513		Components	$1,051,702	$442,598
United Kingdom				**Northwest**		
Segment	Sales Amount	Unit Price		Segment	Sales Amount	Unit Price
Accessories	$43,180	$7,419		Accessories	$53,308	$11,417
Bikes	$3,435,134	$1,094,354		Bikes	$10,484,495	$3,182,041
Clothing	$120,225	$21,981		Clothing	$201,052	$40,055
Components	$712,588	$253,458		Components	$1,784,207	$695,876

FIGURE 2-3:
A spreadsheet report.

Although you could make charts from the report shown in Figure 2-3, it'd be impractical to apply any analysis outside what's already there. For instance, how would you calculate and present the average of all bike sales using this particular report? How would you calculate a list of the top ten best-performing markets?

With this setup, you're forced into very manual processes that are difficult to maintain month after month. Any analysis outside the high-level ones already in the report is basic at best — even with fancy formulas. Furthermore, what happens when you're required to show bike sales by month? When your data model requires analysis with data that isn't in the spreadsheet report, you're forced to search for another data set.

Flat data files lend themselves nicely to data models

Another type of file format is a flat file. *Flat files* are data repositories organized by row and column. Each row corresponds to a set of data elements, or a *record*. Each column is a *field*. A field corresponds to a unique data element in a record. Figure 2-4 contains the same data as the report in Figure 2-3 but expressed in a flat data file format.

⊿	A	B	C	D	E	F
1	Region	Market	Business Segment	Jan Sales Amount	Feb Sales Amount	Mar Sales Amount
2	Europe	France	Accessories	2,628	8,015	3,895
3	Europe	France	Bikes	26,588	524,445	136,773
4	Europe	France	Clothing	6,075	17,172	6,043
5	Europe	France	Components	20,485	179,279	54,262
6	Europe	Germany	Accessories	2,769	6,638	2,615
7	Europe	Germany	Bikes	136,161	196,125	94,840
8	Europe	Germany	Clothing	7,150	12,374	7,159
9	Europe	Germany	Components	46,885	56,611	29,216
10	Europe	United Kingdom	Accessories	4,205	2,579	5,745
11	Europe	United Kingdom	Bikes	111,830	175,522	364,844
12	Europe	United Kingdom	Clothing	7,888	6,763	12,884
13	Europe	United Kingdom	Components	31,331	39,005	124,030
14	North America	Canada	Accessories	2,500	12,350	9,768

FIGURE 2-4:
A flat data file.

Notice that every data field has a column, and every column corresponds to one data element. Furthermore, there's no extra spacing, and each row (or record) corresponds to a unique set of information. But the key attribute that makes this a flat file is that no single field uniquely identifies a record. In fact, you'd have to specify four separate fields (Region, Market, Business Segment, and a month's sales amount) before you could uniquely identify the record.

Flat files lend themselves nicely to data modeling in Excel because they can be detailed enough to hold the data you need and still be conducive to a wide array of analysis with simple formulas — SUM, AVERAGE, VLOOKUP, and SUMIF, just to name a few. Later in this chapter, you explore formulas that come in handy in a reporting data model.

Tabular data sets are perfect for pivot table–driven data models

Many effective data models are driven primarily by pivot tables. Pivot tables (which I cover in Chapter 3) are Excel's premier analysis tools. For those of you who have used pivot tables, you know they offer an excellent way to summarize and shape data for use by reporting components, such as charts and tables.

Tabular data sets are ideal for pivot table–driven data models. Figure 2-5 illustrates a tabular data set. Note that the primary difference between a tabular data set, as shown in Figure 2-5, and a flat data file is that in tabular data sets the column labels don't double as actual data. For instance, in Figure 2-4, the month identifiers are integrated into the column labels. In Figure 2-5, the Sales Period column contains the month identifier. This subtle difference in structure is what makes tabular data sets optimal data sources for pivot tables. This structure ensures that key pivot table functions, such as sorting and grouping, work the way they should.

	A	B	C	D	E
1	Region	Market	Business Segment	Sales Period	Sales Amount
2	Europe	France	Accessories	Jan	1,706
3	Europe	France	Accessories	Feb	3,767
4	Europe	France	Accessories	Mar	1,219
5	Europe	France	Accessories	Apr	3,091
6	Europe	France	Accessories	May	7,057
7	Europe	France	Accessories	Jul	5,930
8	Europe	France	Accessories	Aug	9,628
9	Europe	France	Accessories	Sep	4,279
10	Europe	France	Accessories	Oct	2,504
11	Europe	France	Accessories	Nov	7,493
12	Europe	France	Accessories	Dec	2,268
13	Europe	France	Bikes	Jan	64,895
14	Europe	France	Bikes	Feb	510,102
15	Europe	France	Bikes	Mar	128,806
16	Europe	France	Bikes	Apr	81,301
17	Europe	France	Bikes	May	610,504

FIGURE 2-5:
A tabular data set.

The attributes of a tabular data set are as follows:

» The first row of the data set contains field labels that describe the information in each column.

» The column labels don't pull double duty as data items that can be used as filters or query criteria (such as months, dates, years, regions, or markets).

» There are no blank rows or columns — every column has a heading, and a value is in every row.

» Each column represents a unique category of data.

» Each row represents individual items in each column.

Avoiding turning your data model into a database

In Chapter 1, you might have read that measures used on a dashboard should absolutely support the initial purpose of that dashboard. The same concept applies to the back-end data model. You should only import data that's necessary to fulfill the purpose of your dashboard or report.

In an effort to have as much data as possible at their fingertips, many Excel users bring into their spreadsheets every piece of data they can get their hands on. You can spot these people by the 40-megabyte files they send through email. You've seen these spreadsheets — two tabs that contain some reporting or dashboard interface and then six hidden tabs that contain thousands of lines of data (most of which isn't used). They essentially build a database in their spreadsheet.

What's wrong with utilizing as much data as possible? Well, here are a few issues:

» **Aggregating data within Excel increases the number of formulas.** If you're bringing in all raw data, you have to aggregate that data in Excel. This inevitably causes you to exponentially increase the number of formulas you have to employ and maintain. Remember that your data model is a vehicle for presenting analyses, not processing raw data. The data that works best in reporting mechanisms is what's already been aggregated and summarized into useful views that can be navigated and fed to dashboard components. Importing data that's already been aggregated as much as possible is far better. For example, if you need to report on Revenue by Region and Month, there's no need to import sales transactions into your data model. Instead, use an aggregated table consisting of Region, Month, and Sum of Revenue.

» **Your data model will be distributed with your dashboard.** In other words, because your dashboard is fed by your data model, you need to maintain the model behind the scenes (likely in hidden tabs) when distributing the dashboard. Besides the fact that it causes the file size to be unwieldy, including too much data in your data model can actually degrade the performance of your dashboard. Why? When you open an Excel file, the entire file is loaded into memory to ensure quick data processing and access. The drawback to this behavior is that Excel requires a great deal of RAM to process even the smallest change in your spreadsheet. You may have noticed that when you try to perform an action on a large, formula-intensive data set, Excel is slow to respond, giving you a Calculating indicator on the status bar. The larger your data set is, the less efficient the data crunching in Excel is.

» **Large data sets can cause difficulty in scalability.** Imagine that you're working in a small company and you're using monthly transactions in your data model. Each month holds 80,000 lines of data. As time goes on, you build a robust process complete with all the formulas, pivot tables, and macros you need to analyze the data that's stored on your neatly maintained tab. Now what happens after one year? Do you start a new tab? How do you analyze two data sets on two different tabs as one entity? Are your formulas still good? Do you have to write new macros?

These are all issues that can be avoided by importing only aggregated and summarized data that's useful to the core purpose of your reporting needs.

Using tabs to document and organize your data model

Wanting to keep your data model limited to one worksheet tab is natural. In my mind, keeping track of one tab is much simpler than using different tabs.

However, limiting your data model to one tab has its drawbacks, including the following:

>> **Using one tab typically places limits on your analysis.** Because only so many data sets can fit on a tab, using one tab limits the number of analyses that can be represented in your data model. This in turn limits the analysis your dashboard can offer. Consider adding tabs to your data model to provide additional data and analysis that may not fit on just one tab.

>> **Too much on one tab makes for a confusing data model.** When working with large data sets, you need plenty of staging tables to aggregate and shape the raw data so that it can be fed to your reporting components. If you use only one tab, you're forced to position these staging tables below or to the right of your data sets. Although this may provide all the elements needed to feed your presentation layer, a good deal of scrolling is necessary to view all the elements positioned in a wide range of areas. This makes the data model difficult to understand and maintain. Use separate tabs to hold your analysis and staging tables, particularly in data models that contain large data sets occupying a lot of real estate.

>> **Using one tab limits the amount of documentation you can include.** You'll find that your data models easily become a complex system of intertwining links among components, input ranges, output ranges, and formulas. Sure, it all makes sense while you're building your data model, but try coming back to it after a few months. You'll find you've forgotten what each data range does and how each range interacts with the final presentation layer. To avoid this problem, consider adding a Model Map tab to your data model. The *Model Map* tab essentially summarizes the key ranges in the data model and allows you to document how each range interacts with the reporting components in the final presentation layer. As you can see in Figure 2-6, the model map is nothing fancy — just a table that lists key information about each range in the model.

Tab	Range	Purpose	Linked Component/s
Analysis 1	A2:A11	Provides the data source for the trend graph component.	United States trend 1
Analysis 2	A3:A11	Data source for the List Box component.	List Box 1
Analysis 2	C1	Output range for the selected item in the List Box component.	Conditional trend icon
Analysis 2	D1:R1	Vlookup formulas that reference cell C1. This range also serves as the source data for the Combination Chart component.	Combination Chart 1
Data	C4:R48	Main data set for this data model.	

FIGURE 2-6: A model map allows you to document how each range interacts with your data model.

You can include any information you think appropriate in your model map. The idea is to give yourself a handy reference that guides you through the elements in your data model.

Testing your data model before building reporting components on top of it

This best practice is simple. Make sure your data model does what it's supposed to do before building dashboard components on top of it. In that vein, here are a few things to watch for:

>> **Test your formulas to ensure they're working properly.** Make sure your formulas don't produce errors and that each formula outputs expected results.

>> **Double-check your main data set to ensure it's complete.** Check that your data table was not truncated when transferring to Excel. Also, be sure that each column of data is present with appropriate data labels.

>> **Make sure all numeric formatting is appropriate.** Be sure that the formatting of your data is appropriate for the field. For example, check to see that dates are formatted as dates, currency values are formatted properly, and the correct number of decimal places is displayed where needed.

The obvious goal here is to eliminate easily avoidable errors that may cause complications later.

Excel Functions That Really Deliver

As you discover in this chapter, the optimal data model for any reporting mechanism is one in which data, analysis, and presentation are separated into three layers. Although all three layers are important, the analysis layer is where the real art comes into play. The fundamental task of the analysis layer is to pull information from the data layer and then create staging tables that feed your charts, tables, and other reporting components. To do this effectively, you need to employ formulas that serve as data delivery mechanisms — formulas that deliver data to a destination range.

You see, the information you need lives in the data layer (typically, a table containing aggregated data). *Data delivery formulas* are designed to get that data and deliver it to the analysis layer so it can be analyzed and shaped. The cool thing is that after you've set up the data delivery formulas, the analysis layer automatically updates each time the data layer is refreshed.

Confused? Don't worry — in this section, I show you a few Excel functions that work particularly well in data delivery formulas. As you complete the examples here, you'll start to see how these concepts come together.

The VLOOKUP function

The VLOOKUP function is the king of all lookup functions in Excel. I'd be willing to bet you've at least heard of VLOOKUP, if not used it a few times yourself. The purpose of VLOOKUP is to find a specific value from a column of data where the leftmost row value matches a given criterion.

VLOOKUP basics

Take a look at Figure 2-7 to get the general idea. The table on the left shows sales by month and product number. The bottom table translates those product numbers to actual product names. The VLOOKUP function can help in associating the appropriate name to each respective product number.

To understand how VLOOKUP formulas work, take a moment to review the basic syntax. A VLOOKUP formula requires four arguments:

```
VLOOKUP(Lookup_value, Table_array, Col_index_num, Range_lookup)
```

	Month	Product Number	Sales	Product Name		
3	Feb	5	$ 396	Pinapples	—	#VLOOKUP(C3,$D$16:$E$22,2,FALSE)
4	Feb	2	$ 388	Oranges	—	#VLOOKUP(C4,$D$16:$E$22,2,FALSE)
5	Feb	1	$ 377	Apples	—	#VLOOKUP(C5,$D$16:$E$22,2,FALSE)
6	Feb	3	$ 204	Bananas	—	#VLOOKUP(C6,$D$16:$E$22,2,FALSE)
7	Feb	4	$ 200	Pears	—	#VLOOKUP(C7,$D$16:$E$22,2,FALSE)
8	Feb	6	$ 161	Mangos	—	#VLOOKUP(C8,$D$16:$E$22,2,FALSE)
9	Jan	3	$ 489	Bananas	—	#VLOOKUP(C9,$D$16:$E$22,2,FALSE)
10	Jan	6	$ 465	Mangos	—	#VLOOKUP(C10,$D$16:$E$22,2,FALSE)
11	Jan	1	$ 382	Apples	—	#VLOOKUP(C11,$D$16:$E$22,2,FALSE)
12	Jan	2	$ 285	Oranges	—	#VLOOKUP(C12,$D$16:$E$22,2,FALSE)
13	Jan	4	$ 200	Pears	—	#VLOOKUP(C13,$D$16:$E$22,2,FALSE)
14	Jan	5	$ 113	Pinapples	—	#VLOOKUP(C14,$D$16:$E$22,2,FALSE)

Product Number	Product Name
1	Apples
2	Oranges
3	Bananas
4	Pears
5	Pinapples
6	Mangos

FIGURE 2-7: In this example, the VLOOKUP function helps to look up the appropriate product name for each product number.

Lookup_value: The *Lookup_value* argument identifies the value being looked up. This is the value that needs to be matched to the lookup table. In the example in Figure 2-7, the *Lookup_value* is the product number. Therefore, the first argument for all the formulas shown in Figure 2-7 references column C (the column that contains the product number).

Table_array: The *Table_array* argument specifies the range that contains the lookup values. In Figure 2-7, that range is D16 : E22. Here are a couple of points to keep in mind with this argument. First, for a VLOOKUP to work, the leftmost column of the table must be the matching value. For instance, if you're trying to match product numbers, the leftmost column of the lookup table must contain product numbers. Second, notice that the reference used for this argument is an absolute reference. This means the column and row references are prefixed with dollar ($) signs — as in $D$16 : $E$22. This ensures that the references don't shift while you copy the formulas down or across.

Col_index_num: The *Col_index_num* argument identifies the column number in the lookup table that contains the value to be returned. In the example in Figure 2-7, the second column contains the product name (the value being looked up), so the formula uses the number 2. If the product name column were the fourth column in the lookup table, the number 4 would be used.

Range_lookup: The *Range_lookup* argument specifies whether you're looking for an exact match or an approximate match. If an exact match is needed, you'd enter FALSE for this argument. If the closest match will do, you'd enter TRUE or leave the argument blank.

Applying VLOOKUP formulas in a data model

As you can imagine, there are countless ways to apply a VLOOKUP in all kinds of analyses. Let's take a moment to walk through a scenario where using a VLOOKUP can help enhance your dashboard model.

With a few VLOOKUP formulas and a simple drop-down list, you can create a data model that not only delivers data to the appropriate staging table, but also allows you to dynamically change data views based on a selection you make. Figure 2-8 illustrates the setup.

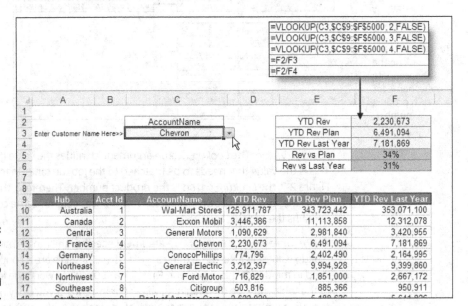

FIGURE 2-8: Using the VLOOKUP function to extract and shape data.

TIP

To see this effect in action, get the Chapter 2 Samples.xlsx workbook from this book's companion website. Open that workbook to see a VLOOKUP tab.

The data layer in the model shown in Figure 2-8 resides in the range A9:F209. The analysis layer is held in range E2:F6. The data layer consists of all formulas that extract and shape the data as needed. As you can see, the VLOOKUP formulas use the Customer Name value in cell C3 to look up the appropriate data from the data layer. So if you entered **Chevron** in cell C3, the VLOOKUP formulas would extract the data for Chevron.

TECHNICAL STUFF

You may have noticed that the VLOOKUP formulas in Figure 2-8 specify a Table_array argument of $C$9:$F$5000. This means that the lookup table they're pointing to stretches from C9 to F5000. That seems strange because the table ends at F209. Why would you force your VLOOKUP formulas to look at a range far past the end of the data table?

Well, remember that the idea behind separating the data layer and the analysis layer is so that the analysis layer can be automatically updated when the data is refreshed. When you get new data next month, you should be able to simply replace the data layer in the model without having to rework the analysis layer. Allowing for more rows than necessary in your VLOOKUP formulas ensures that if the data layer grows, records won't fall outside the lookup range of the formulas.

Later in this chapter, I show you how to automatically keep up with growing data tables by using smart tables.

Using data validation drop-down lists in the data model

In the example illustrated in Figure 2-8, the data model allows you to select customer names from a drop-down list when you click cell C3. The customer name serves as the lookup value for the VLOOKUP formulas. Changing the customer name extracts a new set of data from the data layer. This allows you to quickly switch from one customer to another without having to remember and type the customer name.

Now, as cool as this seems, the reasons for this setup aren't all cosmetic. There are practical reasons for adding drop-down lists to your data models.

Many of your models consist of multiple analytical layers in which each shows a different set of analyses. Although each analysis layer is different, they often need to revolve around a shared dimension, such as the same customer name, the same market, or the same region. For instance, when you have a data model that reports on Financials, Labor Statistics, and Operational Volumes, you want to make certain that when the model is reporting financials for the South region, the Labor Statistics are for the South region as well.

An effective way to ensure this happens is to force your formulas to use the same dimension references. If cell C3 is where you switch customers, every analysis that is customer-dependent should reference cell C3. Drop-down lists allow you to have a predefined list of valid variables located in a single cell. With a drop-down list, you can easily switch dimensions while building and testing multiple analysis layers.

Adding a drop-down list is relatively easy with Excel's Data Validation functionality. To add a drop-down list, follow these steps:

1. **Select the Data tab on the Ribbon.**
2. **Click the Data Validation button.**

3. **Select the Settings tab in the newly activated Data Validation dialog box (see Figure 2-9).**

4. **In the Allow drop-down list, choose List.**

5. **In the Source input box, reference the range of cells that contain your predefined selection list.**

   In our example, this would be the list of customers you want exposed through the dashboard.

6. **Click OK.**

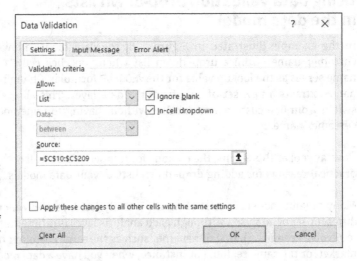

The HLOOKUP function

The HLOOKUP function is the less popular cousin of the VLOOKUP function. The *H* in HLOOKUP stands for *horizontal*. Because Excel data is typically vertically oriented, most situations require a vertical lookup, or VLOOKUP. However, some data structures are horizontally oriented, requiring a horizontal lookup; thus, the HLOOKUP function comes in handy. The HLOOKUP searches a lookup table to find a single value from a row of data where the column label matches a given criterion.

HLOOKUP basics

Figure 2-10 demonstrates a typical scenario in which HLOOKUP formulas are used. The table in C5 requires quarter-end numbers (March and June) for 2021. The HLOOKUP formulas use the column labels to find the correct month columns and then locate the 2021 data by moving down to the specified row. In this case, 2021 data is in row 4, so the number 4 is used in the formulas.

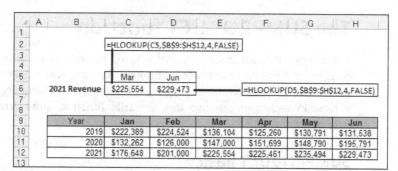

FIGURE 2-10:
HLOOKUP
formulas help to
find March and
June numbers
from the
lookup table.

To get your mind around how this works, take a look at the basic syntax of the HLOOKUP function.

```
HLOOKUP(Lookup_value, Table_array, Row_index_num, Range_lookup)
```

Lookup_value: The *Lookup_value* argument identifies the value being looked up. In most cases, these values are column names. In the example in Figure 2-10, the column labels are being referenced for the *Lookup_value*. This points the HLOOKUP function to the appropriate column in the lookup table.

Table_array: The *Table_array* argument identifies the range that contains the lookup table. In Figure 2-10, that range is B9:H12. Like the VLOOKUP examples earlier in this chapter, notice that the references used for this argument are absolute. This means the column and row references are prefixed with dollar ($) signs — as in $B$9:$H$12. This ensures that the reference doesn't shift while you copy the formula down or across.

Row_index_num: The *Row_index_num* argument identifies the row number that contains the value you're looking for. In the example in Figure 2-10, the 2021 data is located in row 4 of the lookup table. Therefore, the formulas use the number 4.

Range_lookup: The *Range_lookup* argument specifies whether you're looking for an exact match or an approximate match. If an exact match is needed, you'd enter FALSE for this argument. If the closest match will do, you'd enter TRUE or leave the argument blank.

Applying HLOOKUP formulas in a data model

HLOOKUPs are especially handy for shaping data into structures appropriate for charting or other types of reporting. A simple example is demonstrated in Figure 2-11. With HLOOKUPs, the data shown in the raw data table at the bottom of the figure is reoriented in a staging table at the top. When the raw data is changed or refreshed, the staging table captures the changes.

The SUMPRODUCT function

The SUMPRODUCT function is actually listed under the math and trigonometry category of Excel functions. Because the primary purpose of SUMPRODUCT is to calculate the sum product, most people don't know you can actually use it to look up values. In fact, you can use this versatile function quite effectively in most data models.

SUMPRODUCT basics

The SUMPRODUCT function is designed to multiply values from two or more ranges of data and then add the results together to return the sum of the products. Take a look at Figure 2-12 to see a typical scenario in which the SUMPRODUCT function is useful.

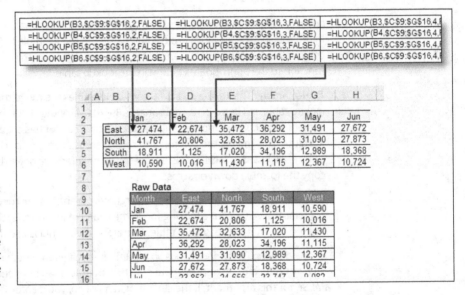

FIGURE 2-11:
In this example, HLOOKUP formulas pull and reshape data without disturbing the raw data table.

In Figure 2-12, you see a common analysis in which you need the total sales for the years 2021 and 2022. As you can see, to get the total sales for each year, you first have to multiply Price by the number of Units to get the total for each Region. Then you have to sum those results to get the total sales for each year.

With the SUMPRODUCT function, you can perform the two-step analysis with just one formula. Figure 2-13 shows the same analysis with SUMPRODUCT formulas. Rather than use 11 formulas, you can accomplish the same analysis with just 3!

FIGURE 2-12:
Without the
SUMPRODUCT
function, getting
the total
sales involves
multiplying price
by units and
then summing
the results.

Year	Region	Price	Units		
2022	North	$40	751	$30,040	=D3*E3
2022	South	$35	483	$16,905	=D4*E4
2022	East	$32	789	$25,248	=D5*E5
2022	West	$41	932	$38,212	=D6*E6
2021	North	$40	877	$35,080	=D7*E7
2021	South	$35	162	$5,670	=D8*E8
2021	East	$32	258	$8,256	=D9*E9
2021	West	$41	517	$21,197	=D10*E10
			2022 total	$110,405	=SUM(F3:F6)
			2021 total	$70,203	=SUM(F7:F10)
			Variance	$40,202	=F12-F13

FIGURE 2-13:
The SUMPRODUCT
function allows
you to perform
the same
analysis with just
3 formulas
instead of 11.

Year	Region	Price	Units	
2012	North	$40	751	
2012	South	$35	483	
2012	East	$32	789	
2012	West	$41	932	
2011	North	$40	877	
2011	South	$35	162	
2011	East	$32	258	
2011	West	$41	517	
2012 total	$110,405			=SUMPRODUCT(D3:D6,E3:E6)
2011 total	$70,203			=SUMPRODUCT(D7:D10, E7:E10)
Variance	$40,202			=E12-E13

The syntax of the SUMPRODUCT function is fairly simple:

```
SUMPRODUCT(Array1, Array2, ...)
```

Array:Array represents a range of data. You can use anywhere from 2 to 255 arrays in a SUMPRODUCT formula. The arrays are multiplied together and then added. The only hard-and-fast rule you have to remember is that all arrays must have the same number of values. That is to say, you can't use the SUMPRODUCT if range X has 10 values and range Y has 11 values. Otherwise, you get the #VALUE! error.

A twist on the SUMPRODUCT function

The interesting thing about the SUMPRODUCT function is that it can be used to filter out values. Take a look at Figure 2-14 to see what I mean.

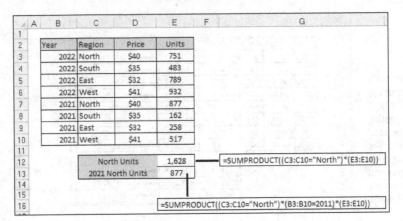

FIGURE 2-14:
The SUMPRODUCT
function can be
used to filter data
based on criteria.

The formula in cell E12 is pulling the sum of total units for just the North region. Meanwhile, cell E13 is pulling the units logged for the North region in the year 2021.

To understand how this works, take a look at the formula in cell E12, shown in Figure 2-14. That formula reads SUMPRODUCT((C3:C10="North")*(E3:E10)).

In Excel, TRUE evaluates to 1 and FALSE evaluates to 0. Every value in column C that equals North evaluates to TRUE or 1. Where the value is not North, it evaluates to FALSE or 0.The part of the formula that reads (C3:C10="North") enumerates through each value in the range C3:C10, assigning a 1 or 0 to each value. Then internally, the SUMPRODUCT formula translates to

```
(1*E3)+(0*E4)+(0*E5)+(0*E6)+(1*E7)+(0*E8)+(0*E9)+(0*E10).
```

This gives you the answer of 1628 because

```
(1*751)+(0*483)+(0*789)+(0*932)+(1*877)+(0*162)+(0*258)+(0*517)
```

equals 1628.

Applying SUMPRODUCT formulas in a data model

As always in Excel, you don't have to hard-code the criteria in your formulas. Rather than explicitly use "North" in the SUMPRODUCT formula, you could reference a cell that contains the filter value. You can imagine that cell A3 contains the word North, in which case you can use (C3:C10=A3) instead of (C3:C10="North"). This way, you can dynamically change your filter criteria, and your formula keeps up.

Figure 2-15 demonstrates how you can use this concept to pull data into a staging table based on multiple criteria. Note that each of the SUMPRODUCT formulas shown here references cells B3 and C3 to filter on Account and Product Line. Again, you can add data validation drop-down lists to cells B3 and C3, allowing you to easily change criteria.

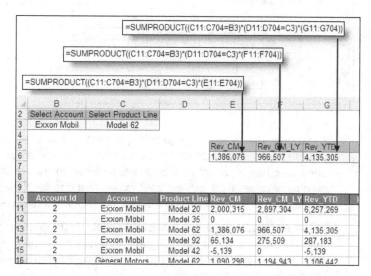

FIGURE 2-15:
The SUMPRODUCT function can be used to pull summarized numbers from the data layer into staging tables.

The CHOOSE function

The CHOOSE function returns a value from a specified list of values based on a specified position number. For instance, if you enter the formulas CHOOSE(3, "Red", "Yellow", "Green", "Blue") into a cell, Excel returns Green because Green is the third item in the list of values. The formula CHOOSE(1, "Red", "Yellow", "Green", "Blue") would return Red. Although this may not look useful on the surface, the CHOOSE function can dramatically enhance your data models.

CHOOSE basics

Figure 2-16 illustrates how CHOOSE formulas can help pinpoint and extract numbers from a range of cells. Note that instead of using hard-coded values, like Red, Green, and so on, you can use cell references to list the choices.

Take a moment to review the basic syntax of the CHOOSE function:

```
CHOOSE(Index_num, Value1, Value2, ...)
```

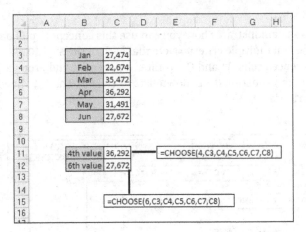

FIGURE 2-16:
The CHOOSE function allows you to find values from a defined set of choices.

Index_num: The *Index_num* argument specifies the position number of the chosen value in the list of values. If the third value in the list is needed, the *Index_num* is 3. The *Index_num* argument must be an integer between one and the maximum number of values in the defined list of values. That is to say, if there are ten choices defined in the CHOOSE formula, the *Index_num* argument can't be more than ten.

Value: Each *Value* argument represents a choice in the defined list of choices for that CHOOSE formula. The *Value* arguments can be hard-coded values, cell references, defined names, formulas, or functions. You can have up to 255 choices listed in your CHOOSE formulas.

Applying CHOOSE formulas in a data model

The CHOOSE function is especially valuable in data models in which multiple layers of data need to be brought together. Figure 2-17 illustrates an example in which CHOOSE formulas help pull data together.

In this example, you have two data tables: one for Revenues and one for Net Income. Each contains numbers for separate regions. The idea is to create a staging table that pulls data from both tables so that the data corresponds to a selected region.

To understand what's going on, focus on the formula in cell F3, shown in Figure 2-17. The formula is CHOOSE($C$2,F7,F8,F9,F10). The *Index_num* argument is actually a cell reference that looks at the value in cell C2, which happens to be the number 2. As you can see, cell C2 is actually a VLOOKUP formula that pulls the appropriate index number for the selected region. The list of defined choices in the CHOOSE formula is essentially the cell references that make up the revenue values for each region: F7, F8, F9, and F10. So the formula in cell F3 translates to CHOOSE(2, 27474, 41767, 18911, 10590). The answer is 41,767.

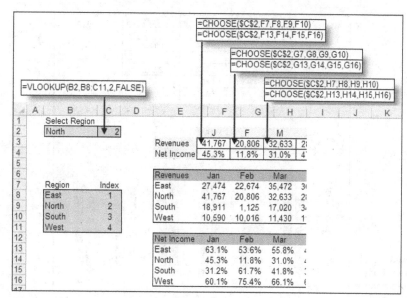

FIGURE 2-17:
The CHOOSE formulas ensure that the appropriate data is synchronously pulled from multiple data feeds.

Using Smart Tables That Expand with Data

One of the challenges you can encounter when building data models is a data table that expands over time. That is to say, the table grows in the number of records it holds due to new data being added. To get a basic understanding of this challenge, take a look at Figure 2-18. In this figure, you see a simple table that serves as the source for the chart. Notice that the table lists data for January through June.

Imagine that next month, this table expands to include July data. You'll have to manually update your chart to include July data. Now imagine you had this same issue across your data model, with multiple data tables that link to multiple staging tables and dashboard components. You can imagine it'd be an extremely painful task to keep up with changes each month.

To solve this issue, you can use Excel's Table feature (you can tell they spent all night coming up with that name). The *Table feature* allows you to convert a range of data into a defined table that's treated independently of other rows and columns on the worksheet. After a range is converted to a table, Excel views the individual cells in the table as a single object with functionality that a typical data range doesn't have.

	2020	2021
Jan	27,474	41,767
Feb	22,674	20,806
Mar	35,472	32,633
Apr	36,292	28,023
May	31,491	31,090
Jun	27,672	27,873

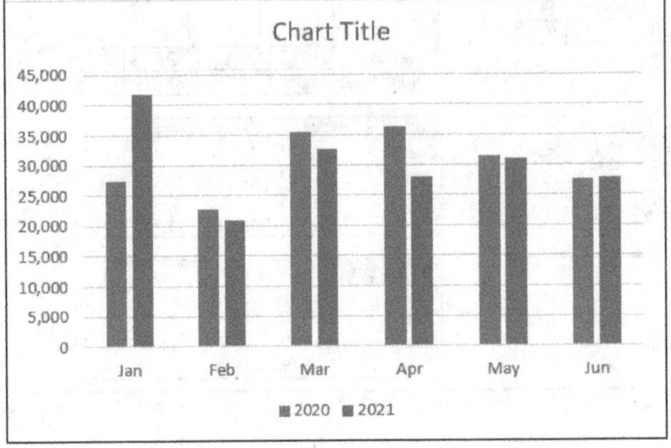

Chart Title

FIGURE 2-18:
The date in both the table and chart ends in June.

For instance, Excel tables offer the following features:

» They're automatically enabled with Filter drop-down headers so that you can filter and sort easily.

» They come with the ability to quickly add a Total row with various aggregate functions.

» You can apply special formatting to Excel tables independent of the rest of the spreadsheet.

» Most important for data modeling purposes, they automatically expand to allow for new data.

Converting a range to an Excel table

To convert a range of data to an Excel table, follow these steps:

1. **Highlight the range of cells that contain the data you want included in your Excel table.**

2. **On the Insert tab of the Ribbon, click the Table button.**

   This step opens the Create Table dialog box, as shown in Figure 2-19.

3. In the Create Table dialog box, verify the range for the table and specify whether the first row of the selected range is a header row.

4. Click OK to apply the changes.

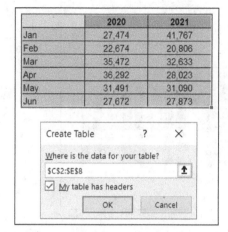

	2020	2021
Jan	27,474	41,767
Feb	22,674	20,806
Mar	35,472	32,633
Apr	36,292	28,023
May	31,491	31,090
Jun	27,672	27,873

Create Table   ?   ✕

Where is the data for your table?

$C$2:$E$8

☑ My table has headers

OK   Cancel

FIGURE 2-19: Converting a range of data to an Excel table.

After the conversion takes place, notice a few small changes. Excel has put auto-filter drop-downs on the header rows and any header that didn't have a value has been named by Excel.

You can use Excel tables as the source for charts, pivot tables, list boxes, or anything else for which you'd typically use a data range. In Figure 2-20, a chart has been linked to the Excel table.

Here's the impressive bit. When data is added to the table, Excel automatically expands the range of the table and incorporates the new range into any linked object. That's just a fancy way of saying that any chart or pivot table tied to an Excel table automatically captures new data without manual intervention.

For example, if I add July and August data to the end of the Excel table, the chart automatically updates to capture the new data. In Figure 2-21, I added July with no data and August with data to show you that the chart captures any new records and automatically plots the data given.

Take a moment to think about what Excel tables mean to a data model. They mean pivot tables that never have to be reconfigured, charts that automatically capture new data, and ranges that automatically keep up with changes.

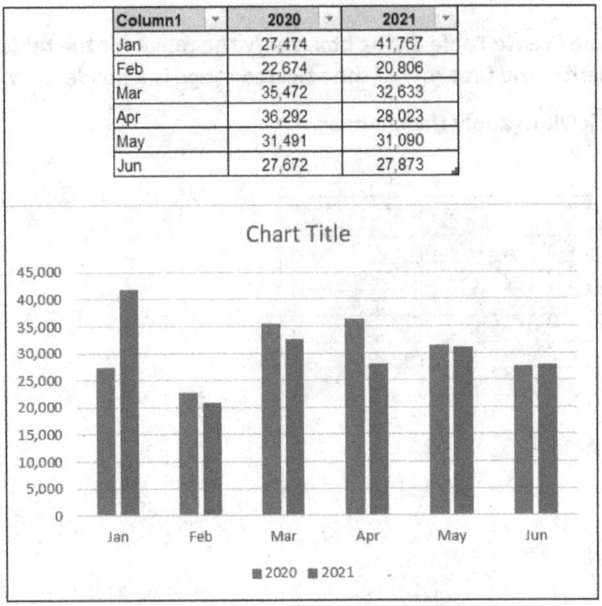

Column1	2020	2021
Jan	27,474	41,767
Feb	22,674	20,806
Mar	35,472	32,633
Apr	36,292	28,023
May	31,491	31,090
Jun	27,672	27,873

Chart Title

FIGURE 2-20:
Excel tables can be used as the source for charts, pivot tables, named ranges, and so on.

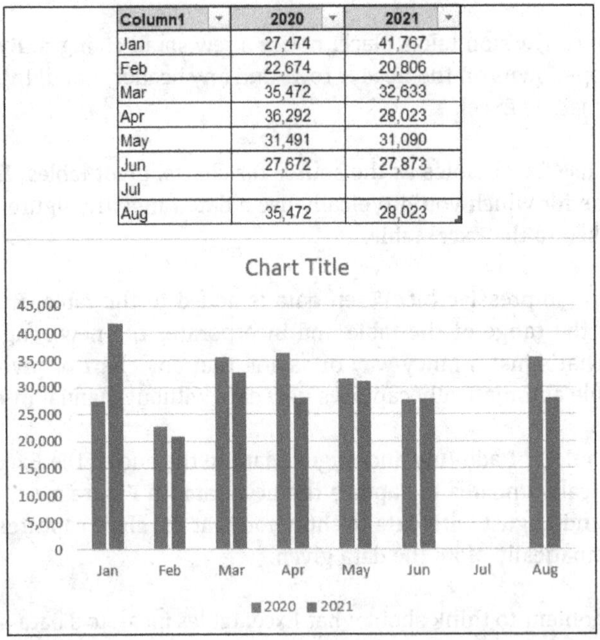

Column1	2020	2021
Jan	27,474	41,767
Feb	22,674	20,806
Mar	35,472	32,633
Apr	36,292	28,023
May	31,491	31,090
Jun	27,672	27,873
Jul		
Aug	35,472	28,023

Chart Title

FIGURE 2-21:
Excel tables automatically expand when new data is added.

Converting an Excel table back to a range

If you want to convert an Excel table back to a range, you can follow these steps:

1. **Place the cursor in any cell inside the Excel table and select the Table Design tab on the Ribbon.**

2. **Click the Convert to Range button, as shown in Figure 2-22.**

3. **When asked if you're sure (via a message box), click the Yes button.**

FIGURE 2-22:
To remove
Excel table
functionality,
convert the table
back to a range.

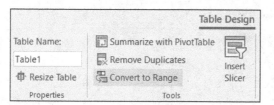

Introducing Dynamic Arrays

The easiest way to grasp the concept of arrays is to imagine a collection of rows and columns. Picture a table containing five rows and one column. On the worksheet, we call that a range of cells, but if we somehow took that range and stored it in memory, it would cease to be a range and be an array. While in memory, any formula operation performed on the array is performed as a collective. That is to say, all items in that array would be touched by the formula in various ways (depending on the formula you're using).

With dynamic arrays, Excel moves into a new era where you no longer need to be a formula guru to leverage the power of arrays. In this section, you'll explore Excel's exciting new dynamic array functions and discover some of the ways these new functions can help you go far beyond the capabilities of traditional formulas.

Getting the basics of dynamic arrays

To see a simple dynamic array in action, take a gander at Figure 2-23 showing a formula that references cells A2:C7.

Simply pressing Enter will automatically propagate the formula to the surrounding cells (see Figure 2-24). The initial formula provides the array dimensions of six rows and three columns. Excel takes that information and outputs the results into a grid equivalent to the dimensions provided.

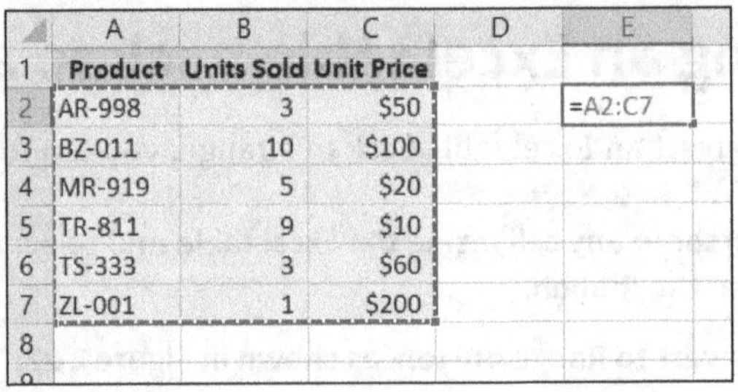

	A	B	C	D	E
1	Product	Units Sold	Unit Price		
2	AR-998	3	$50		=A2:C7
3	BZ-011	10	$100		
4	MR-919	5	$20		
5	TR-811	9	$10		
6	TS-333	3	$60		
7	ZL-001	1	$200		
8					

FIGURE 2-23: A simple formula that references a range.

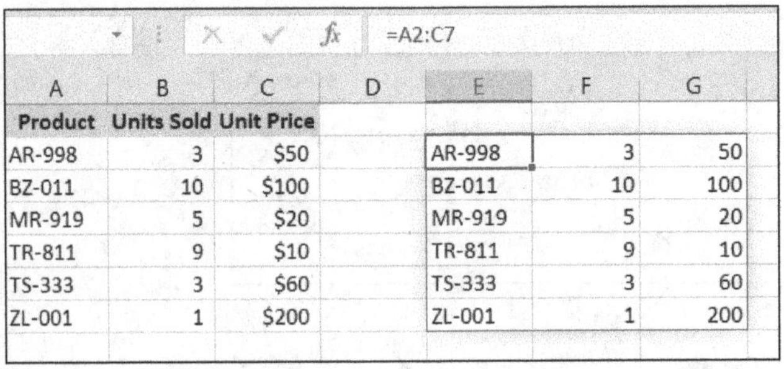

=A2:C7

A	B	C	D	E	F	G
Product	Units Sold	Unit Price				
AR-998	3	$50		AR-998	3	50
BZ-011	10	$100		BZ-011	10	100
MR-919	5	$20		MR-919	5	20
TR-811	9	$10		TR-811	9	10
TS-333	3	$60		TS-333	3	60
ZL-001	1	$200		ZL-001	1	200

FIGURE 2-24: Excel automatically spills the results into the surrounding cells.

This behavior of automatically propagating results to surrounding cells is called *spilling*. The area around an array formula is called the *spill range*. The spill range is determined by dimensions specified in your array formula. In the example shown in Figure 2-24, the array formula references an array that is six rows by three columns. Therefore, no matter where you put the formula, the spill range will be fixed to a grid that is six rows by three columns.

It's important to note that dynamic array behavior is fundamentally part of Excel's calculation engine. When any function uses an array that returns multiple values, the results will be output to a spill range. This even includes older functions that weren't designed to output arrays. For instance, the formula bar in Figure 2-25 shows the following:

```
= SUM(B14:B19*C14:C19)
```

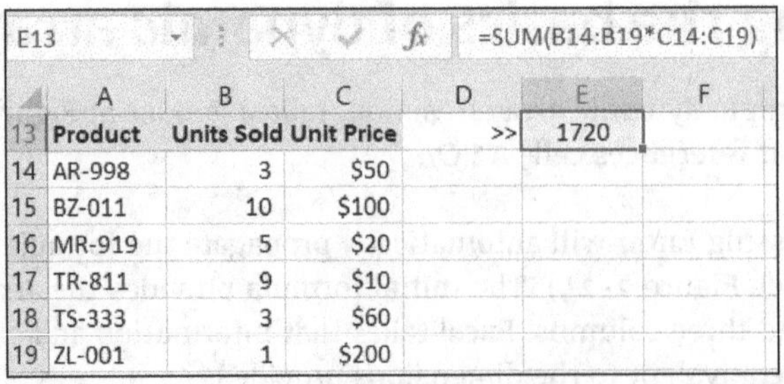

E13 =SUM(B14:B19*C14:C19)

	A	B	C	D	E	F
13	Product	Units Sold	Unit Price	>>	1720	
14	AR-998	3	$50			
15	BZ-011	10	$100			
16	MR-919	5	$20			
17	TR-811	9	$10			
18	TS-333	3	$60			
19	ZL-001	1	$200			

FIGURE 2-25: Dynamic arrays work with any traditional Excel function that accepts arrays as arguments.

DYNAMIC ARRAYS AND COMPATIBILITY

As of this writing, dynamic arrays are only available to those with Office 365 subscriptions and those using the standalone (perpetual license) version of Office/Excel 2022 or later. Dynamic arrays won't be available to those using Excel 2019 or earlier versions. If you save a worksheet with dynamic arrays and open that workbook in an older version of Excel, the dynamic arrays will be converted to legacy array formulas. Excel does its best to retain fidelity, but be aware that the conversion may cause a loss of functionality or unexpected behavior. If your audience is using older versions of Excel, you'll want to fully test your dynamic formulas in their version of Excel to determine how they behave when converted.

This formula uses a simple `SUM` function to multiply the sum of B14:B19 by the sum of C14:C19. Because dynamic arrays are now inherent to the Excel's calculation engine, the arrays are automatically processed without the need to press Ctrl+Shift+Enter like you would need to in older versions of Excel.

Understanding spill ranges

When you enter a dynamic array, the results spill into adjacent cells. Excel visually demarcates a spill range with a solid blue line. All cells inside the spill range are effectively disabled except for the *point of entry* (the cell containing the original formula). Figure 2-26 shows an active spill range containing the results of a dynamic array. The original formula was entered into cell E2. None of the values in the spill range, except for cell E2, can be deleted, moved, or edited in any way.

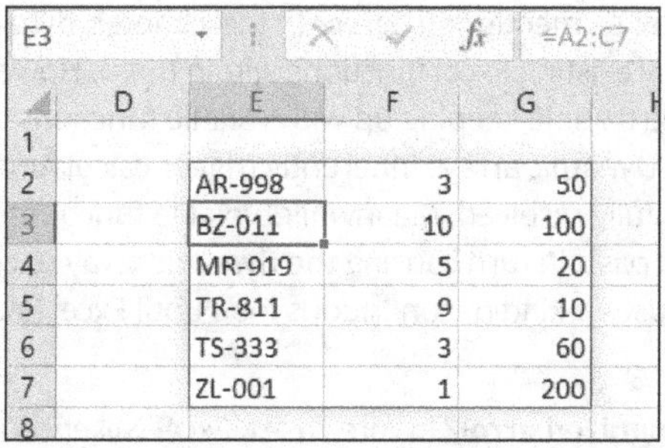

FIGURE 2-26: Spill ranges will visually show a line around them.

Attempting to enter data inside a spill range will cause what is known as a `#SPILL!` error. Figure 2-27 demonstrates a `#SPILL!` error caused by entering a value in the spill range. Removing the obstructing data from the spill range will immediately bring back the array values.

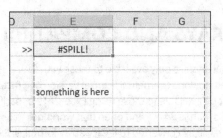

FIGURE 2-27:
A spill error
caused by an
obstruction in the
spill range.

There are several reasons you may see a #SPILL! error:

>> **The spill range contains an obstruction.** This is the most common cause of a #SPILL! error. The spill range must be blank for your dynamic arrays to work. Any cell containing data will cause an error if it's in the path of the spill range.

>> **The spill range extends beyond the worksheet end.** Try selecting cell A2 and entering the formula =B:B. You'll get a # SPILL! error because the spill range needs more room than the worksheet allows.

>> **You're trying to use dynamic arrays in a Table object.** Excel Table objects won't allow other objects inside them. Because spill ranges are essentially a kind of auto-expanding object themselves, you can't use dynamic arrays inside tables.

>> **You're out of memory.** If your dynamic array causes Excel to run out of memory, you'll get a #SPILL! error. In these cases, you'll need to rethink your formula and reference a smaller array.

>> **The spill range has hit a merged cell.** Your spill range can't include merged cells.

>> **Indeterminate size:** As mentioned earlier in this chapter, dynamic arrays allow you to use any existing Excel functions within them. However, dynamic array formulas have trouble keeping up with volatile functions such as RAND and RANDBETWEEN. Dynamic arrays inherently trigger calculation refreshes until the formula is fully resolved. Meanwhile, volatile functions will resize on each calculation pass, in turn causing the dynamic array to continue calculating. This causes a kind of continuous loop until Excel finally throws a #SPILL! error.

>> **There is an unrecognized error.** In rare cases, Excel will encounter an error it can't reconcile, so it throws a #SPILL! error. In these cases, it's best to review your formula to make sure it has all the required arguments.

Referencing spill ranges

It's often useful to reference a spill range in other formulas. However, simply pointing subsequent formulas to a single cell in the spill range won't capture the entirety of the range. You need to use the spill range operator, designated by a hashtag (#). To explore this concept, have a look at Figure 2-28. In the example shown, we want to capture the length of each string value in the spill range found in E2:E7. You can see that entering the formula, LEN(E2) only gives the length for the first value in the spill range.

◢	D	E	F	G	H
1				String Length	
2		AR-90018		8	=Len(E2)
3		BZ-011			
4		MR-9198			
5		TR-81			
6		TS-3333			
7		ZL-001			

FIGURE 2-28: Referencing a single cell in a spill range won't allow you to capture all values.

In Figure 2-29, you can see in the formula bar that I've added the spill range operator (#) to the cell reference, telling Excel to use the entire spill range. This has the effect of carrying the spill range over and effectively creating a new spill range for the LEN function.

G2	▾	⋮	✕	✓	*fx*	=LEN(E2#)

◢	D	E	F	G	H
1				String Length	
2		AR-90018		8	
3		BZ-011		6	
4		MR-9198		7	
5		TR-81		5	
6		TS-3333		7	
7		ZL-001		6	
8					

FIGURE 2-29: Using the spill range operator to apply a function to the entire spill range.

In Figure 2-30, I'm using the spill range operator with the COUNTA function to count all the values in the referenced spill range. Without the spill range operator, you would get a count of 1 for the first cell in the spill range.

WHY DO I SEE AN AT SIGN (@) IN MY FORMULAS?

Traditional Excel formulas had an inherent calculation behavior called *implicit intersection,* in which a single value would be returned from an array of values. This ensured that formulas would always return just one value because, before dynamic arrays came along, a cell could only contain one value.

Now that dynamic arrays exist, Excel is no longer limited to returning single values, so if you have an Office 365 subscription and you're using the standalone (perpetual license) version of Office/Excel 2022, you won't have implicit intersection applied.

However, if you open a workbook created in an older version of Excel, you may see @ in the formulas. The @ is known as the *implicit intersection operator;* it's effectively a visual representation of the previously invisible implicit intersection behavior. Generally speaking, functions that return arrays (INDEX and OFFSET, for instance) will be prefixed with @ if they were authored in an older version of Excel.

If the formula containing the @ operator returns a single value, you can safely remove the @ without effect. If, however, the formula returns an array, removing the @ will cause it to spill to the neighboring cells.

If you remove the @ from a formula that returns an array and later open the workbook in an older version of Excel, the formula will be converted to a legacy array formula.

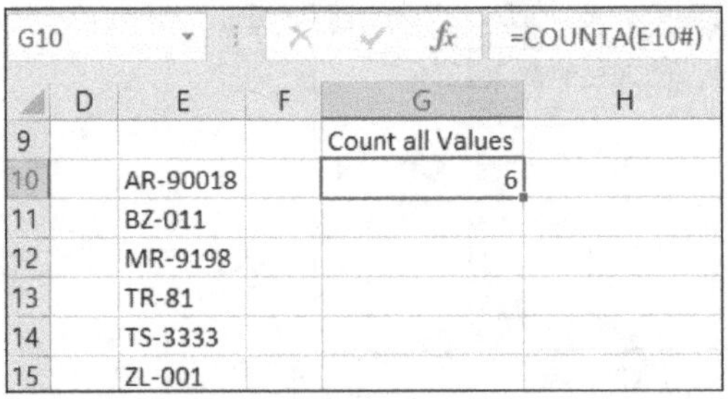

FIGURE 2-30:
Using the spill range operator to count all values in the referenced spill range.

Exploring Dynamic Array Functions

With the introduction of dynamic arrays, Microsoft released new functions that leverage dynamic arrays to improve the ability to carry out complex formula operations with ease. These new functions can remove duplicates, extract unique values, filter data, dynamically sort data, and perform lookups. This section provides an overview of each of the new dynamic array functions.

The SORT function

The SORT function sorts the values in a given range in ascending or descending order with a formula. Results will be output into a spill range that automatically updates when values in the source range change. The SORT function takes four arguments: *Array*, *Sort_index*, *Sort_order*, and *By_col*.

The *Array* argument defines the source range to sort and is the only required argument. The following formula will sort the values in A2:A11 in ascending order.

```
=SORT(A2:A11)
```

The *Sort_index* argument allows you to specify the column to sort by. By default, the SORT function uses the first column in the given range. You can set the *Sort_index* to a different column based on column number. The following formula will sort the values in A2:B11 by column B in ascending order.

```
=SORT(A2:B11,2)
```

The SORT function will sort ascending by default. You can sort descending by adding the *Sort_order* argument. Use −1 as *Sort_order* to sort descending. The following formula will sort the values in A2:B11 by column B in descending order.

```
=SORT(A2:B11,2,−1)
```

Figure 2-31 shows the SORT function in action. Here, I'm sorting students in descending order by the change in test scores.

	F2		▾	⋮	✕	✓	*fx*	=SORT(A2:D15,-1)		

	A	B	C	D	E	F	G	H	I
1	Student	Pre-Test	Post-Test	Change					
2	Andy	56	67	11		Linda	45	68	23
3	Beth	59	74	15		Michelle	71	92	21
4	Cindy	98	92	-6		Eddy	81	100	19
5	Duane	78	79	1		Beth	59	74	15
6	Eddy	81	100	19		Isabel	54	69	15
7	Francis	92	94	2		Andy	56	67	11
8	Georgia	100	100	0		Kent	80	88	8
9	Hilda	92	99	7		Hilda	92	99	7
10	Isabel	54	69	15		Francis	92	94	2
11	Jack	91	92	1		Duane	78	79	1
12	Kent	80	88	8		Jack	91	92	1
13	Linda	45	68	23		Georgia	100	100	0
14	Michelle	71	92	21		Cindy	98	92	-6
15	Nancy	94	83	-11		Nancy	94	83	-11

FIGURE 2-31: Using the SORT function to sort students by the change in test scores.

The SORT function will sort rows by default. The last argument of the SORT function is the `By_col` argument. You can set the `By_col` argument to 1 (see Figure 2-32) to sort by columns instead.

| | | | =SORT(N2:AA3,2,-1,1) | | | | | | | | | | | | |

M	N	O	P	Q	R	S	T	U	V	W	X	Y	Z	AA
Student	Andy	Beth	Cindy	Duane	Eddy	Francis	Georgia	Hilda	Isabel	Jack	Kent	Linda	Michelle	Nancy
Score	56	59	98	78	81	92	100	92	54	91	80	45	71	94
	Georgia	Cindy	Nancy	Francis	Hilda	Jack	Eddy	Kent	Duane	Michelle	Beth	Andy	Isabel	Linda
	100	98	94	92	92	91	81	80	78	71	59	56	54	45

The SORTBY function

The SORTBY function sorts the contents of a range based on the values from other ranges. This function comes in handy when you need to apply sorting based on multiple columns. The SORTBY function takes three arguments: *Array*, *By_array*, and *Sort_order*.

The *Array* argument defines the range to sort, while the *By_array* argument specifies a range to sort by. You can sort ascending or descending using the *Sort_order* argument. Use 1 as *Sort_order* to sort ascending. Use −1 as *Sort_order* to sort descending. For instance, the following formula sorts the values in A2:C18 by the values in C2:18 in descending order.

```
=SORTBY(A2:C18, C2:C18,-1)
```

That's neat, but it's not different than using this SORT function to sort the same range by the third column (column C) in descending order:

```
=SORT(A2:C18,3,-1)
```

Well, the real power of the SORTBY function is the ability to sort by multiple columns. The formula in Figure 2-33 shows the following:

```
=SORTBY(A2:C18, A2:C18,1, C2:C18,-1, B2:B18,1)
```

In this formula, I'm sorting the range first by Market ascending (A2:C18), then by Sales descending (C2:C18), and then by Quarter ascending (B2:B18). The result gives an output containing markets in alphabetical order, sorted by the quarters with the largest sales amount.

	A	B	C	D	E	F	G
		×	✓	fx	=SORTBY(A2:C18, A2:A18,1, C2:C18,-1, B2:B18,1)		
1	Market	Quarter	Sales Amount				
2	BUFFALO	Q2	66,845		C2:C18,-1, B2:	Q3	500,297
3	BUFFALO	Q3	500,297		BUFFALO	Q1	283,337
4	BUFFALO	Q1	283,337		BUFFALO	Q2	66,845
5	CALIFORNIA	Q2	137,401		CALIFORNIA	Q1	1,138,579
6	CALIFORNIA	Q3	78,755		CALIFORNIA	Q2	137,401
7	CALIFORNIA	Q1	1,138,579		CALIFORNIA	Q3	78,755
8	CANADA	Q3	192,717		CANADA	Q1	683,529
9	CANADA	Q1	683,529		CANADA	Q3	192,717
10	CHARLOTTE	Q2	1,170,341		CHARLOTTE	Q2	1,170,341
11	CHARLOTTE	Q3	126,723		CHARLOTTE	Q1	593,458
12	CHARLOTTE	Q1	593,458		CHARLOTTE	Q3	126,723
13	DALLAS	Q2	318,807		DALLAS	Q1	352,632
14	DALLAS	Q3	295,650		DALLAS	Q2	318,807
15	DALLAS	Q1	352,632		DALLAS	Q3	295,650
16	DENVER	Q2	4,312,564		DENVER	Q2	4,312,564
17	DENVER	Q3	116,030		DENVER	Q1	516,989
18	DENVER	Q1	516,989		DENVER	Q3	116,030

FIGURE 2-33: Using the SORTBY function to apply a multi-column sort.

TIP

The SORTBY function does not require that the columns you sort by (specified by the *By_array* arguments) be part of the source data. You can sort by another range in a separate table if you want. However, the range you choose to sort by must have compatible dimensions. For instance, if your source data has 15 rows, the range by which you sort must also have 15 rows.

The UNIQUE function

The UNIQUE function extracts a list of distinct values from a range or array using just three arguments: *Array*, *By_col*, and *Exactly_once*. The *Array* argument is the only required argument. The following formula illustrates the most basic use of the UNIQUE function. This formula will extract the unique values A1:A10 to a spill range, which automatically updates when values in the source range change.

```
=UNIQUE(A1:A10)
```

The UNIQUE function works on rows by default. You can, however, tell Excel to extract unique values from columns setting the *By_col* argument to 1. In the following example, the UNIQUE function is used to extract the unique values from A1:J1 into a new spill range.

```
=UNIQUE(A1:J1,1)
```

The last argument, *Exactly_once*, tells Excel to extract values that appear only once in the given array. Figure 2-34 illustrates the difference between using a basic UNIQUE and using UNIQUE with the *Exactly_once* argument. As you can see, the values in column G show only those markets that appear one time in the source range (CANADA and TULSA).

	A	B	C	D	E	F	G
1	**Market**	**Quarter**	**Sales Amount**		=UNIQUE(A2:A13)		=UNIQUE(A2:A13,,1)
2	BUFFALO	Q2	66,845	>>	BUFFALO	>>	CANADA
3	BUFFALO	Q1	283,337		CALIFORNIA		TULSA
4	CALIFORNIA	Q2	137,401		CANADA		
5	CALIFORNIA	Q3	78,755		CHARLOTTE		
6	CANADA	Q3	192,717		DALLAS		
7	CHARLOTTE	Q3	126,723		DENVER		
8	CHARLOTTE	Q1	593,458		TULSA		
9	DALLAS	Q2	318,807				
10	DALLAS	Q1	352,632				
11	DENVER	Q2	4,312,564				
12	DENVER	Q3	116,030				
13	TULSA	Q1	516,989				

FIGURE 2-34:
Adding the *Exactly_once* argument extracts only values that appear only one time in the given range.

The FILTER function

The FILTER function extracts matching records from a data set based on criteria specified in arguments. Results are output to a spill range and are automatically updated when the source data changes. This function becomes quite useful when building a reporting model using a subset of a larger data table. The FILTER function takes three arguments: *Array*, *Include*, and *If_empty*.

The *Array* argument points to the source data you're extracting from, the *Include* argument specifies the criteria that source records must meet in order to be extracted, and the *If_empty* argument defines what should be returned if no data matches the criteria.

Take a moment to examine Figure 2-35 to see how the FILTER function works. Looking at the formula bar, you'll see I'm extracting all records from A2:D15 (the *Array* argument) if the value D2:D15 is greater than 10 (the *Include* argument). If no records match, then the formula will return No Matches (the *If_empty* argument).

TIP

Although the *If_empty* argument is technically optional, it's a best practice to always specify a value to return if the FILTER function returns no matches. Leaving the *If_empty* argument off can potentially lead to a #CALC error if none of the records in your source range meets the specified criteria.

Instead of hard coding the *Include* argument, you may find it useful to reference a cell that will hold the criteria for your FILTER function. For example, the formula used in Figure 2-36 is essentially the same as the one in Figure 2-35 except I'm getting the criteria from F1. With this setup, I can enter different values in F1 to see the results in the FILTER dynamically change.

F3				f_x	=FILTER(A2:D15,D2:D15>10,"No Matches")			
	A	B	C	D	E	F	G	H	I
1	Student	Pre-Test	Post-Test	Change					
2	Andy	56	67	11					
3	Beth	59	74	15		Andy	56	67	11
4	Cindy	98	92	-6		Beth	59	74	15
5	Duane	78	79	1		Linda P.	45	68	23
6	Linda P.	45	68	23		Michelle	71	92	21
7	Michelle	71	92	21		Linda J.	81	100	19
8	Nancy	94	83	-11		Isabel	54	69	15
9	Linda J.	81	100	19					
10	Francis	92	94	2					
11	Georgia	100	100	0					
12	Roland	91	92	1					
13	Kent	80	88	8					
14	Hilda	92	99	7					
15	Isabel	54	69	15					

FIGURE 2-35: Filtering records where the Change value is greater than 10.

=FILTER(A2:D15,D2:D15>F1,"No Matches")			
E	F	G	H	I
	15			
	Linda P.	45	68	23
	Michelle	71	92	21
	Linda J.	81	100	19

FIGURE 2-36: Getting the FILTER criteria from cell F1.

It's often useful to wrap the FILTER function inside of a SORT function to sort the filtered results. Figure 2-37 demonstrates sorting filtered results by the first column in the filtered array.

In some situations, you may need to filter a data set based on multiple criteria. To do so, you simply need to wrap each criterion in parentheses separated by an asterisk (*). For instance, Figure 2-38 expands on the formula from Figure 2-35 by adding a second criterion for name. Note that each criterion is wrapped in its own set of parentheses.

So, what's exactly going on here? Well, behind the scenes, the two conditions are evaluated for each row of the data set, resulting in a TRUE or FALSE for each respective condition. In Figure 2-39, I've broken the conditions into separate formulas to clearly illustrate the results from each.

=SORT(FILTER(A2:D15,D2:D15>F1,"No Matches"),1)

E	F	G	H	I
	10			
	Andy	56	67	11
	Beth	59	74	15
	Isabel	54	69	15
	Linda J.	81	100	19
	Linda P.	45	68	23
	Michelle	71	92	21

FIGURE 2-37: Combining SORT with FILTER to sort results.

=FILTER(A2:D15,(D2:D15>F1)*(A2:A15=H1),"No Matches")

E	F	G	H	I	J
	10		Beth		
	Beth	59	74	15	

FIGURE 2-38: Using multiple filter conditions.

	A	B	C	D	E	F	G	H
1	Student	Pre-Test	Post-Test	Change		10		Beth
2	Andy	56	67	11		=(D2:D15>F1)		=(A2:A15=H1)
3	Beth	59	74	15		TRUE		FALSE
4	Cindy	98	92	-6		TRUE		TRUE
5	Duane	78	79	1		FALSE		FALSE
6	Linda P.	45	68	23		FALSE		FALSE
7	Michelle	71	92	21		TRUE		FALSE
8	Nancy	94	83	-11		TRUE		FALSE
9	Linda J.	81	100	19		FALSE		FALSE
10	Francis	92	94	2		TRUE		FALSE
11	Georgia	100	100	0		FALSE		FALSE
12	Roland	91	92	1		FALSE		FALSE
13	Kent	80	88	8		FALSE		FALSE
14	Hilda	92	99	7		FALSE		FALSE
15	Isabel	54	69	15		FALSE		FALSE
16						TRUE		FALSE

FIGURE 2-39: Criteria evaluation behind the scenes.

In Excel, TRUE is equivalent to 1 and FALSE is equivalent to 0. The asterisk in the FILTER function (see Figure 2-38) will effectively multiply the TRUE and FALSE (1 and 0) results for each row, resulting in a 1 only for those records that show TRUE for both conditions. The asterisk can be thought of as an AND statement. Return results where the first condition is TRUE and the second condition is TRUE.

To return results if the first condition is TRUE or the second condition is TRUE, use the plus (+) operator. The formula in Figure 2-40 returns all records where the Change value is greater than 20 or the Student is Beth.

	A	B	C	D	E	F	G	H	I	J
F3			f_x	=FILTER(A2:D15,(D2:D15>F1)+(A2:A15=H1),"No Matches")						
1	Student	Pre-Test	Post-Test	Change		20		Beth		
2	Andy	56	67	11						
3	Beth	59	74	15		Beth	59	74	15	
4	Cindy	98	92	-6		Linda P.	45	68	23	
5	Duane	78	79	1		Michelle	71	92	21	
6	Linda P.	45	68	23						
7	Michelle	71	92	21						
8	Nancy	94	83	-11						
9	Linda J.	81	100	19						
10	Francis	92	94	2						
11	Georgia	100	100	0						
12	Roland	91	92	1						
13	Kent	80	88	8						
14	Hilda	92	99	7						
15	Isabel	54	69	15						

FIGURE 2-40: Using the + operator to return results if the first condition is TRUE or the second condition is TRUE.

The XLOOKUP function

The XLOOKUP function is designed to be the successor to the traditional VLOOKUP and HLOOKUP functions you may be used to. With more flexible options like approximate matching and wildcard matching, this function is truly an improved version of Excel's lookup capability. XLOOKUP accepts a whopping six arguments: *Lookup_value*, *Lookup_array*, *Return_array*, *Not_found*, *Match_mode*, and *Search_mode*.

The minimum arguments you need for XLOOKUP to work is a *Lookup_value*, a *Lookup_array*, and a *Return_array*. To understand these arguments, take a gander at Figure 2-41. In this example, I'm attempting to populate the Customer Type column (column C) based on the matching values in the table found in columns E and F. A quick look at the formula bar shows the following formula:

```
=XLOOKUP(B2:B19, E2:E5, F2:F5, "No Match")
```

This formula is telling Excel to look up the values in column B (the *Lookup_value*), match them to the values in column E (the *Lookup_array*), and return the matching value in column F (the *Return_array*). The final argument (*Not_found*) defines what should be returned if no data matches the lookup criteria. Although the *Not_found* argument is optional, it's typically best practice to include it to avoid the ugly #N/A errors you get when a value isn't found.

TIP

When building your XLOOKUP, keep in mind that the *Lookup_array* argument must have the same dimensions as the *Return_array*. That is, the same number of rows/columns.

| C2 | | ▼ | : | × | ✓ | f_x | =XLOOKUP(B2:B19,E2:E5,F2:F5,"No Match") |

◢	A	B	C	D	E	F
1	CustomerName	Revenue	Customer Type		Revenue	Customer Type
2	Communication Connections	$5,000	C		30000	A
3	Aaron Fitz Electrical	$30,000	A		10000	B
4	Astor Suite	$10,000	B		5000	C
5	Blue Yonder Airlines	$9,306	No Match		1000	D
6	Central Communications LTD	$11,975	No Match			
7	Computerized Phone Systems	$59	No Match			
8	Country View Estates	$19	No Match			
9	Lawrence Telemarketing	$50,024	No Match			
10	Leisure & Travel Consultants	$92	No Match			
11	Magnificent Office Images	$9,489	No Match			
12	Mahler State University	$11,161	No Match			

FIGURE 2-41:
A basic XLOOKUP function to find Customer Type based on revenue.

As you look at Figure 2-41, you'll notice that the XLOOKUP function found a Customer Type only for those records that exactly match the revenue in the *Lookup_array* (column E). In many cases, you won't find an exact match, especially when trying to match numbers like revenue. In my example, I want to perform an approximate match on my records to catch even those revenues that don't exactly match the values in my lookup table. To do so, I can add the *Match_mode* argument.

Entering a comma after the *Not_found* argument will bring up a list of choices (see Figure 2-42). The one you choose will depend on what exactly you're trying to achieve. It's best to experiment with each option to see which option is right for you. In this case, I want to apply the option for Exact match or next smaller item. Selecting the appropriate option will immediately retrieve the valid customer types. Figure 2-43 shows the result of the applied approximate matching.

| =XLOOKUP(B2:B19,E2:E5,F2:F5,"No Match",) | | | | | |

G	H	I	J	K	L
			(…)0 - Exact match		
			(…)-1 - Exact match or next smaller item		
			(…)1 - Exact match or next larger item		
			(…)2 - Wildcard character match		

FIGURE 2-42:
Enter a comma to see choices for the next argument.

In rare cases, you can use the *Search_mode* argument to dictate how Excel performs the search for the XLOOKUP. For this argument, you have the following options:

≫ **1:** This is the default search mode and will be the most appropriate in most of your lookup scenarios.

>> **–1:** Search from the last value in the array up (essentially reverse order of the default behavior).

>> **2:** Binary search on values that are already sorted in ascending order. This mode is used to improve performance on very large arrays. Binary searches are fast, but if your data is not sorted as prescribed, your XLOOKUP can return invalid results.

>> **–2:** Binary search on values that are already sorted in descending order. Again, this mode is used to improve performance, but you'll want to ensure your data is sorted as prescribed, or your XLOOKUP will return invalid results.

| C2 | | × | ✓ | *fx* | =XLOOKUP(B2:B19,E2:E5,F2:F5,"No Match",-1) | | |

	A	B	C	D	E	F
1	CustomerName	Revenue	Customer Type		Revenue	Customer Type
2	Communication Connections	$5,000	C		30000	A
3	Aaron Fitz Electrical	$30,000	A		10000	B
4	Astor Suite	$10,000	B		5000	C
5	Blue Yonder Airlines	$9,306	C		1000	D
6	Central Communications LTD	$11,975	B			
7	Computerized Phone Systems	$59	No Match			
8	Country View Estates	$19	No Match			
9	Lawrence Telemarketing	$50,024	A			
10	Leisure & Travel Consultants	$92	No Match			
11	Magnificent Office Images	$9,489	C			
12	Mahler State University	$11,161	B			
13	Metropolitan Fiber Systems	$10,686	B			

FIGURE 2-43: XLOOKUP results using approximate matching.

TIP

When using XLOOKUP to match across workbooks, both workbooks must be open, or Excel will return a #REF! error.

One of the options for the *Match_mode* argument is Wildcard character match (see Figure 2-42). Wildcards are special characters that enable complex searches using approximate matching. Excel allows the use of three different wildcard characters, each with its own purpose.

>> **Asterisk (*):** The asterisk wildcard is used to tell your formula to look for a portion of text no matter what comes before or after. For example, searching for *hotel will look for any value that ends with the word *hotel*, no matter what comes before. Searching for hotel* will look for any value that starts with *hotel*, no matter what comes after. And as you may have guessed, searching for *hotel* will look for any value containing the word *hotel*.

>> **Question mark (?):** The question mark wildcard is used to tell your formula to look for any one character within a text. For instance, searching for p?ace would return both *peace* and *place*. You can use multiple question mark wildcards in a search (??onder and sm?itt?n are both valid searches). In addition, you can combine the asterisk and question mark wildcards to create a more complex search. For example, searching for *vis??* would return any text string containing the word *visor* or *vision*.

>> **Tilde (~):** The tilde wildcard is useful when you need to include a character that is, itself, a wildcard. For example, if you need to search for any text string that ends in a question mark, you'll need to preface the question mark with a tilde because the question mark itself is a wildcard (*~?). The same goes for the asterisk. To search for any text string that starts with an asterisk, you would use ~**.

Figure 2-44 demonstrates the use of wildcard characters. In column J, XLOOKUP searches for the Revenue (B2:B19) where the Customer Name contains the letters *LTD*. In column L, XLOOKUP searches for the Revenue where the Customer Name contains *f?tz*.

J2				f_x	=SUM(XLOOKUP(J1,A2:A19,B2:B19,"no match",2))				
	A	B	D	J	K	L	M	
1	**CustomerName**	**Revenue**		*LTD*		*f?tz*		
2	Communication Connections	$5,000		$11,975		$30,000		
3	Aaron Fitz Electrical	$30,000						
4	Astor Suite	$10,000						
5	Blue Yonder Airlines	$9,306						
6	Central Communications LTD	$11,975						
7	Computerized Phone Systems	$59						

FIGURE 2-44: Using wildcard characters to perform complex searches.

IN THIS CHAPTER

» **Introducing pivot tables**

» **Building your first pivot table**

» **Customizing your pivot tables**

» **Using pivot-driven reports**

» **Creating top and bottom reports**

Chapter **3**

The Pivotal Pivot Table

know what you're thinking: "Am I supposed to be jumping right in with pivot tables?" My answer is an emphatic yes!

In Chapter 2, I introduce the concept of reporting models that separate the data, analysis, and presentation layers. As you discover in this chapter, pivot tables lend themselves nicely to this concept. With pivot tables, you can build reporting models that not only are easy to set up, but can also be refreshed with the simple press of a button. Then you can spend less time maintaining your dashboards and reports and more time doing other useful things. No utility in the whole of Excel allows you to achieve this efficient data model better than a pivot table.

Pivot tables have a reputation for being complicated, but if you're new to pivot tables, relax a bit. After reading this introduction, you'll be pleasantly surprised at how easy it is to create and use pivot tables. Later, you'll find some time-saving techniques to help create useful pivot-driven views for your dashboards and reports.

An Introduction to the Pivot Table

A *pivot table* is a robust tool that allows you to create an interactive view of your data set, commonly referred to as a *pivot table report*. With a pivot table report, you can quickly and easily categorize your data into groups, summarize large amounts of data into meaningful analyses, and interactively perform a wide variety of calculations.

Pivot tables get their name from the way they allow you to drag and drop fields within the pivot table report to dynamically change (or *pivot*) perspective and give you an entirely new analysis using the same data source.

Think of a pivot table as an object you can point at your data set. When you look at your data set through a pivot table, you can see your data from different perspectives. The data set itself doesn't change, and it's not connected to the pivot table. The pivot table is simply a tool you're using to dynamically change analyses, apply varying calculations, and interactively drill down to the detail records.

The reason a pivot table is so well suited for dashboarding and reporting is that you can refresh the analyses shown through the pivot table simply by updating the data set it's pointed to. This allows you to set up your analysis and presentation layers only one time; then, to refresh your reporting mechanism, all you have to do is press a button.

Let's start this exploration of pivot tables with a lesson on the anatomy of a pivot table.

The Four Areas of a Pivot Table

A pivot table is composed of four areas. The data you place in these areas defines both the utility and appearance of the pivot table. Take a moment to understand the function of each of these four areas.

Values area

The *values area*, as shown in Figure 3-1, is the large rectangular area below and to the right of the column and row headings. In the example in Figure 3-1, the values area contains a sum of the values in the Sales Amount field.

The values area calculates and counts data. The data fields that you drag and drop here are typically those that you want to measure — fields such as Sum of Revenue, Count of Units, or Average of Price.

Region	(All)		

Sales Amount	Segment		
Market	Accessories	Bikes	Clothing	Components
Australia	23,974	1,351,873	43,232	203,791
Canada	119,303	11,714,700	383,022	2,246,255
Central	46,551	6,782,978	155,874	947,448
France	48,942	3,597,879	129,508	871,125
Germany	35,681	1,602,487	75,593	337,787
Northeast	51,246	5,690,285	163,442	1,051,702
Northwest	53,308	10,484,495	201,052	1,784,207
Southeast	45,736	6,737,556	165,689	959,337
Southwest	110,080	15,430,281	364,099	2,693,568
United Kingdom	43,180	3,435,134	120,225	712,588

Values Area

FIGURE 3-1: The values area of a pivot table calculates and counts data.

Row area

The *row area* is shown in Figure 3-2. Placing a data field into the row area displays the unique values from that field down the rows of the left side of the pivot table. The row area typically has at least one field, although it's possible to have no fields.

Region	(All)		

Sales Amount	Segment		
Market	Accessories	Bikes	Clothing	Components
Australia	23,974	1,351,873	43,232	203,791
Canada	119,303	11,714,700	383,022	2,246,255
Central	46,551	6,782,978	155,874	947,448
France	48,942	3,597,879	129,508	871,125
Germany	35,681	1,602,487	75,593	337,787
Northeast	51,246	5,690,285	163,442	1,051,702
Northwest	53,308	10,484,495	201,052	1,784,207
Southeast	45,736	6,737,556	165,689	959,337
Southwest	110,080	15,430,281	364,099	2,693,568
United Kingdom	43,180	3,435,134	120,225	712,588

Row Area

FIGURE 3-2: The row area of a pivot table gives you a row-oriented perspective.

The types of data fields that you would drop here include those that you want to group and categorize, such as Products, Names, and Locations.

Column area

The *column area* is composed of headings that stretch across the top of columns in the pivot table.

As you can see in Figure 3-3, the column area stretches across the top of the columns. In this example, it contains the unique list of business segments.

Column Area

Region	(All)			
Sales Amount	Segment			
Market	Accessories	Bikes	Clothing	Components
Australia	23,974	1,351,873	43,232	203,791
Canada	119,303	11,714,700	383,022	2,246,255
Central	46,551	6,782,978	155,874	947,448
France	48,942	3,597,879	129,508	871,125
Germany	35,681	1,602,487	75,593	337,787
Northeast	51,246	5,690,285	163,442	1,051,702
Northwest	53,308	10,484,495	201,052	1,784,207
Southeast	45,736	6,737,556	165,689	959,337
Southwest	110,080	15,430,281	364,099	2,693,568
United Kingdom	43,180	3,435,134	120,225	712,588

FIGURE 3-3: The column area of a pivot table gives you a column-oriented perspective.

Placing a data field into the column area displays the unique values from that field in a column-oriented perspective. The column area is ideal for creating a data matrix or showing trends over time.

Filter area

The *filter area* is an optional set of one or more drop-down menus at the top of the pivot table. In Figure 3-4, the filter area contains the Region field, and the pivot table is set to show all regions.

Filter Area

Region	(All)			
Sales Amount	Segment			
Market	Accessories	Bikes	Clothing	Components
Australia	23,974	1,351,873	43,232	203,791
Canada	119,303	11,714,700	383,022	2,246,255
Central	46,551	6,782,978	155,874	947,448
France	48,942	3,597,879	129,508	871,125
Germany	35,681	1,602,487	75,593	337,787
Northeast	51,246	5,690,285	163,442	1,051,702
Northwest	53,308	10,484,495	201,052	1,784,207
Southeast	45,736	6,737,556	165,689	959,337
Southwest	110,080	15,430,281	364,099	2,693,568
United Kingdom	43,180	3,435,134	120,225	712,588

FIGURE 3-4: The filter area allows you to easily apply filters to a pivot table report.

Placing data fields into the filter area allows you to filter the entire pivot table based on your selections. The types of data fields that you'd drop here include those that you want to isolate and focus on — for example, Region, Line of Business, and Employees.

Creating Your First Pivot Table

If you've followed along in this chapter, you now have a good understanding of the basic structure of a pivot table, so let's quit all the talking and use the following instructions to walk through the creation of your first pivot table.

TIP

You can find the sample file for this chapter on this book's companion website.

Follow these steps:

1. **Click any single cell inside the *data source* — the table you'll use to feed the pivot table.**

2. **Select the Insert tab on the Ribbon and then click the PivotTable icon, as shown in Figure 3-5.**

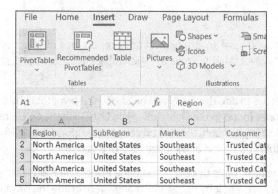

FIGURE 3-5:
Start a pivot table via the Insert tab.

3. **From the drop-down menu that appears, choose PivotTable.**

   This step activates the Create PivotTable dialog box, as shown in Figure 3-6. As you can see, this dialog box asks you to specify the location of your source data and the place you want to put the pivot table.

REMEMBER

   Notice that in the Create PivotTable dialog box, Excel makes an attempt to fill in the range of your data for you. In most cases, Excel gets this right. However, always make sure the correct range is selected.

You will also note in Figure 3-6 that the default location for a new pivot table is New Worksheet. This means the pivot table will be placed in a new worksheet within the current workbook. You can change this by selecting the Existing Worksheet option and specifying the worksheet where you want the pivot table placed.

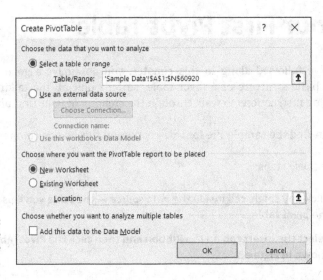

FIGURE 3-6:
The Create PivotTable dialog box.

4. **Click OK.**

   At this point, you have an empty pivot table report on a new worksheet. Next to the empty pivot table, you see the PivotTable Fields task pane, shown in Figure 3-7.

   The idea here is to add the fields you need into the pivot table by using the four *drop zones* found in the PivotTable Field List — Filters, Columns, Rows, and Values. Pleasantly enough, these drop zones correspond to the four areas of the pivot table you review at the beginning of this chapter.

TIP

   If clicking the pivot table doesn't activate the PivotTable Fields task pane, you can manually activate it by right-clicking anywhere inside the pivot table and selecting Show Field List from the menu that appears.

   Now, before you go wild and start dropping fields into the various drop zones, you should ask yourself two questions: "What am I measuring?" and "How do I want to see it?" The answers to these questions give you some guidance when determining which fields go where.

   For your first pivot table report, you measure the dollar sales by market. This automatically tells you that you will need to work with the Sales Amount field and the Market field.

How do you want to see that? You want markets to go down the left side of the report and sales amounts to be calculated next to each market. Remembering the four areas of the pivot table, you'll need to add the Market field to the Rows drop zone and add the Sales Amount field to the Values drop zone.

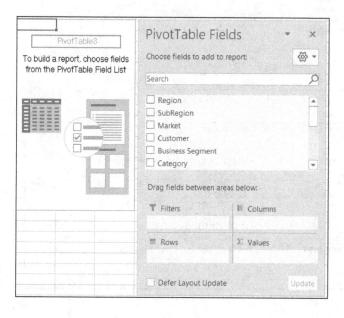

FIGURE 3-7:
The PivotTable
Fields task pane.

5. **Select the Market check box in the list, as demonstrated in Figure 3-8.**

   Now that you have regions in your pivot table, it's time to add the dollar sales.

6. **Select the Sales Amount check box in the list, as demonstrated in Figure 3-9.**

TIP

Selecting a check box that is *nonnumeric* (text or date) automatically places that field into the row area of the pivot table. Selecting a check box that is *numeric* automatically places that field in the values area of the pivot table.

What happens if you need fields in the other areas of the pivot table? Well, instead of selecting the field's check box, you can drag any field directly to the different drop zones.

One more thing: When you add fields to the drop zones, you may find it difficult to see all fields in each drop zone. You can expand the PivotTable Fields task pane by clicking and dragging the borders of the task pane.

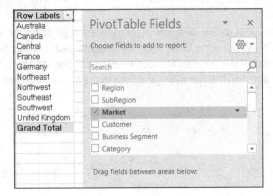

As you can see, you have just analyzed the sales for each market in only six steps! That's an amazing feat, considering that you start with more than 60,000 rows of data. With a little formatting, this modest pivot table can become the starting point for a management dashboard or report.

Changing and rearranging your pivot table

Here's the wonderful thing about pivot tables: You can add as many layers of analysis as made possible by the fields in your source data table. Say that you want to show the dollar sales each market earned by business segment. Because the pivot table already contains the Market and Sales Amount fields, all you have to add is the Business Segment field.

So simply click anywhere on the pivot table to reactivate the PivotTable Fields task pane and then select the Business Segment check box. Figure 3-10 illustrates what the pivot table should look like now.

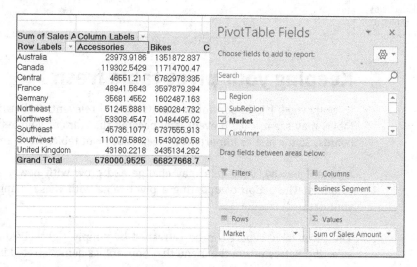

FIGURE 3-10:
Adding a layer of
analysis is as easy
as bringing in
another field.

REMEMBER

If clicking the pivot table doesn't activate the PivotTable Fields task pane, you can manually activate it by right-clicking anywhere inside the pivot table and selecting Show Field List from the menu that appears.

Imagine that your manager says that this layout doesn't work for them. They want to see business segments going across the top of the pivot table report. No problem. Simply drag the Business Segment field from the Rows drop zone to the Columns drop zone. As you can see in Figure 3-11, this instantly restructures the pivot table to their specifications.

FIGURE 3-11:
Your business
segments are
now column-
oriented.

Adding a report filter

Often, you're asked to produce reports for one particular region, market, product, and so on. Instead of working hours and hours building separate reports for every possible analysis scenario, you can leverage pivot tables to help create multiple views of the same data. For example, you can do so by creating a region filter in your pivot table.

Click anywhere on the pivot table to reactivate the PivotTable Fields task pane and then drag the Region field to the Filters drop zone. This adds a drop-down selector to the pivot table, as shown in Figure 3-12. You can then use this selector to analyze one particular region at a time.

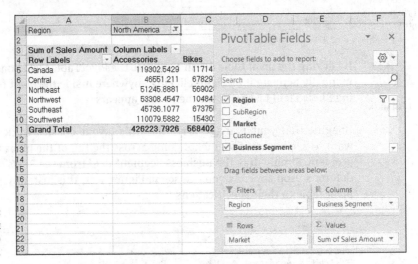

FIGURE 3-12:
Using pivot tables to analyze regions.

Keeping your pivot table fresh

In Hollywood, it's important to stay fresh and relevant. As boring as your pivot tables may seem, they'll eventually become the stars of your reports and dashboards. So it's just as important to keep your pivot tables fresh and relevant.

As time goes by, your data may change and grow with newly added rows and columns. The action of updating a pivot table with these changes is *refreshing* your data.

The pivot table report can be refreshed by simply right-clicking inside it and selecting Refresh from the menu that appears, as demonstrated in Figure 3-13.

Sometimes, *you're* the data source that feeds your pivot table changes in structure. For example, you may have added or deleted rows or columns from your data table. These types of changes affect the range of your data source, not just a few data items in the table.

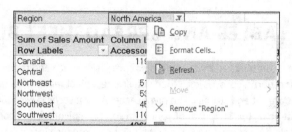

FIGURE 3-13:
Refreshing your
pivot table
captures changes
made to
your data.

In these cases, performing a simple Refresh of the pivot table won't do. You have to update the range being captured by the pivot table. Here's how:

1. **Click anywhere inside the pivot table to activate the PivotTable Analyze contextual tab on the Ribbon.**

2. **Select the PivotTable Analyze tab on the Ribbon.**

3. **Click the tab's Change Data Source icon and choose Change Data Source from the menu that appears, as demonstrated in Figure 3-14.**

   The Change PivotTable Data Source dialog box appears.

4. **Change the range selection to include any new rows or columns (see Figure 3-15).**

5. **Click OK to apply the change.**

FIGURE 3-14:
Changing the
range that feeds
the pivot table.

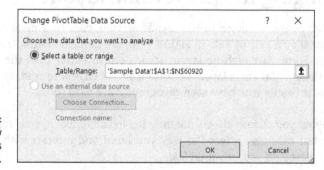

FIGURE 3-15:
Select the new
range that feeds
the pivot table.

PIVOT TABLES AND SPREADSHEET BLOAT

It's important to understand that pivot tables come with space and memory implications for your reporting processes. When you create a pivot table, Excel takes a snapshot of your data set and stores it in a pivot cache. A *pivot cache* is essentially a memory container that holds this snapshot of your data set. Each pivot table report you create from a separate data source creates its own pivot cache, which increases your workbook's memory usage and file size. The increase in memory usage and file size depends on the size of the original data source that's being duplicated to create the pivot cache.

Simple enough, right? Well, here's the rub: You often need to create separate pivot tables from the same data source in order to analyze the same data in different ways. If you create two pivot tables from the data source, a new pivot cache is automatically created even though one may already exist for the data set being used. This means that you're bloating your spreadsheet with redundant data each time you create a new pivot table using the same data set.

To work around this potential problem, you can employ Copy and then Paste. That's right: Simply copying a pivot table and pasting it somewhere else will create another pivot table *without* duplicating the pivot cache. This allows you to create multiple pivot tables that use the same source data, with negligible increases in memory and file size.

Customizing Pivot Table Reports

The pivot tables you create often need to be tweaked to get the look and feel you're looking for. In this section, I cover some of the options you can adjust to customize your pivot tables to suit your reporting needs.

Changing the pivot table layout

Excel gives you a choice in the layout of your data in a pivot table. The three layouts, shown side by side in Figure 3-16, are Compact Form, Outline Form, and Tabular Form. Although no layout stands out as better than the others, I prefer using the Tabular Form layout because it seems easiest to read, and it's the layout that most people who have seen pivot tables are used to.

REMEMBER

The layout you choose affects not only the look and feel of your reporting mechanisms but may also affect the way you build and interact with any dashboard models based on your pivot tables.

Compact Form Layout			Outline Form Layout				Tabular Form Layout		
Row Labels	Sales		Market	Segment	Sales		Market	Segment	Sales
⊟ Australia	1622869.422		⊟ Australia		1622869.422		⊟ Australia	Accessories	23973.9186
Accessories	23973.9186			Accessories	23973.9186			Bikes	1351872.837
Bikes	1351872.837			Bikes	1351872.837			Clothing	43231.6124
Clothing	43231.6124			Clothing	43231.6124			Components	203791.0536
Components	203791.0536			Components	203791.0536		Australia Total		1622869.422
⊟ Canada	14463280.15		⊟ Canada		14463280.15		⊟ Canada	Accessories	119302.5429
Accessories	119302.5429			Accessories	119302.5429			Bikes	11714700.47
Bikes	11714700.47			Bikes	11714700.47			Clothing	383021.7229
Clothing	383021.7229			Clothing	383021.7229			Components	2246255.419
Components	2246255.419			Components	2246255.419		Canada Total		14463280.15
⊟ Central	7932851.609		⊟ Central		7932851.609		⊟ Central	Accessories	46551.211
Accessories	46551.211			Accessories	46551.211			Bikes	6782978.335
Bikes	6782978.335			Bikes	6782978.335			Clothing	155873.9547
Clothing	155873.9547			Clothing	155873.9547			Components	947448.1091
Components	947448.1091			Components	947448.1091		Central Total		7932851.609
⊟ France	4647454.207		⊟ France		4647454.207		⊟ France	Accessories	48941.5643
Accessories	48941.5643			Accessories	48941.5643			Bikes	3597879.394
Bikes	3597879.394			Bikes	3597879.394			Clothing	129508.0548
Clothing	129508.0548			Clothing	129508.0548			Components	871125.1938
Components	871125.1938			Components	871125.1938		France Total		4647454.207
⊟ Germany	2051547.729		⊟ Germany		2051547.729		⊟ Germany	Accessories	35681.4552
Accessories	35681.4552			Accessories	35681.4552			Bikes	1602487.163
Bikes	1602487.163			Bikes	1602487.163			Clothing	75592.5945
Clothing	75592.5945			Clothing	75592.5945			Components	337786.516
Components	337786.516			Components	337786.516		Germany Total		2051547.729

FIGURE 3-16:
The three layouts for a pivot table report.

Changing the layout of a pivot table is easy. Follow these steps:

1. **Click anywhere inside the pivot table to activate the Design contextual tab on the Ribbon.**

2. **Select the Design tab on the Ribbon.**

3. **Click the Report Layout icon and choose the layout you like from the menu that appears (see Figure 3-17).**

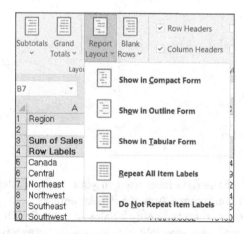

FIGURE 3-17:
Changing the layout of the pivot table.

Customizing field names

Notice that every field in your pivot table has a name. The fields in the row, column, and filter areas inherit their names from the data labels in the source table. The fields in the values area are given a name, such as Sum of Sales Amount.

Sometimes you might prefer the name Total Sales instead of the unattractive default name, like Sum of Sales Amount. In these situations, the ability to change your field names is handy. To change a field name, do the following:

1. **Right-click any value within the target field.**

    For example, if you want to change the name of the field Sum of Sales Amount, you right-click any value under that field.

2. **Select Value Field Settings from the menu that appears, as shown in Figure 3-18.**

    The Value Field Settings dialog box appears.

    Note that if you were changing the name of a field in the row or column area, this selection is Field Settings.

3. **Enter the new name in the Custom Name input box, shown in Figure 3-19.**

4. **Click OK to apply the change.**

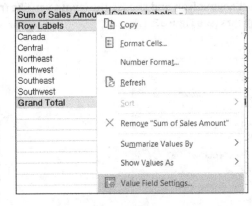

FIGURE 3-18:
Right-click any value in the target field to select the Value Field Settings option.

TIP

If you use the name of the data label used in your source table, you receive an error. For example, if you rename Sum of Sales Amount as Sales Amount, you get an error message because there's already a Sales Amount field in the source data table. Well, this is kinda lame, especially if Sales Amount is exactly what you want to name the field in the your pivot table.

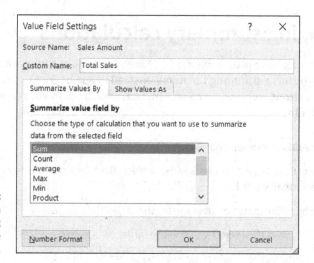

To get around this, you can name the field and add a space to the end of the name. Excel considers Sales Amount (followed by a space) to be different from Sales Amount. This way, you can use the name you want and no one will notice that it's any different.

Applying numeric formats to data fields

Numbers in pivot tables can be formatted to fit your needs — that is, formatted as currency, percentage, or number. You can easily control the numeric formatting of a field using the Value Field Settings dialog box. Here's how:

1. **Right-click any value within the target field.**

   For example, if you want to change the format of the values in the Sales Amount field, right-click any value under that field.

2. **Select Value Field Settings from the menu that appears.**

   The Value Field Settings dialog box appears.

3. **Click the Number Format button.**

   The Format Cells dialog box opens.

4. **Apply the number format you desire, just as you typically would on your spreadsheet.**

5. **Click OK to apply the changes.**

   After you set the formatting for a field, the applied formatting will persist even if you refresh or rearrange the pivot table.

Changing summary calculations

When creating your pivot table report, Excel, by default, summarizes your data by either counting or summing the items. Instead of Sum or Count, you might want to choose functions, such as Average, Min, Max, and so on. In all, 11 options are available, including

>> Sum: Adds all numeric data.

>> Count: Counts all data items within a given field, including numeric-, text-, and date-formatted cells.

>> Average: Calculates an average for the target data items.

>> Max: Displays the largest value in the target data items.

>> Min: Displays the smallest value in the target data items.

>> Product: Multiplies all target data items together.

>> Count Nums: Counts only the numeric cells in the target data items.

>> StdDevP and StdDev: Calculates the standard deviation for the target data items. Use StdDevP if your data set contains the complete population. Use StdDev if your data set contains a sample of the population.

>> VarP and Var: Calculates the statistical variance for the target data items. Use VarP if your data contains a complete population. If your data contains only a sampling of the complete population, use Var to estimate the variance.

You can easily change the summary calculation for any given field by taking the following actions:

1. **Right-click any value within the target field.**

2. **Select Value Field Settings from the menu that appears.**

   The Value Field Settings dialog box appears.

3. **Choose the type of calculation you want to use from the list of calculations (see Figure 3-20).**

4. **Click OK to apply the changes.**

REMEMBER

Did you know that a single blank cell causes Excel to count instead of sum? That's right. If all the cells in a column contain numeric data, Excel chooses Sum. If just one cell is either blank or contains text, Excel chooses Count.

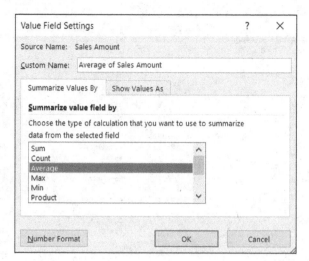

Be sure to pay attention to the fields that you place into the values area of the pivot table. If the field name starts with Count Of, Excel's counting the items in the field instead of summing the values.

Suppressing subtotals

Notice that each time you add a field to your pivot table, Excel adds a subtotal for that field. There may be times however, when the inclusion of subtotals either doesn't make sense or just hinders a clear view of the pivot table report. For example, Figure 3-21 shows a pivot table in which the subtotals inundate the report with totals that hide the real data you're trying to report.

Removing all subtotals at one time

You can remove all subtotals at one time by taking these actions:

1. **Click anywhere inside the pivot table to activate the Design contextual tab on the Ribbon.**

2. **Select the Design tab on the Ribbon.**

3. **Click the Subtotals icon and select Do Not Show Subtotals from the menu that appears, as shown in Figure 3-22.**

	A	B	C	D	E
1	Region	SubRegion	Market	Business Segment	Sum of Sales Amount
2	North America	United States	Central	Accessories	46,551
3				Bikes	6,782,978
4				Clothing	155,874
5				Components	947,448
6			Central Total		7,932,852
7			Northeast	Accessories	51,246
8				Bikes	5,690,285
9				Clothing	163,442
10				Components	1,051,702
11			Northeast Total		6,956,674
12			Northwest	Accessories	53,308
13				Bikes	10,484,495
14				Clothing	201,052
15				Components	1,784,207
16			Northwest Total		12,523,063
17			Southeast	Accessories	45,736
18				Bikes	6,737,556
19				Clothing	165,689
20				Components	959,337
21			Southeast Total		7,908,318
22			Southwest	Accessories	110,080
23				Bikes	15,430,281
24				Clothing	364,099
25				Components	2,693,568
26			Southwest Total		18,598,027
27		United States Total			53,918,934
28	North America Total				53,918,934

FIGURE 3-21:
Subtotals
sometimes
muddle the data
you're trying
to show.

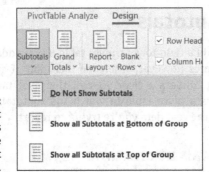

FIGURE 3-22:
Use the Do Not
Show Subtotals
option to remove
all subtotals at
one time.

As you can see in Figure 3-23, the same report without subtotals is much more pleasant to review.

Removing the subtotals for only one field

Maybe you want to remove the subtotals for only one field? In such a case, you can take the following actions:

1. **Right-click any value within the target field.**

2. **Select Field Settings from the menu that appears.**

    The Field Settings dialog box appears.

3. Choose the None option under Subtotals, as demonstrated in Figure 3-24.

4. Click OK to apply the changes.

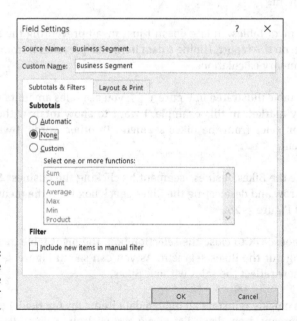

	A	B	C	D	E
1	Region ▼	SubRegion ▼	Market ▼	Business Segment ▼	Sum of Sales Amount
2	⊟ North America	⊟ United States	⊟ Central	Accessories	46,551
3				Bikes	6,782,978
4				Clothing	155,874
5				Components	947,448
6			⊟ Northeast	Accessories	51,246
7				Bikes	5,690,285
8				Clothing	163,442
9				Components	1,051,702
10			⊟ Northwest	Accessories	53,308
11				Bikes	10,484,495
12				Clothing	201,052
13				Components	1,784,207
14			⊟ Southeast	Accessories	45,736
15				Bikes	6,737,556
16				Clothing	165,689
17				Components	959,337
18			⊟ Southwest	Accessories	110,080
19				Bikes	15,430,281
20				Clothing	364,099
21				Components	2,693,568
22	Grand Total				53,918,934

FIGURE 3-23:
The report shown in Figure 3-21, without subtotals.

FIGURE 3-24:
Choose the None option to remove subtotals for one field.

Removing grand totals

There may be instances when you want to remove the grand totals from your pivot table:

1. **Right-click anywhere on the pivot table.**

2. **Select PivotTable Options from the menu that appears.**

   The PivotTable Options dialog box appears.

3. **Click the Totals & Filters tab.**

4. **Click the Show Grand Totals for Rows check box to deselect it.**

5. **Click the Show Grand Totals for Columns check box to deselect it.**

6. **Click OK to apply the changes.**

Showing and hiding data items

A pivot table summarizes and displays all records in the source data table. There may be situations, however, when you want to inhibit certain data items from being included in the pivot table summary. In these situations, you can choose to hide a data item.

In terms of pivot tables, hiding doesn't just mean preventing the data item from being shown on the report. Hiding a data item also prevents it from being factored into the summary calculations.

In the pivot table illustrated in Figure 3-25, you see sales amounts for all business segments by market. In this example, I want to show totals without taking into consideration sales from the Bikes segment. In other words, I want to hide the Bikes segment.

You can hide the Bikes business segment by clicking the Business Segment drop-down list arrow and deselecting the Bikes check box from the menu that appears, as shown in Figure 3-26.

After you choose OK to close the selection box, the pivot table instantly recalculates, leaving out the Bikes segment. As you can see in Figure 3-27, the Market total sales now reflect the sales without Bikes.

I can just as quickly reinstate all hidden data items for my field. I simply click the Business Segment drop-down list arrow and click the Select All check box from the menu that appears, as shown in Figure 3-28.

	A	B	C
1	Market ▾	Business Segment ▾	Sum of Sales Amount
2	⊟ Australia	Accessories	$23,974
3		Bikes	$1,351,873
4		Clothing	$43,232
5		Components	$203,791
6	Australia Total		$1,622,869
7	⊟ Canada	Accessories	$119,303
8		Bikes	$11,714,700
9		Clothing	$383,022
10		Components	$2,246,255
11	Canada Total		$14,463,280
12	⊟ Central	Accessories	$46,551
13		Bikes	$6,782,978
14		Clothing	$155,874
15		Components	$947,448
16	Central Total		$7,932,852
17	⊟ France	Accessories	$48,942

FIGURE 3-25:
To remove Bikes from this analysis . . .

FIGURE 3-26:
. . . deselect the Bikes check box.

	A	B	C
1	Market ▾	Business Segment 🔽	Sum of Sales Amount
2	⊟ Australia	Accessories	$23,974
3		Clothing	$43,232
4		Components	$203,791
5	Australia Total		$270,997
6	⊟ Canada	Accessories	$119,303
7		Clothing	$383,022
8		Components	$2,246,255
9	Canada Total		$2,748,580
10	⊟ Central	Accessories	$46,551
11		Clothing	$155,874
12		Components	$947,448
13	Central Total		$1,149,873
14	⊟ France	Accessories	$48,942

FIGURE 3-27:
The analysis from Figure 3-25, without the Bikes segment.

FIGURE 3-28:
Clicking the Select
All check box
forces all data
items in that field
to become
unhidden.

Hiding or showing items without data

By default, the pivot table shows only data items that have data. This inherent behavior may cause unintended problems for your data analysis.

Look at Figure 3-29, which shows a pivot table with the SalesPeriod field in the row area and the Region field in the filter area. Note that the Region field is set to (All) and that every sales period appears in the report.

	A	B
1	Region	(All)
2		
3	SalesPeriod	Sum of Sales Amount
4	01/01/08	$713,230
5	02/01/08	$1,900,797
6	03/01/08	$1,455,282
7	04/01/08	$883,011
8	05/01/08	$2,269,722
9	06/01/08	$1,137,250
10	07/01/08	$2,411,569
11	08/01/08	$3,615,926

FIGURE 3-29:
All sales periods
are showing.

If I choose Europe in the filter area, only a portion of all the sales periods will show (see Figure 3-30). The pivot table will show only those sales periods that apply to the Europe region.

Displaying only those items with data could cause trouble if I plan to use this pivot table as the feeder for my charts or other dashboard components. From a dashboarding-and-reporting perspective, it wouldn't be ideal if half the year's data disappeared every time customers selected Europe.

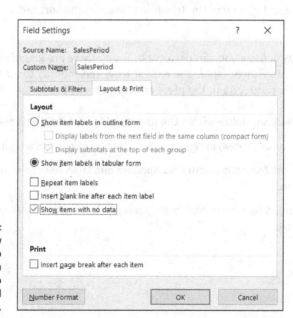

	A	B
1	Region	Europe
2		
3	SalesPeriod	Sum of Sales Amount
4	07/01/08	$180,241
5	08/01/08	$448,373
6	09/01/08	$373,122
7	10/01/08	$119,384
8	11/01/08	$330,026
9	12/01/08	$254,011
10	01/01/09	$71,313
11	02/01/09	$264,487

FIGURE 3-30:
Filtering for the Europe region causes some sales periods to disappear.

Here's how you can prevent Excel from hiding pivot items without data:

1. **Right-click any value within the target field.**

   In this example, the target field is the SalesPeriod field.

2. **Select Field Settings from the menu that appears.**

   The Field Settings dialog box appears.

3. **Select the Layout & Print tab in the Field Settings dialog box.**

4. **Select the Show Items with No Data option, as shown in Figure 3-31.**

5. **Click OK to apply the change.**

FIGURE 3-31:
Click the Show Items with No Data option to force Excel to display all data items.

As you can see in Figure 3-32, after you choose the Show Items with No Data option, all sales periods appear whether the selected region had sales that period or not.

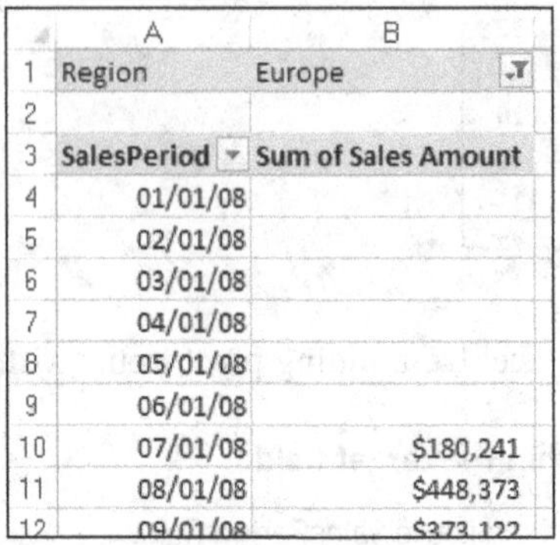

FIGURE 3-32:
All sales periods
are now
displayed, even if
there is no data
to be shown.

	A	B
1	Region	Europe
2		
3	SalesPeriod	Sum of Sales Amount
4	01/01/08	
5	02/01/08	
6	03/01/08	
7	04/01/08	
8	05/01/08	
9	06/01/08	
10	07/01/08	$180,241
11	08/01/08	$448,373
12	09/01/08	$373,122

After you're confident that the structure of the pivot table is locked down, you can use it to feed charts and other components on the dashboard.

Sorting your pivot table

By default, items in each pivot field are sorted in ascending sequence based on the item name. Excel gives you the freedom to change the sort order of the items in a pivot table.

As with many actions you can perform in Excel, there are lots of different ways to sort data within a pivot table. The easiest way, and the way that I use the most, is to apply the sort directly in the pivot table. Here's how:

1. **Right-click any value within the *target field* — the field you need to sort.**

   In the example shown in Figure 3-33, I want to sort by sales amount.

2. **Select Sort from the menu that appears and then select the sort direction.**

   The changes take effect immediately and persist while you work with the pivot table.

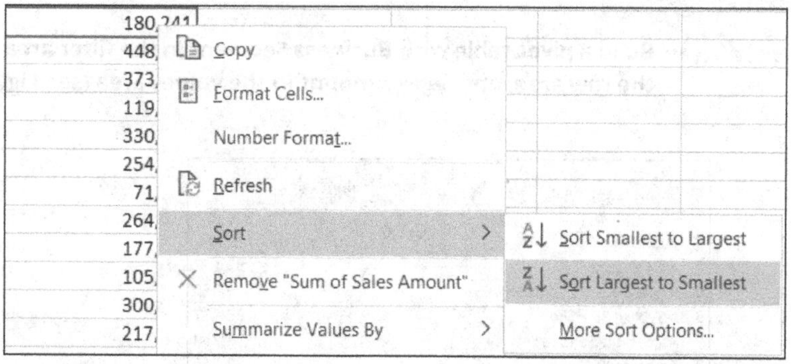

FIGURE 3-33:
Applying a sort to
a pivot table field.

Creating Useful Pivot-Driven Views

At this point in your exploration of pivot tables, you have covered enough of the fundamentals to start creating your own pivot table reports. In this last section, I share with you a few of the techniques I use to create some of the more useful report views. Although you could create these views by hand, creating them with pivot tables helps save you hours of work and allows you to more easily update and maintain them.

Producing top and bottom views

You'll often find that managers are interested in the top and bottom of things: the top 50 customers, the bottom 5 sales reps, the top 10 products. Although you may think this is because managers have the attention span of a 4-year-old, there's a more logical reason for focusing on the outliers.

Dashboarding and reporting is often about showing actionable data. If you, as a manager, know who the bottom ten revenue-generating accounts are, you could apply your effort and resources in building up those accounts. Because you most likely wouldn't have the resources to focus on all accounts, viewing a manageable subset of accounts would be more useful.

Luckily, pivot tables make it easy to filter your data for the top five, the bottom ten, or any conceivable combination of top or bottom records.

Here's an example. Imagine that in your company, the Accessories business segment is a high-margin business — you make the most profit for each dollar of sales in the Accessories segment. To increase sales, your manager wants to focus on the 50 customers who spend the least amount of money on accessories. They obviously want to spend their time and resources on getting those customers to buy more accessories. Here's what to do:

1. **Build a pivot table with Business Segment in the filter area, Customer in the row area, and Sales Amount in the values area (see Figure 3-34).**

	A	B
1	Business Segment	(All)
2		
3	**Customer**	**Sum of Sales Amount**
4	A Bike Store	85,177
5	A Great Bicycle Company	9,055
6	A Typical Bike Shop	83,457
7	Acceptable Sales & Service	1,258
8	Accessories Network	2,216
9	Acclaimed Bicycle Company	7,682
10	Ace Bicycle Supply	3,749
11	Action Bicycle Specialists	328,503
12	Active Cycling	1,805
13	Active Life Toys	200,013
14	Active Systems	643
15	Active Transport Inc.	88,246
16	Activity Center	42,804
17	Advanced Bike Components	363,131
18	Aerobic Exercise Company	2,677
19	Affordable Sports Equipment	311,446

FIGURE 3-34: Build this pivot table to start.

2. **For cosmetic value, change the layout to Tabular Form by choosing Design ⇨ Report Layout ⇨ Show in Tabular Form.**

REMEMBER

You can find the sample file for this chapter on this book's companion website.

3. **Right-click any customer name in the Customer field, select Filter, and then Top 10 — as demonstrated in Figure 3-35.**

REMEMBER

Don't let the label *Top 10* confuse you. You can use the Top 10 option to filter both top and bottom records.

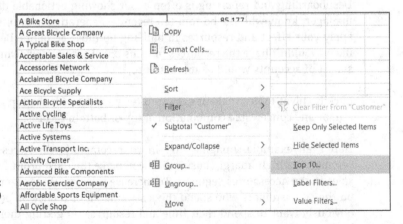

FIGURE 3-35: Select the Top 10 filter option.

4. **In the Top 10 Filter dialog box, as illustrated in Figure 3-36, you simply have to define the view you're looking for.**

   In this example, you want the bottom 50 items (customers), as defined by the Sum of Sales Amount field.

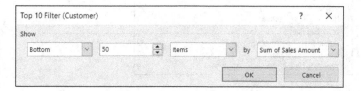

FIGURE 3-36: Specify the filter you want to apply.

5. **Click OK to apply the filter.**

6. **In the filter area, click the drop-down button for the Business Segment field and select the check box for the filter item Accessories in the menu that appears, as shown in Figure 3-37.**

   At this point, you have exactly what your manager asked for — the 50 customers who spend the least amount of money on accessories (see Figure 3-38).

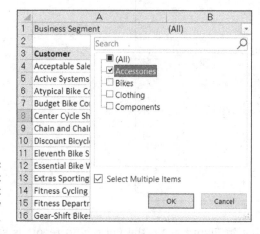

FIGURE 3-37: Filter your pivot table report to show Accessories.

Note that because you built this view using a pivot table, you can easily adapt the newly created report to create a whole new view. For example, you can add the SubRegion field — shown in Figure 3-39 — to the filter area to get the 50 United Kingdom customers who spend the least amount of money on accessories. This, my friends, is the power of using pivot tables for the basis of your dashboards and reports. Continue to play around with the Top 10 filter option to see what kind of reports you can come up with.

	A	B
1	Business Segment	Accessories ▼
2		
3	**Customer** ▼	**Sum of Sales Amount**
4	Running and Cycling Gear	21
5	Local Sales and Rental	21
6	Futuristic Bikes	21
7	Instruments and Parts Company	21
8	New Bikes Company	20
9	Daring Rides	20
10	Non-Slip Pedal Company	20
11	Extended Tours	20
12	Traditional Department Stores	20
13	Blue Bicycle Company	20
14	Noiseless Gear Company	20

FIGURE 3-38:
The final report.

	A	B
1	Business Segment	Accessories ▼
2	SubRegion	United Kingdom ▼
3		
4	**Customer** ▼	**Sum of Sales Amount**
5	Vigorous Sports Store	3
6	Closest Bicycle Store	3
7	Exclusive Bicycle Mart	15
8	Extended Tours	20
9	Instruments and Parts Company	21
10	Tachometers and Accessories	23
11	Metropolitan Bicycle Supply	26
12	Number One Bike Co.	30
13	Nearby Cycle Shop	36
14	Metro Metals Co.	46
15	Cycles Wholesaler & Mfg.	376
16	Cycling Goods	433
17	Exceptional Cycle Services	758
18	Channel Outlet	918
19	Express Bike Services	1,718
20	Downhill Bicycle Specialists	1,915
21	Uttermost Bike Shop	3,807
22	Bulk Discount Store	4,067
23	Commerce Bicycle Specialists	4,436
24	Action Bicycle Specialists	4,861
25	Exhibition Showroom	5,723
26	Riding Cycles	6,459
27	Prosperous Tours	7,487

FIGURE 3-39:
You can easily
adapt this report
to produce any
combination
of views.

**TECHNICAL
STUFF**

You may notice that in Figure 3-39, the Bottom 50 report is showing only 27 records. This is because there are fewer than 50 customers in the United Kingdom market that have accessories sales. Because I asked for the bottom 50, Excel shows as many as 50 accounts, but fewer if there are fewer than 50. If there's a tie for any rank in the bottom 50, Excel shows you all the tied records.

You can remove the applied filters in your pivot tables by taking these actions:

1. **Click anywhere inside your pivot table and then select the PivotTable Analyze contextual tab on the Ribbon.**

2. **Click the Clear icon and select Clear Filters from the menu that appears, as demonstrated in Figure 3-40.**

FIGURE 3-40:
Select Clear
Filters to clear the
applied filters
in a field.

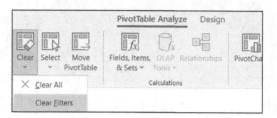

Creating views by month, quarter, and year

Raw transactional data is rarely aggregated by month, quarter, or year for you. This type of data is often captured by the day. However, managers often want reports by month or quarters instead of detail by day. Fortunately, pivot tables make it easy to group date fields into various time dimensions.

Figure 3-41 illustrates a pivot table with Order Date in the row area and Sales Amount in the values area. There are a couple of interesting things to note about the pivot table. First, notice that Quarters and Years have been added to the field list. Keep in mind that your source data hasn't changed to include these new fields; instead, these fields are now part of the pivot table. Another interesting thing to note is that, by default, the Years and Quarters fields are automatically added next to the Order Date field in the pivot table layout.

You can use the plus and minus icons to expand or collapse the grouped time periods. As you can see in Figure 3-42, expanding each grouping will expose the next layer of data all the way down to months.

In some scenarios, you may not want Excel to group individual dates at all. After adding a date field to a pivot table, you can right-click the field name and select the Ungroup option (see Figure 3-43). After ungrouping, the Years and Quarters fields will be removed from both the pivot table and the field list. Figure 3-44 illustrates the ungrouped Order Date field.

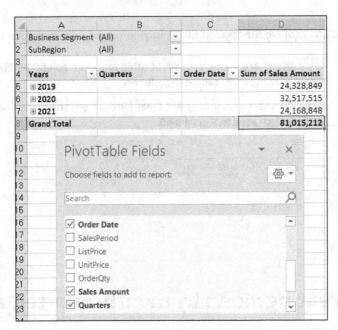

FIGURE 3-41:
Adding date fields will automatically group data by Years and Quarters.

	A	B		C	D
1	Business Segment	(All)	▾		
2	SubRegion	(All)	▾		
3					
4	Years ▾	Quarters ▾		Order Date ▾	Sum of Sales Amount
5	⊞ 2019				24,328,849
6	⊞ 2020				32,517,515
7	⊞ 2021	⊟ Qtr1		Jan	1,670,606
8				Feb	2,521,878
9				Mar	2,929,133
10		⊟ Qtr2		Apr	2,168,448
11				May	3,380,604
12				Jun	1,536,545
13		⊞ Qtr3			5,058,264
14		⊞ Qtr4			4,903,371
15	Grand Total				81,015,212

FIGURE 3-42:
Click the plus and minus icons to expand or collapse time periods.

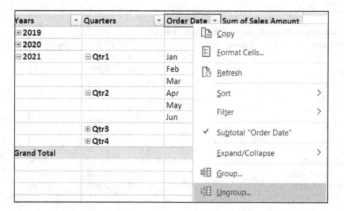

FIGURE 3-43:
Ungrouping a
date field to show
individual dates.

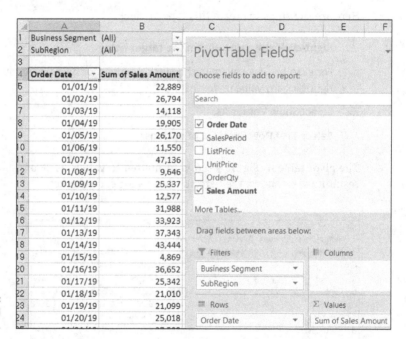

FIGURE 3-44:
The ungrouped
Order Date field.

Creating a percent distribution view

A *percent distribution* (or *percent contribution*) view allows you to see how much of
the total is made up of a specific data item. This view is useful when you're trying
to measure the general impact of a particular item.

The pivot table, as shown in Figure 3-45, gives you a view into the percent of sales
that comes from each business segment. Here, you can tell that bikes make up
81 percent of Canada's sales, whereas only 77 percent of France's sales come
from bikes.

	A	B	C	D	E
1	Sum of Sales Amount	Business Segment			
2	Market	Accessories	Bikes	Clothing	Components
3	Australia	1.48%	83.30%	2.66%	12.56%
4	Canada	0.82%	81.00%	2.65%	15.53%
5	Central	0.59%	85.50%	1.96%	11.94%
6	France	1.05%	77.42%	2.79%	18.74%
7	Germany	1.74%	78.11%	3.68%	16.46%
8	Northeast	0.74%	81.80%	2.35%	15.12%
9	Northwest	0.43%	83.72%	1.61%	14.25%
10	Southeast	0.58%	85.20%	2.10%	12.13%
11	Southwest	0.59%	82.97%	1.96%	14.48%
12	United Kingdom	1.00%	79.68%	2.79%	16.53%
13	Grand Total	0.71%	82.49%	2.22%	14.57%

FIGURE 3-45: This view shows percent of total for the row.

Here are the steps to create this type of view:

1. **Right-click any value within the target field.**

   For example, if you want to change the settings for the Sales Amount field, right-click any value under that field.

2. **Select Show Values As.**

3. **Select % of Row Total list of options.**

The pivot table in Figure 3-46 is formatted to values as % of Column Total. The resulting view shows the percent of sales for each market.

	A	B	C	D	E
1	Sum of Sales Amount	Business Segment			
2	Market	Accessories	Bikes	Clothing	Components
3	Australia	4.15%	2.02%	2.40%	1.73%
4	Canada	20.64%	17.53%	21.26%	19.02%
5	Central	8.05%	10.15%	8.65%	8.02%
6	France	8.47%	5.38%	7.19%	7.38%
7	Germany	6.17%	2.40%	4.20%	2.86%
8	Northeast	8.87%	8.51%	9.07%	8.91%
9	Northwest	9.22%	15.69%	11.16%	15.11%
10	Southeast	7.91%	10.08%	9.20%	8.12%
11	Southwest	19.04%	23.09%	20.21%	22.81%
12	United Kingdom	7.47%	5.14%	6.67%	6.03%
13	Grand Total	100.00%	100.00%	100.00%	100.00%

FIGURE 3-46: Showing the percent of total for the column.

Sometimes it's useful to capture a running-totals view to analyze the movement of numbers on a year-to-date (YTD) basis. Figure 3-47 illustrates a pivot table that shows values as a running total of revenue by month for each year. In this view, you can see where the YTD sales stand at any given month in each year. For example, you can see that in August 2021, revenues were about a million dollars lower than at the same point in 2009.

⊿	A	B	C	D
1	Sum of Sales Amount	Years	▾	
2	Order Date ▾	2019	2020	2021
3	Jan	713,230	1,318,597	1,670,606
4	Feb	2,395,549	3,484,749	4,192,484
5	Mar	4,069,309	5,268,979	7,121,616
6	Apr	4,941,877	7,098,366	9,290,064
7	May	7,222,042	10,020,068	12,670,668
8	Jun	8,324,063	11,952,318	14,207,214
9	Jul	10,770,861	14,741,281	16,588,415
10	Aug	14,386,786	19,055,823	18,128,489
11	Sep	17,213,226	23,036,113	19,265,477
12	Oct	19,085,628	25,506,056	20,139,655
13	Nov	22,025,413	28,833,967	22,408,366
14	Dec	24,328,849	32,517,515	24,168,848

FIGURE 3-47: This view shows a running total of sales for each month.

To create a view showing running totals, take these actions:

1. **Right-click any value within the target field.**

   For example, if you want to change the settings for the Sales Amount field, right-click any value under that field.

2. **Select Show Values As.**

3. **Select Running Total In.**

   The dialog box in Figure 3-48 opens, asking you to define the base field.

4. **In the Base Field list, select the field that you want the running totals to be calculated against.**

5. **Click OK to apply the change.**

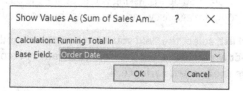

FIGURE 3-48: Applying a running total based on the Order Date field.

Show Values As (Sum of Sales Am...   ?   ✕

Calculation: Running Total In

Base Field: Order Date   ▾

OK   Cancel

Creating a month-over-month variance view

Another commonly requested view is a month-over-month variance. How did this month's sales compare to last month's sales? The best way to create these types of views is to show the raw numbers and the percent variance together.

In that light, you can start creating this view by building a pivot table similar to the one shown in Figure 3-49. Notice that you bring in the Sales Amount field twice. One of these remains untouched, showing the raw data. The other is changed to show the month-over-month variance.

	A	B	C
1		Values	
2	Order Date ▾	Sum of Sales Amount	Sum of Sales Amount2
3	Jan	3,702,433	3702433.28
4	Feb	6,370,348	6370347.689
5	Mar	6,387,124	6387123.637
6	Apr	4,870,403	4870402.742
7	May	8,582,470	8582470.413
8	Jun	4,570,817	4570816.936
9	Jul	7,616,962	7616962.393
10	Aug	9,470,541	9470540.56
11	Sep	7,943,719	7943718.637
12	Oct	5,216,523	5216523
13	Nov	8,536,406	8536405.542
14	Dec	7,747,467	7747467.262
15	**Grand Total**	**81,015,212**	**81015212.09**

FIGURE 3-49: Build a pivot table that contains the Sum of Sales Amount twice.

To create the month-over-month view, take these actions:

1. **Right-click any value within the target field.**

   In this case, the target field is the second Sum of Sales Amount field.

2. **Select Show Values As.**

3. **Select Running Total In.**

   The dialog box in Figure 3-50 opens, asking you to define the base field and the item you want to compare against when calculating the percent variance.

4. **In the Base Field list, select the field you want compared, and from the Base Item drop-down menu, select the item you want to compare against when calculating the percent variance.**

   In this example, you want to calculate each month's variance to the previous month. Therefore, select the (Previous) item.

5. **Click OK to apply the change.**

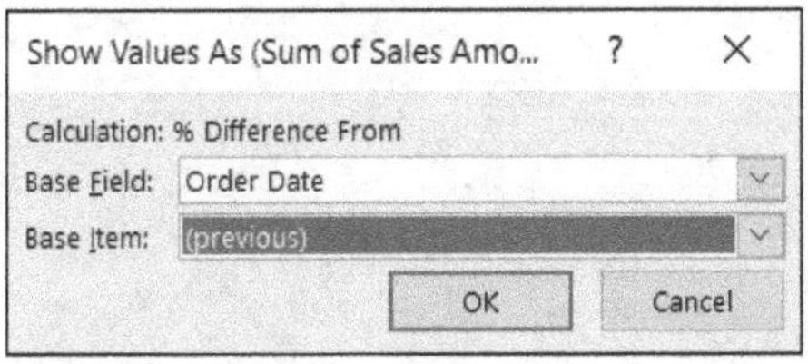

FIGURE 3-50:
Comparing each
Order Date
month with the
previous item.

Figure 3-51 illustrates the resulting pivot table view of raw sales dollars and the variance over last month. You can obviously change the field names (see the section "Customizing field names," earlier in this chapter) to reflect the appropriate labels for each column.

	A	B	C
1		Values	
2	Order Date ▾	Sum of Sales Amount	Sum of Sales Amount2
3	Jan	3,702,433	
4	Feb	6,370,348	72.06%
5	Mar	6,387,124	0.26%
6	Apr	4,870,403	-23.75%
7	May	8,582,470	76.22%
8	Jun	4,570,817	-46.74%
9	Jul	7,616,962	66.64%
10	Aug	9,470,541	24.33%
11	Sep	7,943,719	-16.12%
12	Oct	5,216,523	-34.33%
13	Nov	8,536,406	63.64%
14	Dec	7,747,467	-9.24%
15	Grand Total	81,015,212	

FIGURE 3-51:
The second Sum
of Sales Amount
field now displays
the month-over-
month variance
for each month.

Chapter **4**

Using External Data for Your Dashboards and Reports

Wouldn't it be wonderful if all the data you come across could be neatly packed into one easy-to-use Excel table? The reality is that sometimes the data you need comes from external data sources. *External data* is exactly what it sounds like: data that isn't located in the Excel workbook in which you're operating. Some examples of external data sources are text files, Access tables, SQL Server tables, and even other Excel workbooks.

This chapter explores some efficient ways to get external data into your Excel data models. Before jumping in, however, this humble author wants to throw out one disclaimer: There are numerous ways to get data into Excel. In fact, between the functionality found in the user interface and the VBA/code techniques, Excel has too many techniques to focus on in one chapter. Instead, then, in this chapter I focus on a handful of techniques that can be implemented in most situations and don't come with a lot of pitfalls and gotchas.

Leveraging Power Query to Extract and Transform Data

Every day, millions of Excel users manually pull data from some source location, manipulate that data, and integrate it into their pivot table reporting.

This process of extracting, manipulating, and integrating data is called ETL. ETL refers to the three separate functions typically required in order to integrate disparate data sources:

>> **Extract:** The extraction function involves reading data from a specified source and extracting a desired subset of data.

>> **Transform:** The transformation function involves cleaning, shaping, and aggregating data to convert it to the desired structure.

>> **Load:** The loading function involves actually importing or using the resulting data.

In an attempt to empower Excel analysts to develop robust and reusable ETL processes, Microsoft created Power Query. Power Query enhances the ETL experience by offering an intuitive mechanism to extract data from a wide variety of sources, perform complex transformations on that data, and then load the data into a workbook or the internal data model.

In this section, you see how Power Query works and how you can use it to help save time and automate the steps for importing data into your reporting models.

Reviewing Power Query basics

Although Power Query is relatively intuitive, it's worth taking the time to walk through a basic scenario to understand its high-level features. To start this basic look at Power Query, pretend that your job entails creating reports that show trending for Microsoft stock prices. As a part of your job, you frequently need to pull stock data from the web.

To start the query, follow these steps:

1. **In Excel, select the Get Data command in the Get & Transform Data group on the Data tab and then select From Other Sources ⇨ From Web (see Figure 4-1).**

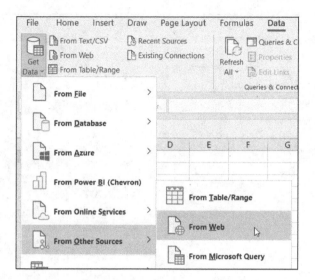

FIGURE 4-1:
Starting a Power
Query web query.

WARNING

Excel has another From Web command button, on the Data tab in the Get External Data group. This unfortunate duplicate command is the legacy web-scraping capability found in all Excel versions since Excel 2000. The Power Query version of the From Web command (found under the Get Data drop-down) goes beyond simple web scraping. Power Query is able to pull data from advanced web pages and manipulate the data. Make sure you're using the correct feature when pulling data from the web.

2. **In the dialog box that appears, enter the URL for the data you need, as shown in Figure 4-2.**

In this example, you type `http://finance.yahoo.com/q/hp?s=MSFT`.

After a bit of gyrating, the Navigator pane (shown in Figure 4-3) appears. You can select the data source that you want to extract. Click each table to see a preview of the data.

FIGURE 4-2:
Enter the target
URL containing
the data
you need.

From Web

○ Basic   ○ Advanced

URL

`http://finance.yahoo.com/q/hp?s=MSFT`

[OK]   [Cancel]

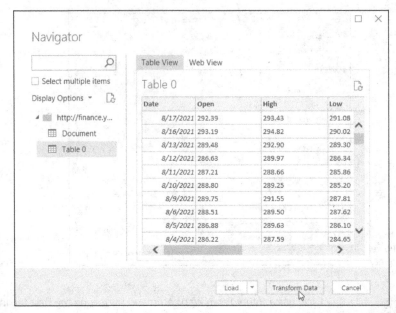

FIGURE 4-3:
Select the correct
data source and
then click the
Transform
Data button.

When you click the Transform Data button, Power Query activates a new
Query Editor window, which contains its own ribbon and a preview pane that
shows a preview of the data (see Figure 4-4). You can apply certain actions to
shape, clean, and transform the data before importing.

3. **In this case, Table 0 holds the historical stock data you need, so click
Table 0 in the list box on the left and then click the Transform Data
button.**

You may have noticed that the Navigator pane, shown in Figure 4-3, offers a
Load button (next to the Transform Data button). You can use this button to
skip any editing and import your targeted data as is. If you're sure that you
won't need to transform or shape your data in any way, click the Load button
to import the data directly into the data model or a spreadsheet in your
workbook.

The idea is to work with each column shown in the Query Editor, applying the
necessary actions that will give you the data and structure you need. You can
dive deeper into column actions later in this chapter. For now, continue toward
the goal of getting the last 30 days of stock prices for Microsoft Corporation.

Formula Bar

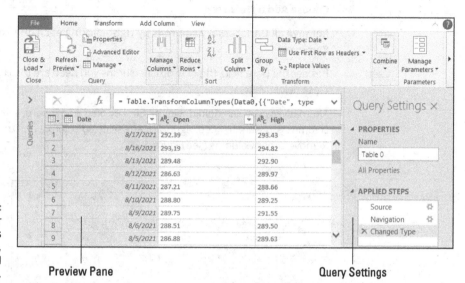

FIGURE 4-4:
The Query Editor
window allows
you to shape,
clean, and
transform data.

Preview Pane

Query Settings

4. **Click the High field, hold down Ctrl, click the Low field and the Close fields, and then right-click and select Change Type ➪ Currency, as shown in Figure 4-5.**

This ensures that the Date field is formatted as a proper date. Power Query asks if you want to replace the current step or add a new step.

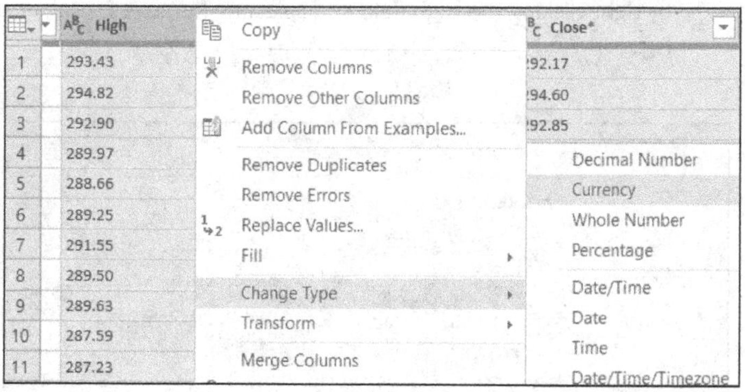

FIGURE 4-5:
Change the data
type of the
High, Low, and
Close fields to
currency format.

5. **Choose Add a New Step.**

6. **Remove all unnecessary columns by right-clicking each one and selecting Remove.**

   Besides the Date field, the only other columns you need are the High, Low, and Close fields.

   Alternatively, you can hold down the Ctrl key on the keyboard, select the columns you want to keep, right-click any selected column, and then choose Remove Other Columns (see Figure 4-6).

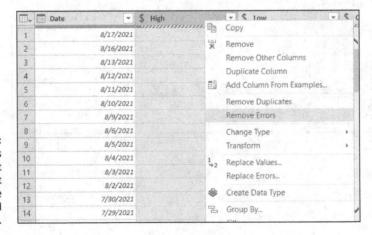

FIGURE 4-6:
Select unneeded columns, and then select Remove Other Columns to get rid of them.

TIP

You may notice that some of the rows show the word *Error*. These are rows that contained text values that couldn't be converted. Remove the Error rows by right-clicking the High field and selecting Remove Errors, as shown in Figure 4-7.

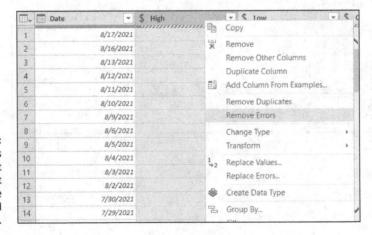

FIGURE 4-7:
Removing errors caused by text values that couldn't be converted to currency.

7. After all the errors are removed, add a Week Of field that displays the week to which each date in the table belongs.

To do this, right-click the Date field and select the Duplicate Column option. A new column (named Date - Copy) is added to the preview.

8. Right-click the newly added column, select the Rename option, and then rename the column Week Of.

9. Right-click the Week Of column you just created and select Transform ⇨ Week ⇨ Start of Week, as shown in Figure 4-8.

Excel transforms the date to display the start of the week for a given date.

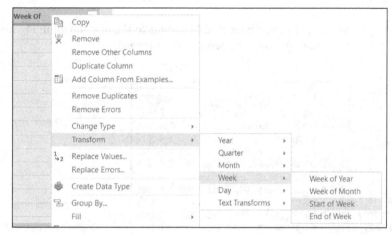

FIGURE 4-8:
You can use the
Power Query
Editor to apply
transformation
actions such as
displaying the
start of the week
for a given date.

10. When you've finished configuring your Power Query feed, save and output the results.

To do this, click the Close & Load drop-down found on the Home tab of the Power Query Ribbon to reveal the two options:

- *Close & Load:* Saves your query and outputs the results to a new worksheet in your workbook as an Excel table. The Close & Load To option activates the Import Data dialog box, where you can choose to output the results to a specific worksheet or to the internal data model.

- *Close & Load To:* Activates the Import Data dialog box (see Figure 4-9) where you have more control over how the query results are used. You can choose to send results to a pivot table or to a table in a new worksheet in the active workbook. Alternatively, you can save the query as a query connection only, which means you'll be able to use the query in various in-memory processes without needing to output the results anywhere.

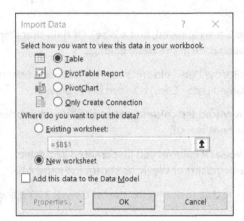

FIGURE 4-9:
The Load To
dialog box gives
you more control
over how the
results of queries
are used.

At this point, you have a table similar to the one shown in Figure 4-10, which can be used to produce the pivot table you need.

	A	B	C	D	E
1	Date	High	Low	Close*	Week Of
2	8/17/2021	293.43	291.08	292.86	8/15/2021
3	8/16/2021	294.82	290.02	294.6	8/15/2021
4	8/13/2021	292.9	289.3	292.85	8/8/2021
5	8/12/2021	289.97	286.34	289.81	8/8/2021
6	8/11/2021	288.66	285.86	286.95	8/8/2021
7	8/10/2021	289.25	285.2	286.44	8/8/2021
8	8/9/2021	291.55	287.81	288.33	8/8/2021
9	8/6/2021	289.5	287.62	289.46	8/1/2021
10	8/5/2021	289.63	286.1	289.52	8/1/2021
11	8/4/2021	287.59	284.65	286.51	8/1/2021
12	8/3/2021	287.23	284	287.12	8/1/2021
13	8/2/2021	286.77	283.74	284.82	8/1/2021
14	7/30/2021	286.66	283.91	284.91	7/25/2021
15	7/29/2021	288.62	286.08	286.5	7/25/2021
16	7/28/2021	290.15	283.83	286.22	7/25/2021
17	7/27/2021	289.58	282.95	286.54	7/25/2021

FIGURE 4-10:
Your final query
pulled from
the Internet:
transformed, put
into an Excel
table, and ready
to use in a
pivot table.

Take a moment to appreciate what Power Query allowed you to do just now. With a few clicks, you searched the Internet, found some base data, shaped the data to keep only the columns you needed, and even manipulated that data to add an extra Week Of dimension to the base data. This is what Power Query is about: enabling you to easily extract, filter, and reshape data without the need for any programmatic coding skills.

TIP

You can get back to the Power Query Editor window for any query by activating the Queries & Connections task pane. On the Excel Ribbon, click Data and then click Queries & Connections. From here, you can simply right-click your target query and select Edit.

MANAGING EXTERNAL DATA PROPERTIES

When you import external data into a table, you can control a few adjustable properties via the Properties dialog box. You can get to the properties of a particular external data table by clicking anywhere inside the target table and then clicking the Properties command under the Table Design tab.

This activates the External Data Properties dialog box. The properties found in this dialog box allow you to further customize your query tables to suit your needs. Take a moment to familiarize yourself with some of the more useful options in this dialog box.

- **Include Row Numbers:** This property is deselected by default. Selecting this property creates a dummy column that contains row numbers. The first column of your data set will be this row number column upon refresh.

- **Adjust Column Width:** This property is selected by default, telling Excel to adjust the column widths every time the data is refreshed. Deselecting this option causes the column widths to remain the same.

- **Preserve Column/Sort/Filter/Layout:** If this property is selected, the order of the columns and rows of the Excel range remains unchanged. This way, you can rearrange and sort the columns and rows of the external data in your worksheet without worrying about blowing away your formatting every time you refresh. Deselecting this property makes the Excel range look like the query.

- **Preserve Cell Formatting:** This property is selected by default, telling Excel to keep the applied cell formatting when you refresh.

- **Insert Cells for New Data, Delete Unused Cells:** This is the default setting for data range changes. This option inserts cells (not rows) when the imported table grows and deletes cells (not rows) when it shrinks.

- **Insert Entire Rows for New Data, Clear Unused Cells:** This option inserts whole rows when the imported table grows and clears cells (not deletes rows) when it shrinks.

- **Overwrite Cells for New Data, Clear Unused Cells:** This option overwrites cells when the imported table grows and clears cells (not deletes rows) when it shrinks.

Understanding query steps

Power Query uses its own formula language (known as the M language) to codify your queries. As with macro recording, each action you take when working with Power Query results in a line of code being written into a query step. Query steps are embedded M code that allow your actions to be repeated each time you refresh your Power Query data.

To explore this concept, open the Power Query Editor for the table you just created. Right-click anywhere in the table shown in Figure 4-10 and choose Table ⇨ Edit Query. You can see the query steps for your queries in the Query Settings pane (see Figure 4-11).

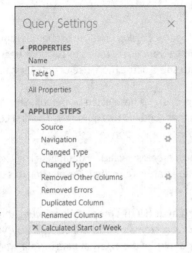

FIGURE 4-11:
Query steps can
be viewed and
managed in the
Applied Steps
section of
the Query
Settings pane.

Each query step represents an action you took to get to a data table. You can click any step to see the underlying M code in the Power Query formula bar. For example, clicking the step called Removed Errors reveals the code for that step in the formula bar.

TIP

If you don't see the Query Settings pane, click the Query Settings command on the View tab of the Power Query Editor Ribbon. The View tab also contains the Formula Bar check box, allowing you to display the formula bar, which shows the M syntax for each given step.

When you click a query step, the data shown in the preview pane shows you what the data looked like up to and including the step you clicked. For example, in Figure 4-11, clicking the step before the Removed Other Columns step lets you see what the data looked like before you removed the nonessential columns.

You can right-click any step to see a menu of options for managing your query steps. Figure 4-12 illustrates the following options:

>> **Edit Settings:** Edit the arguments or parameters that define the selected step.

>> **Rename:** Give the selected step a meaningful name.

- >> **Delete:** Remove the selected step. Be aware that removing a step can cause errors if subsequent steps depend on the deleted step.

- >> **Delete Until End:** Remove the selected step and all following steps.

- >> **Insert Step After:** Insert a step after the selected step.

- >> **Move Up:** Move the selected step up in the order of steps.

- >> **Move Down:** Move the selected step down in the order of steps.

- >> **Extract Previous:** Create a new query using the steps prior to the selected step.

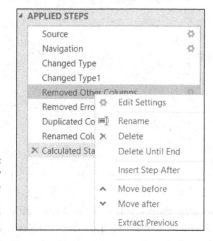

FIGURE 4-12:
Right-click any query step to edit, rename, delete, or move the step.

Importing Data from Files

Organizational data is often stored in files such as text files, comma-separated value (CSV) files, and even other Excel workbooks. It's not uncommon to use these kinds of files as data sources for data analysis. Power Query offers several connection types that enable the importing of data from external files.

REMEMBER

The files you import don't necessarily have to be on your own PC. You can import files on network drives, as well as in cloud repositories such as Google Drive and Microsoft OneDrive.

Getting data from Excel workbooks

You can import data from other Excel workbooks by choosing Data ⇨ Get Data ⇨ From File ⇨ From Workbook from the Excel Ribbon.

Excel opens a dialog box where you can browse for the Excel file you want to work with. Note that you can import any kind of Excel file, including macro-enabled workbooks and template workbooks.

After you've selected a file, the Navigator pane activates (see Figure 4-13), showing you all the data sources available in the workbook.

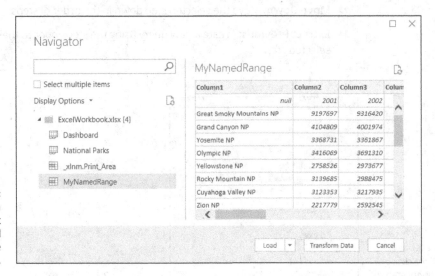

FIGURE 4-13:
Select the data sources you want to work with, and then click the Load button.

The idea here is to select the data source you want and then either load or transform the data using the buttons at the bottom of the Navigator pane. Click the Load button to skip any editing and import your targeted data as is to a table in a new worksheet. Click the Transform Data button if you want to transform or shape before completing the import.

In terms of Excel workbooks, a *data source* is either a worksheet or a defined named range. The icons next to each data source let you distinguish which sources are worksheets and which are named ranges. In Figure 4-13, the source named MyNamedRange is a defined named range, and the source named National Parks is a worksheet.

You can import multiple sources at a time by selecting the Select Multiple Items check box and then placing a check mark next to each worksheet and named range that you want imported.

REMEMBER

Power Query won't bring in charts, pivot tables, shapes, VBA code, or any other objects that may exist within a workbook. Power Query simply imports the data found in the used cell ranges of the workbook.

Getting data from CSV and text files

Text files are commonly used to store and distribute data because of their inherent ability to hold many thousands of bytes of data without having an inflated file size. Text files can do this by foregoing all the fancy formatting, leaving only the text.

TECHNICAL STUFF

A CSV file is a kind of text file that contains commas to delimit (separate) values into columns of data.

To import a text file, choose Data⇨ Get Data⇨ From File⇨ From Text/CSV on the Excel Ribbon. Excel opens the Import Data dialog box, where you can browse for, and select, a text or CSV file.

Power Query opens the dialog box shown in Figure 4-14. Here, you can preview the contents and specify how the file should be imported. Note the drop-down options at the top of the dialog:

>> **File Origin:** Define what encoding standards to use. This option is useful when handling data that comes from different regions of the world.

>> **Delimiter:** Specify how the contents are delimited (separated). Some text files are *tab delimited,* meaning they contain tab characters that separate text values into columns of data. Other text files are *comma delimited,* while others are delimited by another character such as a space or colon. Use the Delimiter option to tell Power Query which delimiter to look for when separating values into columns.

>> **Data Type Detection:** When you import text files, Power Query uses the first 200 rows to guess the data types for each of the columns in the data. For instance, if the first 200 rows of a particular column are made up of numbers, Power Query automatically changes the data type of that column to numeric after importing the file. The Data Type Detection option allows you to tell Power Query to analyze the entire file (as opposed to the first 200 rows) when guessing the data types. You also have the option of telling Power Query not to change any data types.

Click the Load button to import the data directly into your workbook. Click the Transform Data button to bring the data source into the Query Editor, where you can apply your edits and then click the Close & Load command to complete the import.

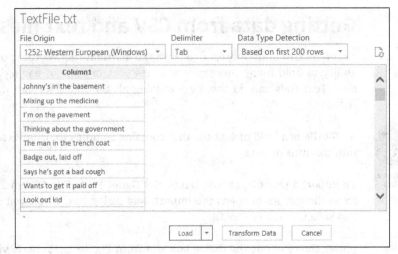

FIGURE 4-14:
Preview the data and use the option drop-down menus to tell Power Query how to import the data.

Importing Data from Database Systems

In smart organizations, the task of data management is not performed by Excel; instead, it's performed primarily by database systems such as Microsoft Access and SQL Server. Databases like these not only store millions of rows of data, but also ensure data integrity and allow for the rapid search and retrieval of data by way of queries and views.

Power Query has the ability to connect to virtually any database commonly used today: Microsoft Access, MySQL, Oracle, SQL Server, and so on.

Choose Data ⇨ Get Data ⇨ From Database and you see the list of database types you can leverage to supplement the data in your Excel reports.

Importing data from Microsoft Access

Walking through the process of connection to every type of database available would be redundant. However, it would be useful to walk through the basic steps of connecting a Microsoft Access database.

Microsoft Access is used in many organizations to manage a series of tables that interact with each other, such as a Customers table, an Orders table, and an Invoices table. Managing data in Access provides the benefit of a relational database in which you can ensure data integrity, prevent redundancy, and easily generate data sets via queries.

Here are the steps for connecting to a Microsoft Access database:

1. **Choose Data ⇨ Get Data ⇨ From Database ⇨ From Microsoft Access Database.**

2. **Browse for your target database.**

   After Power Query connects to the database, the Navigator pane, shown in Figure 4-15, activates. There, you see all database objects available to you, including tables and views (or *queries,* in Access lingo).

3. **Click the Sales_By_Employee view.**

   The Navigator pane displays a preview of the Sales_By_Employee data. If you want to transform or shape this data, click the Transform Data button. In this case, the data looks fine as is.

4. **Click the Load button to complete the import.**

   After a bit of processing, Power Query loads the data to a new Excel worksheet and adds the new query to the Workbook Queries pane, as shown in Figure 4-16.

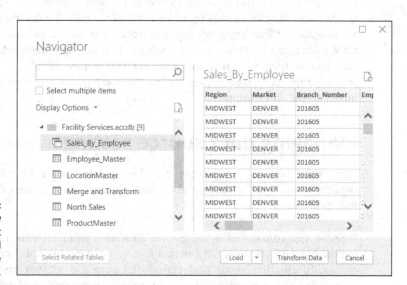

REMEMBER

You can select multiple tables and views by selecting the Select Multiple Items check box and then placing a check mark next to each database object you want imported.

	A	B	C	D	E	F	G	H
1	Region	Market	Branch	Employee	Last_Name	First_Name	Busine	SumOf	Sum
2	MIDWEST	DENVER	201605	160512	FILLIR	V			
3	MIDWEST	DENVER	201605	160512	FILLIR	V			
4	MIDWEST	DENVER	201605	164264	DEYIL	J.			
5	MIDWEST	DENVER	201605	164264	DEYIL	J.			
6	MIDWEST	DENVER	201605	164465	LEWRINSEN	N			
7	MIDWEST	DENVER	201605	164465	LEWRINSEN	N			
8	MIDWEST	DENVER	201605	164466	HOFMIASTIR	C			
9	MIDWEST	DENVER	201605	2522	BROEKS	H			
10	MIDWEST	DENVER	201605	2522	BROEKS	H			
11	MIDWEST	DENVER	201605	52361	BIHRINS	K			
12	MIDWEST	DENVER	201605	52361	BIHRINS	K			
13	MIDWEST	DENVER	201605	5445	NISSLIR	R			
14	MIDWEST	DENVER	201605	64006	HALL	N			
15	MIDWEST	DENVER	201605	64006	HALL	N			
16	MIDWEST	DENVER	202605	160153	KILLIY	N			
17	MIDWEST	DENVER	202605	160153	KILLIY				

Queries & Connections

Queries | Connections

1 query

Sales_By_Employee
1,346 rows loaded.

FIGURE 4-16:
The final imported database data.

REMEMBER

The icon next to each database object distinguishes whether that object is a table or a view. Views have an icon that looks like two overlapping grids. See the icon for the Sales_By_Employee view, shown in Figure 4-15, to get the idea.

TIP

It's a best practice to use views whenever possible. Views are often cleaner data sets because they're already optimized to include only the columns and data that are necessary. (This improves query performance and helps minimize the workbook's file size.) In addition, you don't need an intimate knowledge of the database architecture. Someone with that knowledge has already done the work for you — joined the correct tables, applied the appropriate business rules, and optimized output, for example.

Managing data source settings

Every time you connect to any web-based data source or data source that requires some level of credentials, Power Query *caches* (stores) the settings for that data source.

Suppose you connect to a SQL Server database, enter all your credentials, and import the data you need. At the moment of successful connection, Power Query caches information about that connection in a file located on your local PC. It includes the connection string, username, password, and privacy settings, for example.

The purpose of all this caching is so you don't have to reenter credentials every time you need to refresh your queries. That's nifty, but what happens when your credentials are changed? Well, the short answer is those queries will fail until the data source settings are updated.

You can edit data source settings by activating the Data Source Settings dialog box. To do so, choose Data ⇨ Get Data ⇨ Data Source Settings.

The Data Source Settings dialog box, shown in Figure 4-17, contains a list of all credentials-based data sources previously used in queries. Select the data source you need to change, and then click the Edit Permissions button.

FIGURE 4-17: Edit a data source by selecting it and clicking the Edit Permissions button.

The Edit Permissions dialog box opens — this time, specific to the data source you selected (see Figure 4-18). This dialog box enables you to edit credentials, as well as other data privacy settings.

Click the Edit button to make changes to the credentials for the data source. The credentials editing screen will differ based on the data source you're working with, but again, the input dialog boxes are relatively intuitive and easy to update.

Power Query caches data source settings in a file located on your local PC. Even though you may have deleted a particular query, the data source setting is retained for possible future use. This can lead to a cluttered list of old and current data sources. You can clean out old items by selecting the data source in the Data Source Settings dialog box and clicking the Clear Permissions button.

FIGURE 4-18:
Click the Edit button in the Edit Permissions dialog box to change permissions for a data source.

2

Building Basic Dashboard Components

IN THIS PART . . .

Uncover the best practices for designing effective
data tables.

See how you can leverage the Sparkline functionality
found in Excel.

Look at the various techniques you can use to visualize
data without the use of charts or graphs.

Chapter **5**

Dressing Up Your Data Tables

The Excel table is the perfect way to consolidate and relay information. Data tables are quite common — you'll find one in any Excel report. Yet the concept of making tables easier to read and more visually appealing escapes most of us.

Maybe it's because the nicely structured rows and columns of a table lull us into believing that the data is already presented in the best way possible. Maybe the options of adding color and borders make the table seem nicely packaged. Excel makes table creation easy, but even so, you can use several design principles to make your Excel table a more effective platform for conveying your data.

In this chapter, you explore how easy it is to apply a handful of table design best practices. The tips found here ultimately help you create visually appealing tables that make the data within them easier to consume and comprehend.

Table Design Principles

Table design is one of the most underestimated endeavors in Excel reporting. How a table is designed has a direct effect on how well an audience absorbs and interprets the data in that table. Unfortunately, putting together a data table with an eye for economy and ease of consumption is an uncommon skill.

For example, the table shown in Figure 5-1 is similar to many found in Excel reports. The thick borders, the variety of colors, and the poorly formatted numbers are all unfortunate trademarks of tables that come from the average Excel analyst.

Top 10 Domestic Routes by Revenue

From	To	Revenue Dollars	Revenue Percent	Margin Dollars	Margin Percent	Revenue per Passenger	Margin per Passenger
		Revenue		**Margin**		**Per Passenger**	
Atlanta	New York	$3,602,000	8.09%	$955,000	9%	245	65
Chicago	New York	$4,674,000	10.50%	$336,000	3%	222	16
Columbus (Ohio)	New York	$2,483,000	5.58%	$1,536,000	14%	202	125
New York	Detroit	$12,180,000	27.35%	$2,408,000	23%	177	35
New York	Washington	$6,355,000	14.27%	$1,230,000	12%	186	36
New York	Philadelphia	$3,582,000	8.04%	-$716,000	-7%	125	-25
New York	San Francisco	$3,221,000	7.23%	$1,856,000	18%	590	340
New York	Phoenix	$2,846,000	6.39%	$1,436,000	14%	555	280
New York	Toronto	$2,799,000	6.29%	$1,088,000	10%	450	175
New York	Seattle	$2,792,000	6.27%	$467,000	4%	448	75
Total Domestic routes		**$44,534,000**		**$10,596,000**		**272**	**53**

FIGURE 5-1:
A poorly designed table.

Throughout this chapter, you improve on this table by applying these four basic design principles:

» **Use colors sparingly,** reserving them for information about key data points.

» **De-emphasize borders,** using the natural white space between the components to partition your dashboard.

» **Use effective number formatting** to avoid inundating your table with too much ink.

» **Subdue your labels and headers.**

Use colors sparingly

Color is most often used to separate the various sections of a table. The basic idea is that the colors applied to a table suggest the relationship between the rows and columns. The problem is that colors often distract and draw attention away from the important data. In addition, printed tables with dark-colored cells are notoriously difficult to read (especially on black-and-white printers). They are also hard on the toner budget, if that holds any importance to you.

Colors in general should be used sparingly, reserved for providing information about key data points. The headers, labels, and natural structure of your table are more than enough to guide your audience. There is no real need to add a layer of color as demarcation for your rows and columns.

Figure 5-2 shows the table from Figure 5-1 with the colors removed. As you can see, it's already easier to read.

Top 10 Domestic Routes by Revenue		Revenue		Margin		Per Passenger	
From	To	Revenue Dollars	Revenue Percent	Margin Dollars	Margin Percent	Revenue per Passenger	Margin per Passenger
Atlanta	New York	$3,602,000	8.09%	$955,000	9%	245	65
Chicago	New York	$4,674,000	10.50%	$336,000	3%	222	16
Columbus (Ohio)	New York	$2,483,000	5.58%	$1,536,000	14%	202	125
New York	Detroit	$12,180,000	27.35%	$2,408,000	23%	177	35
New York	Washington	$6,355,000	14.27%	$1,230,000	12%	186	36
New York	Philadelphia	$3,582,000	8.04%	-$716,000	-7%	125	-25
New York	San Francisco	$3,221,000	7.23%	$1,856,000	18%	590	340
New York	Phoenix	$2,846,000	6.39%	$1,436,000	14%	555	280
New York	Toronto	$2,799,000	6.29%	$1,088,000	10%	450	175
New York	Seattle	$2,792,000	6.27%	$467,000	4%	448	75
Total Domestic routes		$44,534,000		$10,596,000		272	53

FIGURE 5-2: Remove unnecessary cell coloring.

TIP

If you're working with a table that contains colored cells, you can quickly remove the color by highlighting the cells and choosing the No Fill option under the Theme Colors drop-down menu on the Home tab (see Figure 5-3).

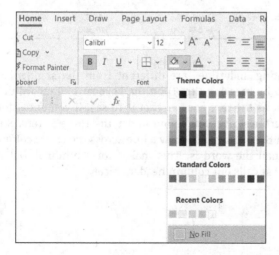

FIGURE 5-3: Use the No Fill option to clear cell colors.

De-emphasize borders

Believe it or not, borders get in the way of quickly reading the data in a table. Because borders help separate data in nicely partitioned sections, this may seem counterintuitive, but the reality is that a table's borders are the first thing your eyes see when you look at a table. Don't believe it? Stand back a bit from an Excel table and squint. The borders will come popping out at you.

You should always endeavor to de-emphasize borders and gridlines wherever you can. Try to use the natural white space between the columns to partition sections. If borders are necessary, format them to lighter hues than your data; light grays are typically ideal. The idea is to indicate sections without distracting from the information displayed.

Figure 5-4 demonstrates these concepts with the table from Figure 5-1. Notice how the numbers are no longer caged in gridlines and that headings now jump out at you with the addition of Single Accounting underlines.

Top 10 Domestic Routes by Revenue

From	To	Revenue		Margin		Per Passenger	
		Revenue Dollars	Revenue Percent	Margin Dollars	Margin Percent	Revenue per Passenger	Margin per Passenger
Atlanta	New York	$3,602,000	8.09%	$955,000	9%	245	65
Chicago	New York	$4,674,000	10.50%	$336,000	3%	222	16
Columbus (Ohio)	New York	$2,483,000	5.58%	$1,536,000	14%	202	125
New York	Detroit	$12,180,000	27.35%	$2,408,000	23%	177	35
New York	Washington	$6,355,000	14.27%	$1,230,000	12%	186	36
New York	Philadelphia	$3,582,000	8.04%	-$716,000	-7%	125	-25
New York	San Francisco	$3,221,000	7.23%	$1,856,000	18%	590	340
New York	Phoenix	$2,846,000	6.39%	$1,436,000	14%	555	280
New York	Toronto	$2,799,000	6.29%	$1,088,000	10%	450	175
New York	Seattle	$2,792,000	6.27%	$467,000	4%	448	75
Total Domestic routes		**$44,534,000**		**$10,596,000**		272	53

FIGURE 5-4: Minimize the use of borders and use the single accounting underlines to accent the column headers.

TIP

Single accounting underlines are different from the standard underlining you typically apply by pressing Ctrl+U on the keyboard. Standard underlines draw a line only as far as the text goes — that is to say, if you underline the word YES, standard underlines give you a line under the three letters. Single accounting underlines, on the other hand, draw a line across the entire column, regardless of how big or small the word is. This makes for a minimal, but apparent, visual demarcation that calls out column headers nicely.

You can format borders by first highlighting the cells you are working with and then pressing Ctrl+1 on the keyboard. This will activate the Format Cells dialog box shown in Figure 5-5. From here, take the following steps:

1. **Select an appropriate line thickness.**

   Typically, you should select the line with the lightest weight.

2. **Select an appropriate color.**

   Again, lighter hues are the best options.

3. **Use the border buttons to control where the borders are placed.**

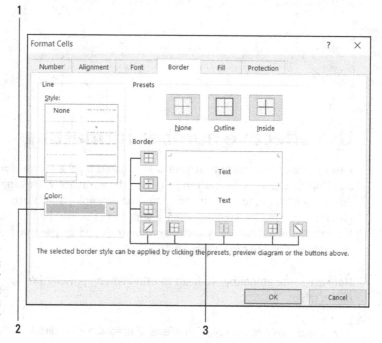

FIGURE 5-5:
Use the Border
tab of the Format
Cells dialog box
to customize your
borders.

To apply the single accounting underline, right-click the column headings and select Format Cells. Click the Font tab of the Format Cells dialog box and in the Underline drop-down menu, choose the Single Accounting option, as demonstrated in Figure 5-6.

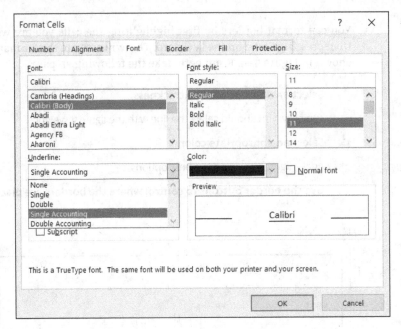

Use effective number formatting

Every piece of information in your table should have a reason for being there. In an effort to clarify, tables often inundate the audience with superfluous ink that doesn't add value to the information. For example, you'll often see tables that show a number like $145.57 when a simple 145 would be just fine. Why include the extra decimal places, which serve only to add to the mass of numbers that the audience has to plow through?

Here are some guidelines to keep in mind when applying formats to the numbers in the table:

- ❯❯ Use decimal places only if that level of precision is required.

- ❯❯ In percentages, use only the minimum number of decimals required to represent the data effectively.

- ❯❯ Rather than use currency symbols (like $ or £), let labels clarify that you are referring to monetary values.

- ❯❯ Format very large numbers to the thousands or millions place.

- ❯❯ Right-align numbers so that they are easier to read and compare.

Figure 5-7 shows the table from Figure 5-1 with appropriate number formatting applied. Notice that the large revenue and margin dollar amounts have been converted to the thousands place. In addition, the labels above the numbers now clearly indicate as such.

Top 10 Domestic Routes by Revenue		Revenue		Margin		Per Passenger	
From	To	Revenue $ (000's)	Revenue %	Margin $ (000's)	Margin %	$ per Passenger	Margin $per Passenger
Atlanta	New York	3,602	8%	955	9%	245	65
Chicago	New York	4,674	10%	336	3%	222	16
Columbus (Ohio)	New York	2,483	6%	1,536	14%	202	125
New York	Detroit	12,180	27%	2,408	23%	177	35
New York	Washington	6,355	14%	1,230	12%	186	36
New York	Philadelphia	3,582	8%	-716	-7%	125	-25
New York	San Francisco	3,221	7%	1,856	18%	590	340
New York	Phoenix	2,846	6%	1,436	14%	555	280
New York	Toronto	2,799	6%	1,088	10%	450	175
New York	Seattle	2,792	6%	467	4%	448	75
Total Domestic routes		44,534		10,596		272	53

The percentages have been truncated to show no decimal places. Also, the color coding draws attention to the Margin % column, the key metric in this table.

Amazingly, all of these improvements have been made simply with number formatting. That's right: No formulas were used to convert large numbers to the thousands place, no conditional formatting was used to color code the Margin % field, and there were no other peripheral tricks of any kind.

Subdue your labels and headers

No one would argue that the labels and headers of a table aren't important. On the contrary, they provide the audience with the guidance and structure needed to make sense of the data within. However, many of us have a habit of overemphasizing labels and headers to the point that they overshadow the data within the table. How many times have you seen a bold or oversized font applied to headers? The reality is that your audience will benefit more with subdued labels.

De-emphasizing labels by formatting them to lighter hues actually makes the table easier to read and draws more attention to the data within the table. Lightly colored labels give users the information they need without distracting them from the information being presented. Ideal colors to use for labels are soft grays, light browns, soft blues, and greens.

Font size and alignment also factor into the effective display of tables. Aligning column headers to the same alignment as the numbers beneath them helps reinforce the column structures in your table. Keeping the font size of your labels close to that of the data within the table helps keep your eyes focused on the data — not the labels.

Figure 5-8 illustrates how the original table from Figure 5-1 looks with subdued headers and labels. Note how the data now becomes the focus while the muted labels work in the background.

FIGURE 5-8:
Send your labels
and headers to
the background
by subduing their
colors and
keeping their font
sizes in line with
the data.

Top 10 Domestic Routes by Revenue

From	To	Revenue $ (000's)	Revenue %	Margin $ (000's)	Margin %	$ per Passenger	Margin $ per Passenger
New York	Detroit	12,180	27%	2,408	23%	177	35
New York	Washington	6,355	14%	1,230	12%	186	36
Chicago	New York	4,674	10%	336	3%	222	16
Atlanta	New York	3,602	8%	955	9%	245	65
New York	Philadelphia	3,582	8%	-716	-7%	125	-25
New York	San Francisco	3,221	7%	1,856	18%	590	340
New York	Phoenix	2,846	6%	1,436	14%	555	280
New York	Toronto	2,799	6%	1,088	10%	450	175
New York	Seattle	2,792	6%	467	4%	448	75
Columbus (Ohio)	New York	2,483	6%	1,536	14%	202	125
Total Domestic routes		44,534		10,596		272	53

Sorting is another key factor in the readability of your data. Many tables sort based on labels (alphabetical by route, for example). Sorting the table based on a key data point within the data helps establish a pattern the audience can use to quickly analyze the top and bottom values. Note in Figure 5-8 that the data has been sorted by the Revenue dollars. This again adds a layer of analysis, providing a quick look at the top- and bottom-generating routes.

Figure 5-9 illustrates the difference these simple improvements can make in the readability of your data tables. It's easy to see how a few table design principles can greatly enhance your ability to present table-driven data.

If possible, consider using modern-looking fonts such as Calibri and Segoe UI in your reports and dashboards. Fonts such as Times New Roman or Arial can make your reports look old compared with the rounded edges of the more trendy fonts used now. This change in font perception is primarily driven by popular online sites that often use fonts with rounded edges.

Top 10 Domestic Routes by Revenue

From	To	Revenue		Margin		Per Passenger	
		Revenue Dollars	Revenue Percent	Margin Dollars	Margin Percent	Revenue per Passenger	Margin per Passenger
Atlanta	New York	$3,602,000	8.09%	$955,000	9%	245	65
Chicago	New York	$4,674,000	10.50%	$336,000	3%	222	16
Columbus (Ohio)	New York	$2,483,000	5.58%	$1,536,000	14%	202	125
New York	Detroit	$12,180,000	27.35%	$2,408,000	23%	177	35
New York	Washington	$6,355,000	14.27%	$1,230,000	12%	186	36
New York	Philadelphia	$3,582,000	8.04%	-$716,000	-7%	125	-25
New York	San Francisco	$3,221,000	7.23%	$1,856,000	18%	590	340
New York	Phoenix	$2,846,000	6.39%	$1,436,000	14%	555	280
New York	Toronto	$2,799,000	6.29%	$1,088,000	10%	450	175
New York	Seattle	$2,792,000	6.27%	$467,000	4%	448	75
Total Domestic routes		**$44,534,000**		**$10,596,000**		**272**	**53**

Top 10 Domestic Routes by Revenue

From	To	Revenue		Margin		Per Passenger	
		Revenue $ (000's)	Revenue %	Margin $ (000's)	Margin %	$ per Passenger	Margin $ per Passenger
New York	Detroit	12,180	27%	2,408	23%	177	35
New York	Washington	6,355	14%	1,230	12%	186	36
Chicago	New York	4,674	10%	336	3%	222	16
Atlanta	New York	3,602	8%	955	9%	245	65
New York	Philadelphia	3,582	8%	-716	-7%	125	-25
New York	San Francisco	3,221	7%	1,856	18%	590	340
New York	Phoenix	2,846	6%	1,436	14%	555	280
New York	Toronto	2,799	6%	1,088	10%	450	175
New York	Seattle	2,792	6%	467	4%	448	75
Columbus (Ohio)	New York	2,483	6%	1,536	14%	202	125
Total Domestic routes		*44,534*		*10,596*		*272*	*53*

FIGURE 5-9: Before and after applying table design principles.

Getting Fancy with Custom Number Formatting

You can apply number formatting to cells in several ways. Most people simply use the convenient number commands found on the Home tab. By using these commands, you can quickly apply some default formatting (number, percent, currency, and so on) and just be done with it, but a better way is to use the Format Cells dialog box, in which you have the ability to create your own custom number formatting.

Number formatting basics

Follow these steps to apply basic number formatting:

1. **Right-click a range of cells and select Format Cells from the menu that appears.**

   The Format Cells dialog box appears.

2. **Open the Number tab and choose a starting format that makes the most sense for your scenario.**

In Figure 5-10, the format chosen is Number and the selected options are not to use a comma separator, to include no decimal places, and to enclose negative numbers in parentheses.

3. **Click the Custom option, as shown in Figure 5-11.**

Excel takes you to a screen that exposes the syntax that makes up the format you selected. Here, you can edit the syntax in the Type input box to customize the number format.

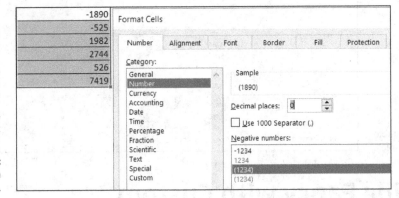

FIGURE 5-10:
Choose a base format.

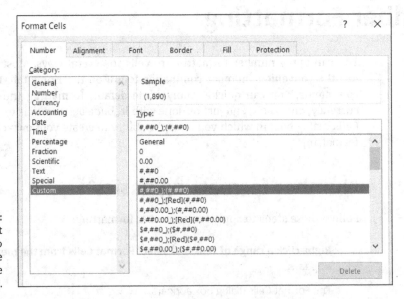

FIGURE 5-11:
The Type input box allows you to customize the syntax for the number format.

The number formatting syntax tells Excel how a number should look in various scenarios. Number formatting syntax consists of different individual number formats separated by semicolons.

In this case, you see

```
#,##0_);(#,##0)
```

Here, you see two different formats: the format to the left of the semicolon and the format to the right of the semicolon.

By default, any formatting to the left of the first semicolon is applied to positive numbers and any formatting to the right of the first semicolon is applied to negative numbers. So with this choice, positive numbers will be formatted as a simple number, whereas negative numbers will be formatted with parentheses, like this:

```
(1,890)
1,982
```

REMEMBER

Note that the syntax for the positive formatting in the previous example ends with an underscore and a closing parenthesis: _). This tells Excel to leave a space the width of a parenthesis character at the end of positive numbers, which ensures that positive and negative numbers align nicely when negative numbers are wrapped in parentheses.

You can edit the syntax in the Type input box so that the numbers are formatted differently. For example, try changing the syntax to

```
+#,##0;-#,##0
```

When this syntax is applied, positive numbers will start with the + symbol and negative numbers will start with the – symbol, like so:

```
+1,200
-15,000
```

This comes in handy when formatting percentages. For instance, you can apply a custom percent format by entering the following syntax into the Type input box:

```
+0%;-0%
```

This syntax gives you percentages that look like this:

```
+43%
–54%
```

You can get fancy and wrap your negative percentages with parentheses with this syntax:

```
0%_);(0%)
```

This syntax gives you percentages that look like this:

```
43%
(54%)
```

REMEMBER

If you include only one format syntax (meaning you don't add a second formatting option with the use of a semicolon separator), that single format will be applied to all numbers — negative or positive.

Formatting numbers in thousands and millions

Earlier in this chapter, you format your revenue numbers to appear in thousands. This allows you to present cleaner numbers and avoid inundating the audience with overlarge numbers. To show your numbers in thousands, highlight them, right-click, and select Format Cells from the menu that appears.

After the Format Cells dialog box opens, click the Custom option to get to the screen shown in Figure 5-12.

In the Type input box, add a comma after the format syntax:

```
#,##0,
```

After confirming your changes, your numbers will automatically appear in the thousands place!

The beautiful thing here is that this technique doesn't change the integrity or truncate the numeric values in any way. Excel is simply applying a cosmetic effect to the number. To see what this means, take a look at Figure 5-13.

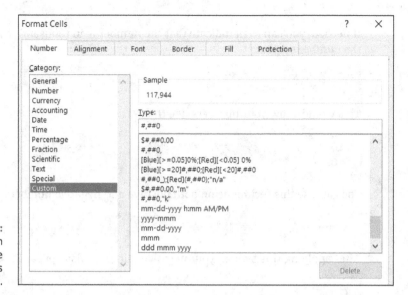

FIGURE 5-12:
Go to the Custom screen of the Format Cells dialog box.

FIGURE 5-13:
Formatting numbers applies only a cosmetic look. Look on the formula bar to see the real, unformatted number.

	A	B	C	D	E
				f_x	117943.605787004
6		North	118	380k	463k
7		Northeast	24k	803k	328k
8		East	313k	780k	904k
9		Southeast	397k	466k	832k
10		South	840k	118k	800k
11		Southwest	623k	977k	808k
12		West	474k	79k	876k

The selected cell has been formatted to show in thousands; you see 118. But if you look on the formula bar above it, you'll see the real unformatted number (117943.605787004). The 118 you are seeing in the cell is a cosmetically formatted version of the real number shown on the formula bar.

REMEMBER

Custom number formatting has obvious advantages over using other techniques to format numbers to thousands. For instance, many beginning analysts would convert numbers to thousands by dividing them by 1,000 in a formula. But that changes the integrity of the number dramatically. When you perform a mathematical operation into a cell, you are literally changing the value represented in that cell. This forces you to carefully keep track of and maintain the formulas you introduced to simply achieve a cosmetic effect. Using custom number formatting avoids that by changing only how the number looks, keeping the actual number intact.

If needed, you can even indicate that the number is in thousands by adding `"k"` to the number syntax:

```
#,##0,"k"
```

This would show your numbers like this:

```
118k
318k
```

You can use this technique on both positive and negative numbers:

```
#,##0,"k"; (#,##0,"k")
```

After applying this syntax, your negative numbers also appear in thousands:

```
118k
(318k)
```

Need to show numbers in millions? Easy. Simply add two commas to the number format syntax in the Type input box:

```
#,##0.00,, "m"
```

Note the use of the extra decimal places (`.00`). When converting numbers to millions, it's often useful to show additional precision points, as in

```
24.65 m
```

Hiding and suppressing zeroes

In addition to formatting positive and negative numbers, Excel allows you to provide a format for zeroes. You do this by adding another semicolon to your custom number syntax. By default, any format syntax placed after the second semicolon is applied to any number that evaluates to zero.

For example, the following syntax applies a format that shows n/a for any cells that contain zeroes:

```
#,##0_);(#,##0);"n/a"
```

You can also use this to suppress zeroes entirely. If you add the second semicolon but don't follow it with any syntax, cells containing zeroes will appear blank:

```
#,##0_);(#,##0);
```

Again, custom number formatting only affects the cosmetic look of the cell. The actual data in the cell is not affected. Figure 5-14 demonstrates this. The selected cell is formatted so that zeroes appear as n/a, but if you look at the formula bar, you can see the actual unformatted cell contents.

FIGURE 5-14: Custom number formatting that shows zeroes as n/a.

B	C	D	E
Printers	37,000	64,000	24,000
Copiers	18,000	29,000	58,000
Scanners	n/a	77,000	88,000
Service Contr	16,000	12,000	n/a
Warranties	65,000	88,000	16,000

Applying custom format colors

Have you ever set the formatting on a cell so that negative numbers appear in red? If you have, you essentially applied a custom format color. In addition to controlling the look of your numbers with custom number formatting, you can control their color.

In this example, you format the percentages so that positive percentages appear blue with a + symbol, whereas negative percentages appear red with a – symbol. Enter this syntax in the Type input box shown in Figure 5-11:

```
[Blue]+0%;[Red]-0%
```

Notice that all it takes to apply a color is to enter the color name wrapped in square brackets [ ].

Now, there are only certain colors — the eight Visual Basic colors — you can call out by name like this. These colors make up the first eight colors of the default Excel color palette:

[Black]

[Blue]

[Cyan]

[Green]

[Magenta]

[Red]

[White]

[Yellow]

Formatting dates and times

Custom number formatting isn't just for numbers. You can also format dates and times. As you can see in Figure 5-15, you use the same dialog box to apply date and time formats using the Type input box.

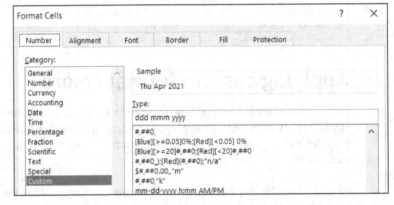

Figure 5-15 demonstrates that date and time formatting involves little more than stringing together date-specific or time-specific syntax. The syntax used is fairly intuitive. For example, ddd is the syntax for the 3-letter day, mmm is the syntax for the 3-letter month, and yyyy is the syntax for the 4-digit year.

There are several variations on the format for days, months, years, hours, and minutes. It's worthwhile to take some time and experiment with different combinations of syntax strings.

Table 5-1 lists some common date and time format codes you can use as starter syntax for your reports and dashboards.

TABLE 5-1
Common Date and Time Format Codes

Format Code	1/31/2021 7:42:53 PM Displays As
m	1
mm	01
mmm	Jan
mmmm	January
mmmmm	J
dd	31
ddd	Sun
dddd	Sunday
yy	21
yyyy	2021
mmm-yy	Jan-21
dd/mm/yyyy	31/01/2021
dddd mmm yyyy	Sunday Jan 2021
mm-dd-yyyy h:mm AM/PM	01-31-2021 7:42 PM
h AM/PM	7 PM
h:mm AM/PM	7:42 PM
h:mm:ss AM/PM	7:42:53 PM

Chapter **6**

Sparking Inspiration with Sparklines

This chapter introduces you to *sparklines*. These magically named visualizations are essentially mini word-size charts placed in and among the textual data in tables. Sparklines enable you to see, at a glance, trends and patterns within your data using minimal real estate on your dashboard.

Before getting into the nuts and bolts of using sparklines, you should understand exactly how they can enhance your reporting. This chapter introduces you to the concept of sparklines and then shows you how to customize and add them to tables.

Introducing Sparklines

As I mention in Chapter 5, much of the reporting done in Excel is table-based, in which precise numbers are more important than pretty charts. However, in table-based reporting, you often lose the ability to show important aspects of the data such as trends. The number of columns needed to show adequate trend data in a table makes it impractical to do so. Any attempt to add trend data to a table usually does nothing more than render your report unreadable.

In the example in Figure 6-1, the data represents a compact KPI (key performance indicator) summary designed to be an at-a-glance view of key metrics. Although the table compares various time periods (in columns D, E, and F), it does so only by averaging, which tells you nothing about trends over time. It quickly becomes evident that seeing a full-year trend would be helpful.

	A	B	C	D	E	F	H	I
1	Compact KPI Summary			Current Month	Last 3 Mo Avg	Last 12 mo Avg	Target	% of Target
2		Finance Metrics	$ Revenues	$18,134 K	$17,985 K	$17,728 K	$18,000 K	101%
3			$ Expenses	$11,358 K	$11,186 K	$11,580 K	$12,600 K	90%
4			$ Profits	$6,776 K	$6,799 K	$6,147 K	$5,400 K	125%
5			% Market Share	44%	46%	45%	52%	85%
6		Flight Metrics	Flights	446	447	449	500	89%
7			Passengers	63 K	62 K	61 K	65 K	97%
8			Miles	346 K	347 K	349 K	395 K	88%
9			Passenger Miles	31,206 K	31,376 K	31,510 K	36,000 K	87%
10			Cancelled Flights	9	9	10	15	60%
11			Late Arrivals	63	71	64	45	141%
12			Minutes Late	1,302	1,472	1,337	1,000	130%
13			$ Fuel Costs	$1,293 K	$1,332 K	$1,326 K	$1,080 K	120%
14			Customer Satisfaction	4.52	4.5	4.5	4.80	94%
15			Flight Utilization	92%	91%	91%	94%	98%

FIGURE 6-1: Although this KPI summary is useful, it cannot show a full-year trend.

Figure 6-2 illustrates the same KPI summary with Excel sparklines added to visually show the 12-month trend. With the sparklines added, you can see the broader story behind each metric. For example, based solely on the numbers, the Passengers metric appears to be up slightly from the average. But the sparkline tells the story of a heroic comeback from a huge hit at the beginning of the year.

Again, it's not about adding flash and pizzazz to your tables. It's about building the most effective message in the limited space you have. Sparklines are another tool you can use to add another dimension to your table-based reports.

	Compact KPI Summary		Current Month	Last 3 Mo Avg	Last 12 mo Avg	12 Month Trend	Target	% of Target
Finance Metrics		$ Revenues	$18,134 K	$17,985 K	$17,728 K		$18,000 K	101%
		$ Expenses	$11,358 K	$11,186 K	$11,580 K		$12,600 K	90%
		$ Profits	$6,776 K	$6,799 K	$6,147 K		$5,400 K	125%
		% Market Share	44%	46%	45%		52%	85%
Flight Metrics		Flights	446	447	449		500	89%
		Passengers	63 K	62 K	61 K		65 K	97%
		Miles	346 K	347 K	349 K		395 K	88%
		Passenger Miles	31,206 K	31,376 K	31,510 K		36,000 K	87%
		Cancelled Flights	9	9	10		15	60%
		Late Arrivals	63	71	64		45	141%
		Minutes Late	1,302	1,472	1,337		1,000	130%
		$ Fuel Costs	$1,293 K	$1,332 K	$1,326 K		$1,080 K	120%
		Customer Satisfaction	4.52	4.5	4.5		4.80	94%
		Flight Utilization	92%	91%	91%		94%	98%

FIGURE 6-2: Sparklines allow you to add trending in a compact space, enabling you to see a broader picture for each metric.

Understanding Sparklines

Although sparklines look like miniature charts (and can sometimes take the place of a chart), this feature is completely separate from the Excel chart feature (covered in Chapters 7, 8, and 9 of this book). For example, charts are placed on a worksheet's drawing layer, and a single chart can display several series of data. In contrast, a sparkline is displayed inside a worksheet cell and displays only one series of data.

Excel supports three types of sparklines: Line, Column, and Win/Loss. Figure 6–3 shows examples of each type of sparkline graphic, displayed in column H. Each sparkline depicts the six data points to the left.

>> **Line:** Similar to a line chart, the Line type of sparkline can appear with or without a marker for each data point. The first group in Figure 6-3 shows Line sparklines with markers. A quick glance reveals that with the exception of Fund Number W-91, the funds have been losing value over the 6-month period.

>> **Column:** Similar to a column chart, the second group shows the same data with Column sparklines.

>> **Win/Loss:** A Win/Loss sparkline is a binary-type chart that displays each data point as a high block or a low block. The third group shows Win/Loss sparklines. Notice that the data is different. Each cell displays the change from the

previous month. In the sparkline, each data point is depicted as a high block (win) or a low block (loss). In this example, a positive change from the previous month is a win, and a negative change from the previous month is a loss.

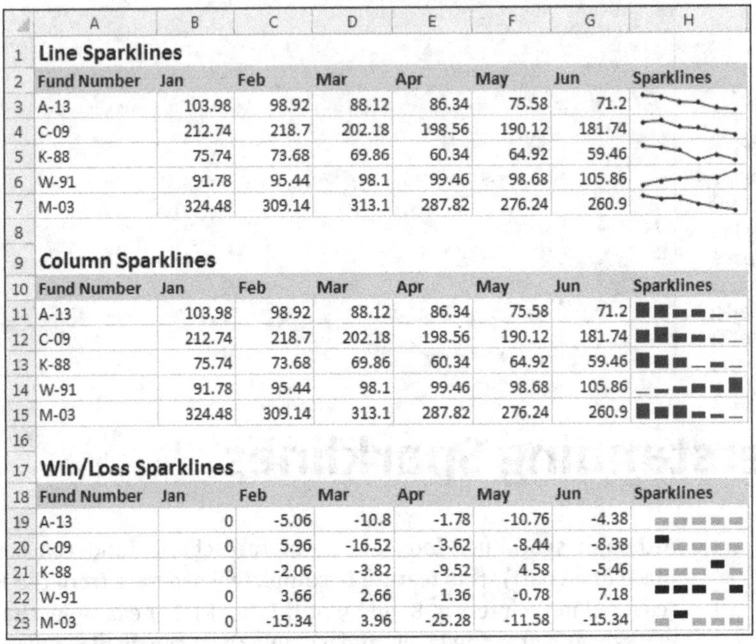

	A	B	C	D	E	F	G	H
1	**Line Sparklines**							
2	**Fund Number**	**Jan**	**Feb**	**Mar**	**Apr**	**May**	**Jun**	**Sparklines**
3	A-13	103.98	98.92	88.12	86.34	75.58	71.2	
4	C-09	212.74	218.7	202.18	198.56	190.12	181.74	
5	K-88	75.74	73.68	69.86	60.34	64.92	59.46	
6	W-91	91.78	95.44	98.1	99.46	98.68	105.86	
7	M-03	324.48	309.14	313.1	287.82	276.24	260.9	
8								
9	**Column Sparklines**							
10	**Fund Number**	**Jan**	**Feb**	**Mar**	**Apr**	**May**	**Jun**	**Sparklines**
11	A-13	103.98	98.92	88.12	86.34	75.58	71.2	
12	C-09	212.74	218.7	202.18	198.56	190.12	181.74	
13	K-88	75.74	73.68	69.86	60.34	64.92	59.46	
14	W-91	91.78	95.44	98.1	99.46	98.68	105.86	
15	M-03	324.48	309.14	313.1	287.82	276.24	260.9	
16								
17	**Win/Loss Sparklines**							
18	**Fund Number**	**Jan**	**Feb**	**Mar**	**Apr**	**May**	**Jun**	**Sparklines**
19	A-13	0	-5.06	-10.8	-1.78	-10.76	-4.38	
20	C-09	0	5.96	-16.52	-3.62	-8.44	-8.38	
21	K-88	0	-2.06	-3.82	-9.52	4.58	-5.46	
22	W-91	0	3.66	2.66	1.36	-0.78	7.18	
23	M-03	0	-15.34	3.96	-25.28	-11.58	-15.34	

FIGURE 6-3: Three types of sparklines.

Creating sparklines

Figure 6-4 shows some weather data that you can summarize with sparklines. To create sparkline graphics for the values in these nine rows, follow these steps:

1. **Select the data range that you want to summarize. In this example, select B4:M12.**

   If you are creating multiple sparklines, select all the data.

2. **With the data selected, click the Insert tab on the Ribbon and find the Sparklines group.**

3. **On the Insert tab, select any one of the three sparkline types — Line, Column, or Win/Loss — from the Sparklines group. In this case, select the Column option.**

   Excel displays the Create Sparklines dialog box, as shown in Figure 6-5.

4. **Specify the data range and the location for the sparklines. For this example, specify N4:N12 as the Location Range.**

Typically, you put the sparklines next to the data, but that's not required. Most of the time, you use an empty range to hold the sparklines. However, Excel does not prevent you from inserting sparklines into filled-in cells. The sparkline location that you specify must match the source data in terms of number of rows or number of columns.

5. **Click OK.**

Excel creates the sparklines graphics of the type you specified, as shown in Figure 6-6.

The sparklines are linked to the data, so if you change any of the values in the data range, the sparkline graphic will update.

REMEMBER

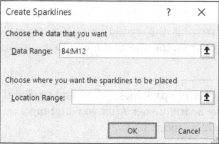

	A	B	C	D	E	F	G	H	I	J	K	L	M
1	**Average Monthly Precipitation (Inches)**												
2													
3		Jan	Feb	Mar	Apr	May	Jun	Jul	Aug	Sep	Oct	Nov	Dec
4	ASHEVILLE, NC	4.06	3.83	4.59	3.50	4.41	4.38	3.87	4.30	3.72	3.17	3.82	3.39
5	BAKERSFIELD, CA	1.18	1.21	1.41	0.45	0.24	0.12	0.00	0.08	0.15	0.30	0.59	0.76
6	BATON ROUGE, LA	6.19	5.10	5.07	5.56	5.34	5.33	5.96	5.86	4.84	3.81	4.76	5.26
7	BILLINGS, MT	0.81	0.57	1.12	1.74	2.48	1.89	1.28	0.85	1.34	1.26	0.75	0.67
8	DAYTONA BEACH, FL	3.13	2.74	3.84	2.54	3.26	5.69	5.17	6.09	6.61	4.48	3.03	2.71
9	EUGENE, OR	7.65	6.35	5.80	3.66	2.66	1.53	0.64	0.99	1.54	3.35	8.44	8.29
10	HONOLULU,HI	2.73	2.35	1.89	1.11	0.78	0.43	0.50	0.46	0.74	2.18	2.26	2.85
11	ST. LOUIS, MO	2.14	2.28	3.60	3.69	4.11	3.76	3.90	2.98	2.96	2.76	3.71	2.86
12	TUCSON, AZ	0.99	0.88	0.81	0.28	0.24	0.24	2.07	2.30	1.45	1.21	0.67	1.03

FIGURE 6-4:
Data that you want to summarize with sparkline graphics.

Create Sparklines ? ×

Choose the data that you want

Data Range: B4:M12

Choose where you want the sparklines to be placed

Location Range:

OK   Cancel

FIGURE 6-5:
Use the Create Sparklines dialog box to specify the data range and the location for the sparkline graphics.

TIP

Most of the time, you'll create sparklines on the same sheet that contains the data. If you want to create sparklines on a different sheet, start by activating the sheet where the sparklines will be displayed. Then, in the Create Sparklines dialog box, specify the source data either by selecting the cell range or by typing the complete sheet reference (for example, **Sheet1!A1:C12**). The Create Sparklines dialog box lets you specify a different sheet for the Data Range, but not for the Location Range.

	A	Jan	Feb	Mar	Apr	May	Jun	Jul	Aug	Sep	Oct	Nov	Dec	N
1	Average Monthly Precipitation (Inches)													
2														
3		Jan	Feb	Mar	Apr	May	Jun	Jul	Aug	Sep	Oct	Nov	Dec	
4	ASHEVILLE, NC	4.06	3.83	4.59	3.50	4.41	4.38	3.87	4.30	3.72	3.17	3.82	3.39	
5	BAKERSFIELD, CA	1.18	1.21	1.41	0.45	0.24	0.12	0.00	0.08	0.15	0.30	0.59	0.76	
6	BATON ROUGE, LA	6.19	5.10	5.07	5.56	5.34	5.33	5.96	5.86	4.84	3.81	4.76	5.26	
7	BILLINGS, MT	0.81	0.57	1.12	1.74	2.48	1.89	1.28	0.85	1.34	1.26	0.75	0.67	
8	DAYTONA BEACH, FL	3.13	2.74	3.84	2.54	3.26	5.69	5.17	6.09	6.61	4.48	3.03	2.71	
9	EUGENE, OR	7.65	6.35	5.80	3.66	2.66	1.53	0.64	0.99	1.54	3.35	8.44	8.29	
10	HONOLULU,HI	2.73	2.35	1.89	1.11	0.78	0.43	0.50	0.46	0.74	2.18	2.26	2.85	
11	ST. LOUIS, MO	2.14	2.28	3.60	3.69	4.11	3.76	3.90	2.98	2.96	2.76	3.71	2.86	
12	TUCSON, AZ	0.99	0.88	0.81	0.28	0.24	0.24	2.07	2.30	1.45	1.21	0.67	1.03	

FIGURE 6-6:
Column sparklines summarize the precipitation data for nine cities.

Understanding sparkline groups

Most of the time, you'll probably create a group of sparklines — one for each row or column of data. A worksheet can hold any number of sparkline groups. Excel remembers each group, and you can work with the group as a single unit. For example, you can select one sparkline in a group and then modify the formatting of all sparklines in the group. When you select one sparkline cell, Excel displays an outline around all other sparklines in the group.

You can, however, perform some operations on an individual sparkline in a group:

>> **Change the sparkline's data source.** Click the sparkline cell and go to the Sparkline tab on the Ribbon. There, you can choose Sparkline ⇨ Edit Data ⇨ Edit Single Sparkline's Data. Excel displays a dialog box that lets you change the data source for the selected sparkline.

>> **Delete the sparkline.** Click the sparkline, click the Sparkline tab on the Ribbon, and then choose Clear ⇨ Clear Selected Sparklines.

REMEMBER

Both operations — changing the sparkline's data source and deleting the sparkline — are available from the shortcut menu that appears when you right-click a sparkline cell.

You can also ungroup a set of sparklines. Select any sparkline in the group and choose Ungroup from the Sparkline tab. After you ungroup a set of sparklines, you can work with each sparkline individually.

TIP

You can add a new sparkline to an existing group by first selecting any sparkline in the existing group and then choosing Edit Data ⇨ Edit Group Location & Data. This opens the Edit Sparklines dialog box. Simply edit the Data Range and Location Range to include the new data you want to add.

Customizing Sparklines

When you activate a cell that contains a sparkline, Excel displays an outline around all sparklines in its group. You can then use the commands on the Sparkline tab to customize the group of sparklines.

Sizing and merging sparkline cells

When you change the width or height of a cell that contains a sparkline, the sparkline adjusts to fill the new cell size. In addition, you can put a sparkline into merged cells. To merge cells, select at least two cells and choose Home ⇨ Merge & Center from the Ribbon.

Figure 6-7 shows the same sparkline displayed in four sizes, resulting from changing column width and row height and from merging cells.

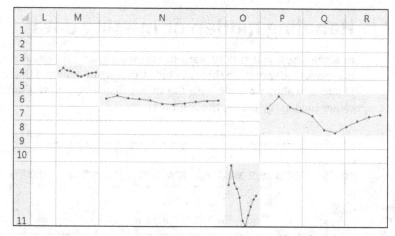

FIGURE 6-7:
A sparkline at various sizes.

It's important to note that a skewed aspect ratio can distort your visualizations, exaggerating the trend in sparklines that are too tall and flattening the trend in sparklines that are too wide. Generally speaking, the most appropriate aspect ratio for a chart is one where the width of the chart is about twice as long as the height. In Figure 6-7, the sparkline with the most appropriate aspect ratio is the one located in cell M4.

REMEMBER

If you merge cells and the merged cells occupy more than one row or one column, Excel doesn't let you insert a group of sparklines into those merged cells. Rather, you need to insert the sparklines into a normal range (with no merged cells) and then merge the cells.

You can also put a sparkline in non-empty cells, including merged cells. Figure 6-8 shows two sparklines that occupy merged cells alongside text that describes the graphics.

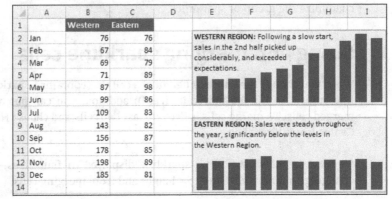

FIGURE 6-8:
Sparklines in
merged cells
(E2:I7 and E9:I14).

Handling hidden or missing data

In some cases, you simply want to present a sparkline visualization without the numbers. One way to do this is to hide the rows or columns that contain the data. Figure 6-9 shows a table with the values displayed and the same table with the values hidden (by hiding the columns).

FIGURE 6-9:
Sparklines can
use data in
hidden rows
or columns.

By default, if you hide rows or columns that contain data used in a sparkline graphic, the hidden data does not appear in the sparkline. In addition, blank cells are displayed as a gap in the graphic.

To change these default settings, go to the Sparkline tab on the Ribbon and select Edit Data ⇨ Hidden & Empty Cells. In the Hidden and Empty Cell Settings dialog box, you can specify how to handle hidden data and empty cells.

Changing the sparkline type

As mentioned earlier in this chapter, Excel supports three sparkline types: Line, Column, and Win/Loss. After you create a sparkline or group of sparklines, you can easily change the type by clicking the sparkline and selecting one of the three icons located in the Type group on the Sparkline tab. If the selected sparkline is part of a group, all sparklines in the group are changed to the new type.

TIP

If you've customized the appearance, Excel remembers the customization settings for each sparkline type if you switch among different ones.

Changing sparkline colors and line width

After you create a sparkline, changing the color is easy. Simply click to select the sparkline, click to open the Sparkline tab on the Ribbon, and select Style. There, you find various options to change the color and style of the sparkline.

For Line sparklines, you can also specify the line width. Choose Sparkline ⇨ Sparkline Color ⇨ Weight.

REMEMBER

Colors used in sparkline graphics are tied to the document theme. If you change the theme (by choosing Page Layout ⇨ Themes), the sparkline colors then change to the new theme colors.

Using color to emphasize key data points

Use the commands in the Show group on the Sparkline tab to customize the sparklines to emphasize key aspects of the data. These options are in the Show group:

>> **High Point:** Apply a different color to the highest data point in the sparkline.

>> **Low Point:** Apply a different color to the lowest data point in the sparkline.

>> **Negative Points:** Apply a different color to negative values in the sparkline.

>> **First Point:** Apply a different color to the first data point in the sparkline.

>> **Last Point:** Apply a different color to the last data point in the sparkline.

>> **Markers:** Show data markers in the sparkline. This option is available only for Line sparklines.

You can control the color of sparkline markers by using the Marker Color control in the Sparkline ⇨ Style group. Unfortunately, you cannot change the size of the markers in Line sparklines.

Adjusting sparkline axis scaling

When you create one or more sparklines, they all use (by default) automatic axis scaling. In other words, Excel determines the minimum and maximum vertical axis values for each sparkline in the group based on the numeric range of the sparkline data.

The Sparkline ⇨ Axis drop-down lets you override this automatic behavior and control the minimum and maximum values for each sparkline or for a group of sparklines. For even more control, you can use the Custom Value option and specify the minimum and maximum for the sparkline group.

Axis scaling can make a huge difference in the sparklines. Figure 6-10 shows two groups of sparklines. The group at the bottom uses the default axis settings (Automatic For Each Sparkline option). Each sparkline in this group shows the 6-month trend for the product but not the magnitude of the values.

FIGURE 6-10: The bottom group of sparklines shows the effect of using the same axis minimum and maximum values for all sparklines in a group.

	A	B	C	D	E	F	G	H
1								
2		Jan	Feb	Mar	Apr	May	Jun	Sparklines
3	Product A	100	103	103	115	122	125	
4	Product B	300	295	300	312	307	322	
5	Product C	600	597	599	606	620	618	
6								
7								
8								
9		Jan	Feb	Mar	Apr	May	Jun	Sparklines
10	Product A	100	103	103	115	122	125	
11	Product B	300	295	300	312	307	322	
12	Product C	600	597	599	606	620	618	

The sparkline group at the bottom (which uses the same data) uses the Same for All Sparklines setting for the minimum and maximum axis values. With these settings in effect, the magnitude of the values across the products is apparent — but the trend across the months within a product is not apparent.

The axis scaling option you choose depends on what aspect of the data you want to emphasize.

Faking a reference line

One useful feature that's missing in sparklines is a reference line. For example, it might be useful to show performance relative to a goal. If the goal is displayed as a reference line in a sparkline, the viewer can quickly see whether the performance for a period exceeded the goal.

One approach is to write formulas that transform the data and then use a sparkline axis as a fake reference line. Figure 6-11 shows an example. Students have a monthly reading goal of 500 pages. The range of data shows the actual pages read, with sparklines in column H. The sparklines show the 6-month page data, but it's impossible to tell who exceeded the goal or when they did it.

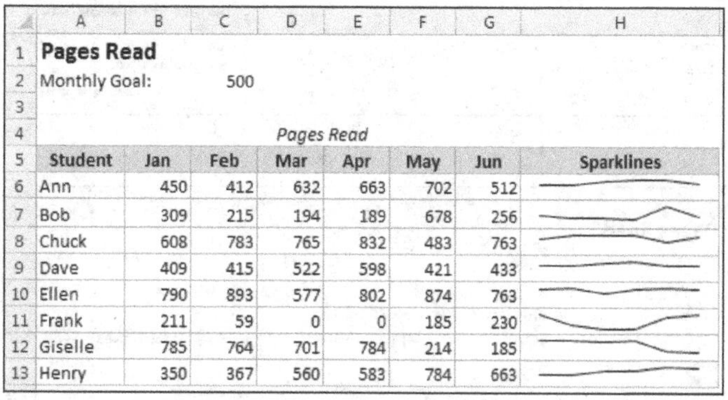

FIGURE 6-11:
Sparklines display the number of pages read per month.

The lower set of sparklines in Figure 6-12 shows another approach: Transform the data such that meeting the goal is expressed as a 1, and failing to meet the goal is expressed as a −1. The following formula (in cell B18) transforms the original data:

```
=IF(B6>$C$2,1,-1)
```

This formula was copied to the other cells in the B18:G25 range.

Using the transformed data, Win/Loss sparklines are used to visualize the results. This approach is better than the original, but it doesn't convey magnitude differences. For example, you cannot tell whether the student missed the goal by 1 page or by 500 pages.

Figure 6-13 shows a better approach. Here, the original data is transformed by subtracting the goal from the pages read. The formula in cell B30 is

```
=B6-C$2
```

	A	B	C	D	E	F	G	H
4				Pages Read				
5	Student	Jan	Feb	Mar	Apr	May	Jun	Sparklines
6	Ann	450	412	632	663	702	512	
7	Bob	309	215	194	189	678	256	
8	Chuck	608	783	765	832	483	763	
9	Dave	409	415	522	598	421	433	
10	Ellen	790	893	577	802	874	763	
11	Frank	211	59	0	0	185	230	
12	Giselle	785	764	701	784	214	185	
13	Henry	350	367	560	583	784	663	
14								
15								
16				Pages Read (Did or Did Not Meet Goal)				
17	Student	Jan	Feb	Mar	Apr	May	Jun	Sparklines
18	Ann	-1	-1	1	1	1	1	
19	Bob	-1	-1	-1	-1	1	-1	
20	Chuck	1	1	1	1	-1	1	
21	Dave	-1	-1	1	1	-1	-1	
22	Ellen	1	1	1	1	1	1	
23	Frank	-1	-1	-1	-1	-1	-1	
24	Giselle	1	1	1	1	-1	-1	
25	Henry	-1	-1	1	1	1	1	

FIGURE 6-12: Using Win/Loss sparklines to display goal status.

	A	B	C	D	E	F	G	H
1	**Pages Read**							
2	Monthly Goal:		500					
3								
28				Pages Read (Relative to Goal)				
29	Student	Jan	Feb	Mar	Apr	May	Jun	Sparklines
30	Ann	-50	-88	132	163	202	12	
31	Bob	-191	-285	-306	-311	178	-244	
32	Chuck	108	283	265	332	-17	263	
33	Dave	-91	-85	22	98	-79	-67	
34	Ellen	290	393	77	302	374	263	
35	Frank	-289	-441	-500	-500	-315	-270	
36	Giselle	285	264	201	284	-286	-315	
37	Henry	-150	-133	60	83	284	163	

FIGURE 6-13: The axis in the sparklines represents the goal.

This formula was copied to the other cells in the B30:G37 range, and a group of Line sparklines displays the resulting values. This group has the Show Axis setting enabled and also uses Negative Point markers so that the negative values (failure to meet the goal) clearly stand out.

Specifying a date axis

By default, data displayed in a sparkline is assumed to be at equal intervals. For example, a sparkline might display a daily account balance, sales by month, or profits by year. But what if the data isn't at equal intervals?

Figure 6-14 shows data, by date, along with a sparklines graphic created from column B. Notice that some dates are missing but that the sparkline shows the columns as though the values were spaced at equal intervals.

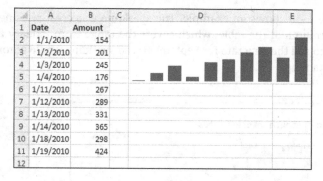

FIGURE 6-14:
The sparkline displays the values as though they are at equal time intervals.

To better depict this type of time-based data, the solution is to specify a Date axis. Select the sparkline and choose Sparkline ⇨ Axis ⇨ Date Axis Type.

Excel displays a dialog box asking for the range that contains the corresponding dates. In this example, specify range A2:A11.

Click OK, and the sparkline displays gaps for the missing dates, as shown in Figure 6-15.

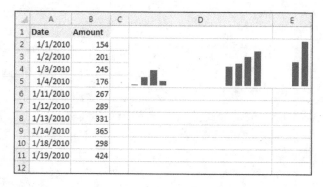

FIGURE 6-15:
After you specify a date axis, the sparkline shows the values accurately.

Autoupdating sparkline ranges

If a sparkline uses data in a normal range of cells, adding new data to the beginning or end of the range does not force the sparkline to use the new data. You need to use the Edit Sparklines dialog box to update the data range (Sparkline ⇨ Edit Data).

However, if the sparkline data is in a column within a table object (created using Insert ⇨ Table, as described in Chapter 2), the sparkline uses new data that's added to the end of the table without requiring an update.

Figure 6-16 shows an example. The sparkline was created using the data in the Rate column of the table, which covers the range from January to August. If you were to add the new rate for September, the sparkline would automatically update its data range.

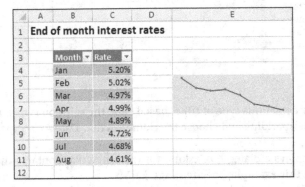

FIGURE 6-16:
Creating a
sparkline from
data in a table.

IN THIS CHAPTER

» **Using conditional formatting**

» **Working with symbols in formulas**

» **Using the Camera tool**

» **Using shapes to enhance Excel reports**

Chapter **7**

Formatting Your Way to Visualizations

isualization is the presentation of abstract concepts or data in visual terms through some sort of graphical imagery. A traffic light, for example, is a visualization of the abstract concepts of stop-and-go.

In the business world, visualizations help us communicate and process the meaning of data faster than simple tables of numbers. Excel offers business analysts a wide array of features that can be used to add visualizations to dashboards and reports.

In this chapter, you explore some of the formatting techniques you can leverage to add layers of visualizations that can turn your data into meaningful views.

Enhancing Reports with Conditional Formatting

Conditional formatting is the term given to Excel's capability to dynamically change the formatting of a value, cell, or range of cells based on a set of conditions you define. Conditional formatting adds a level of visualization that allows you to look at your Excel reports and make split-second determinations on which values are "good" and which are "bad," simply based on formatting.

In this section, you enter the world of conditional formatting as you see how to leverage this functionality to enhance your reports and dashboards.

Applying basic conditional formatting

Thanks to the many predefined scenarios that Excel offers, you can apply some basic conditional formatting with a few clicks of the mouse. To get a first taste of what you can do, click the Conditional Formatting button found on the Home tab of the Ribbon, as shown in Figure 7-1.

FIGURE 7-1:
The predefined conditional formatting scenarios available in Excel.

As you can see, Excel has five categories of predefined scenarios: Highlight Cells Rules, Top/Bottom Rules, Data Bars, Color Scales, and Icon Sets.

Take a moment to review what you can do by using each category of predefined scenario.

Using the Highlight Cells Rules

The formatting scenarios under the Highlight Cells Rules category, shown in Figure 7-2, allow you to highlight those cells whose values meet a specific condition.

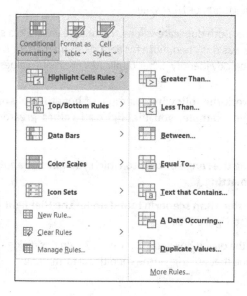

FIGURE 7-2:
The Highlight
Cells Rules
scenarios apply
formats if specific
conditions
are met.

The thing to remember about these scenarios is that they work much like an If...then...else statement. That is to say, if the condition is met, the cell is formatted, and if the condition is not met, the cell remains untouched.

The scenarios under the Highlight Cells Rules category are self-explanatory. Here's a breakdown of what you can conditionally format with each scenario:

» **Greater Than:** A cell whose value is greater than a specified amount. For instance, you can tell Excel to format those cells that contain a value greater than 50.

» **Less Than:** A cell whose value is less than a specified amount. For instance, you can tell Excel to format those cells that contain a value less than 100.

» **Between:** A cell whose value is between two given amounts. For example, you can tell Excel to format those cells that contain a value between 50 and 100.

» **Equal To:** A cell whose value is equal to a given amount. For example, you can tell Excel to format those cells that contain a value that is exactly 50.

>> **Text That Contains:** A cell whose contents contain any form of a given text you specify as a criterion. For example, you can tell Excel to format those cells that contain the text *North*.

>> **A Date Occurring:** A cell whose contents contain a date occurring in a specified period relative to today's date. For example, Yesterday, Last Week, Last Month, Next Month, or Next Week.

>> **Duplicate Values:** Both duplicate values and unique values in a given range of cells. This rule was designed more for data clean-up than for dashboarding, enabling you to quickly identify either duplicates or unique values in your data set.

Take a moment to work the following example of how to apply one of these scenarios. In this simple example, you highlight all values greater than a certain amount.

1. **Start by selecting the range of cells to which you need to apply the conditional formatting.**

2. **Choose the Greater Than scenario found under the Highlight Cells Rules category (refer to Figure 7-2).**

   This step opens the dialog box shown in Figure 7-3. In this dialog box, the idea is to define a value that will trigger the conditional formatting.

FIGURE 7-3:
Each scenario has its own dialog box you can use to define the trigger values and the format for each rule.

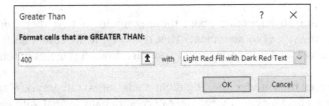

3. **Either type the value (400 in this example) or reference a cell that contains the trigger value, and then use the box's drop-down menu to specify the format you want applied.**

4. **Click the OK button.**

   Immediately, Excel applies the formatting rule to the selected cells (see Figure 7-4).

The benefit of a conditional formatting rule is that Excel automatically reevaluates the rule every time a cell is changed (as long as that cell has a conditional formatting rule applied to it). For instance, if I were to change any of the low values to 450, the formatting for that value would automatically change because all cells in the data set have the formatting applied to them.

	Greater Than 400
Jan	100
Feb	-100
Mar	200
Apr	250
May	-50
Jun	350
Jul	400
Aug	450
Sep	500
Oct	550
Nov	600
Dec	650

FIGURE 7-4:
Cells greater
than 400 are
formatted.

Applying Top/Bottom Rules

The formatting scenarios under the Top/Bottom Rules category, shown in Figure 7-5, allow you to highlight those cells whose values meet a given threshold.

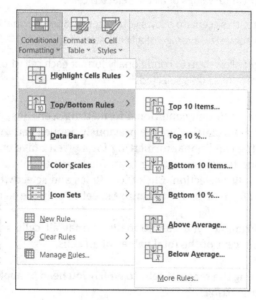

FIGURE 7-5:
The Top/Bottom
Rules scenarios
apply formats
if specific
thresholds
are met.

Like the Highlight Cells Rules, these scenarios work like If...then...else statements: If the condition is met, the cell is formatted; if the condition is not met, the cell remains untouched.

Here is a breakdown of each scenario under the Top/Bottom Rules category:

>> **Top 10 Items:** Although the name doesn't suggest it, this scenario allows you to specify any number of cells to highlight based on individual cell values

(not just ten). For example, you can highlight the top five cells whose values are among the five largest numbers of all selected cells.

>> **Top 10 %:** This scenario is similar to the Top 10 Items scenario: Only the selected cells are evaluated on a percentage basis. Again, don't let the name fool you: The percent selection does not have to be ten. For instance, you can highlight the cells whose values make up the top 20 percent of the total values of all selected cells.

>> **Bottom 10 Items:** You can use this scenario to specify the number of cells to highlight based on the lowest individual cell values. Again, don't let the name fool you: You can specify any number of cells to highlight — not just 10. For example, you can highlight the bottom 15 cells whose values are within the 15 smallest numbers among all selected cells.

>> **Bottom 10 %:** Though this scenario is similar to the Bottom 10 Items scenario, in this one, only selected cells are evaluated on a percentage basis. For instance, you can highlight the cells whose values make up the bottom 15 percent of the total values of all the selected cells.

>> **Above Average:** This scenario allows you to conditionally format each cell whose value is above the average of all cells selected.

>> **Below Average:** Allows you to conditionally format each cell whose value is below the average of all cells selected.

REMEMBER

To avoid overlapping different conditional formatting scenarios, you may want to clear any conditional formatting you've previously applied before applying a new scenario. To clear the conditional formatting for a given range of cells, select the cells and select Conditional Formatting from the Home tab of the Ribbon. There, you find the Clear Rules selection. Click Clear Rules and select whether you want to clear conditional formatting for the entire sheet or only the selected workbook.

In the following example, you conditionally format all cells whose values are within the top 40 percent of the total values of all cells.

1. **Start by selecting the range of cells to which you need to apply the conditional formatting.**

2. **Choose the Top 10 % scenario found under the Top/Bottom Rules category (refer to Figure 7-5).**

   This step opens the Top 10% dialog box shown in Figure 7-6. The idea here is to define the threshold that that will trigger the conditional formatting.

3. **In this example, enter 40 and then use the box's drop-down menu to specify the format you want applied.**

FIGURE 7-6:
Each scenario has
its own dialog
box you can use
to define the
trigger values and
the format for
each scenario.

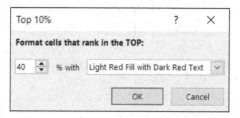

4. **Click OK.**

   Immediately, Excel applies the formatting scenario to the selected cells (see Figure 7-7).

FIGURE 7-7:
With conditional
formatting, you
can easily see
that September
through
December makes
up 40 percent of
the total value in
this data set.

	Within Top 40%
Jan	100
Feb	-100
Mar	200
Apr	250
May	-50
Jun	350
Jul	400
Aug	450
Sep	500
Oct	550
Nov	600
Dec	650

Creating Data Bars

Data Bars fill each cell you are formatting with mini-bars in varying length, indicating the value in each cell relative to other formatted cells. Excel essentially takes the largest and smallest values in the selected range and calculates the length for each bar. To apply Data Bars to a range, do the following:

1. **Select the target range of cells to which you need to apply the conditional formatting.**

2. **Choose Data Bars from the Conditional Formatting menu on the Home tab, as demonstrated in Figure 7-8.**

   As you can see in Figure 7-9, the result is essentially a mini-chart within the cells you selected. Also note that by default, the Data Bars scenario accounts for negative numbers nicely by changing the direction of the bar and inverting the color to red.

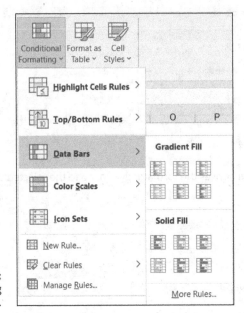

FIGURE 7-8:
Applying
Data Bars.

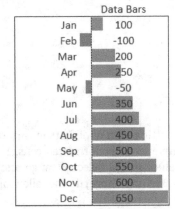

FIGURE 7-9:
Conditional
formatting
with Data Bars.

Applying Color Scales

Color Scales fill each cell you are formatting with a color varying in scale based on the value in each cell relative to other formatted cells. Excel essentially takes the largest and smallest values in the selected range and determines the color for each cell. To apply Color Scales to a range, do the following:

1. **Select the target range of cells to which you need to apply the conditional formatting.**

2. **Choose Color Scales from the Conditional Formatting menu on the Home tab (see Figure 7-10).**

As you can see in Figure 7-11, the result is a kind of heat-map within the cells you selected.

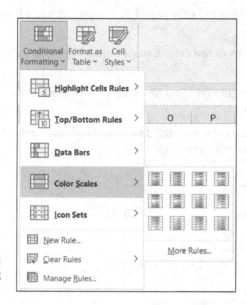

FIGURE 7-10:
Applying
Color Scales.

Color Scales

Jan	100
Feb	-100
Mar	200
Apr	250
May	-50
Jun	350
Jul	400
Aug	450
Sep	500
Oct	550
Nov	600
Dec	650

FIGURE 7-11:
Conditional
formatting with
Color Scales.

Using Icon Sets

Icon Sets are sets of symbols that are inserted in each cell you are formatting. Excel determines which symbol to use based on the value in each cell relative to other formatted cells. To apply an Icon Set to a range, do the following:

1. **Select the target range of cells to which you need to apply the conditional formatting.**

2. **Choose Icon Sets from the Conditional Formatting menu on the Home tab.**

   As you can see in Figure 7-12, you can choose from a menu of Icon Sets varying in shape and color.

   Figure 7-13 illustrates how each cell is formatted with a symbol indicating each cell's value based on the other cells.

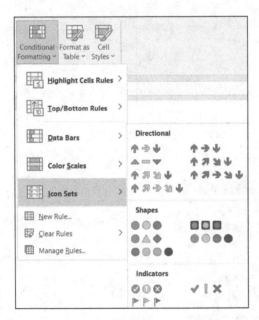

FIGURE 7-12: Applying Icon Sets.

Adding your own formatting rules manually

You don't have to use one of the predefined scenarios offered by Excel. Excel gives you the flexibility to create your own formatting rules manually. Creating your own formatting rules helps you better control how cells are formatted and allows you to do things you wouldn't be able to do with the predefined scenarios.

Jan	✖	100
Feb	✖	-100
Mar	▌	200
Apr	▌	250
May	✖	-50
Jun	▌	350
Jul	▌	400
Aug	✔	450
Sep	✔	500
Oct	✔	550
Nov	✔	600
Dec	✔	650

FIGURE 7-13:
Conditional
formatting with
Icon Sets.

For example, a useful conditional formatting rule is to tag all above-average values with a Check icon and all below-average values with an X icon. Figure 7-14 demonstrates this rule.

	A	B		C
1	REGION	MARKET		Sales
2	North	Great Lakes	✖	70,261
3	North	New England	✔	217,858
4	North	New York North	✖	157,774
5	North	New York South	✖	53,670
6	North	North Carolina	✖	124,600
7	North	Ohio	✖	100,512
8	North	Shenandoah Valley	✖	149,742
9	South	Florida	✖	111,606
10	South	Gulf Coast	✔	253,703
11	South	Illinois	✖	129,148
12	South	Indiana	✖	152,471
13	South	Kentucky	✔	224,524
14	South	South Carolina	✔	249,535
15	South	Tennessee	✔	307,490
16	South	Texas	✔	180,167
17	West	California	✔	190,264
18	West	Central	✖	133,628

FIGURE 7-14:
With a custom
formatting rule,
you can tag the
above-average
values with a
check mark and
the below-
average values
with an X.

REMEMBER

Although it's true that the Above Average and Below Average scenarios built into Excel allow you to format cell and font attributes, they don't enable the use of Icon Sets. You can imagine why Icon Sets would be better on a dashboard than simply color variances. Icons and shapes do a much better job of conveying your message, especially when the dashboard is printed in black-and-white.

To get started in creating your first custom formatting rule, open the Chapter 7 Samples.xlsx file found among the sample files on this book's companion website. After the file is open, go to the Create Rule by Hand tab, and then follow these steps:

1. **Select the target range of cells to which you need to apply the conditional formatting, and select New Rule from the Conditional Formatting menu, as demonstrated in Figure 7-15.**

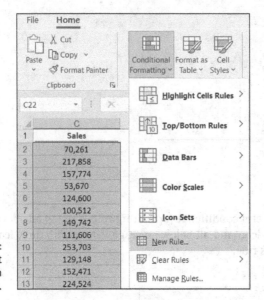

FIGURE 7-15:
Select the target
range and then
select New Rule.

This step opens the New Formatting Rule dialog box shown in Figure 7-16. As you look at the rule types at the top of the dialog box, you may recognize some of them from the predefined scenario choices discussed earlier in this chapter. Here's what each type does:

- *Format All Cells Based on Their Values:* Measures the values in the selected range against each other. This selection is handy for finding general anomalies in your data set.

- *Format Only Cells That Contain:* Applies conditional formatting to those cells that meet specific criteria you define. This selection is perfect for comparing values against a defined benchmark.

- *Format Only Top or Bottom Ranked Values:* Applies conditional formatting to those cells that are ranked in the top or bottom Nth number or percent of all values in the range.

- *Format Only Values That Are Above or Below Average:* Applies conditional formatting to those values that are mathematically above or below the average of all values in the selected range.

- *Use a Formula to Determine Which Cells to Format:* Evaluates values based on a formula you specify. If a particular value evaluates to true, the conditional formatting is applied to that cell. This selection is typically used when applying conditions based on the results of an advanced formula or mathematical operation.

Data Bars, Color Scales, and Icon Sets can be used only with the Format All Cells Based on Their Values rule type.

TIP

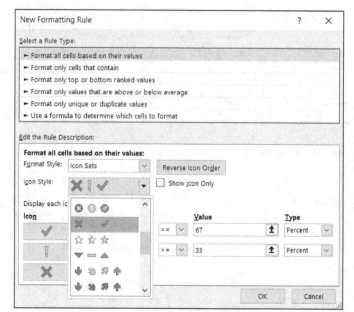

FIGURE 7-16:
Select the Format
All Cells Based on
Their Values rule
and then use the
Format Style
drop-down menu
to switch to
Icon Sets.

2. **Ensure that the Format All Cells Based on Their Values rule type is selected and then use the Format Style drop-down menu to switch to Icon Sets.**

3. **Click the Icon Style drop-down menu to select an Icon Set.**

4. **Change both Type drop-down menus to Formula.**

5. **In each Value box, enter =Average($C$2:$C$22).**

   This step tells Excel that the value in each cell must be greater than the average of the entire data set in order to get the Check icon.

   At this point, the dialog box looks similar to the one in Figure 7-17.

6. **Click OK to apply your conditional formatting.**

It's worth taking some time to understand how this conditional formatting rule works. Excel assesses every cell in the target range to see whether its contents match, in order (top box first), the logic in each Value box. As Excel evaluates the values in the target range, it will apply the specified icon for each cell that meets the specified condition. Any cell that does not fit any of the logic placed in the Value boxes, will apply the last icon.

In this example, you want a cell to get a Check icon only if the value of the cell is greater than (or equal to) the average of the total values. Otherwise, you want Excel to skip directly to the X icon and apply the X.

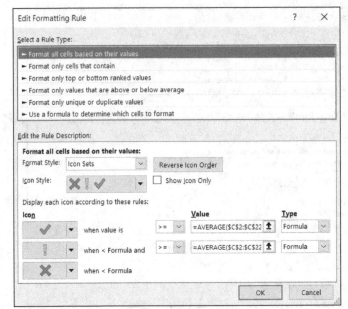

FIGURE 7-17:
Change the Type
drop-down boxes
to Formula and
enter the
appropriate
formulas in the
Value boxes.

Showing only one icon

In many cases, you may not need to show all icons when applying the Icon Set. In fact, showing too many icons at one time may serve only to obstruct the data you're trying to convey on the dashboard.

In the earlier example, you apply a Check icon to values above the average for the range and apply an X icon to all below-average values (see Figure 7-18). However, in the real world, you often need to bring attention to only the below-average values. This way, your eyes aren't inundated with superfluous icons.

	A	B	C
1	REGION	MARKET	Sales
2	North	Great Lakes	✖ 70,261
3	North	New England	✔ 217,858
4	North	New York North	✖ 157,774
5	North	New York South	✖ 53,670
6	North	North Carolina	✖ 124,600
7	North	Ohio	✖ 100,512
8	North	Shenandoah Valley	✖ 149,742
9	South	Florida	✖ 111,606
10	South	Gulf Coast	✔ 253,703
11	South	Illinois	✖ 129,148
12	South	Indiana	✖ 152,471
13	South	Kentucky	✔ 224,524
14	South	South Carolina	✔ 249,535
15	South	Tennessee	✔ 307,490
16	South	Texas	✔ 180,167
17	West	California	✔ 190,264
18	West	Central	✖ 133,628

FIGURE 7-18:
Too many icons
can hide the
items you want to
draw attention to.

Excel provides a clever mechanism to allow you to stop evaluating and formatting values if a condition is true.

In this example, you want to remove the Check icons. The cells that contain those icons all have values above the average for the range. Therefore, you first need to add a condition for all cells whose values are above average. To do so, follow these steps:

1. **Select the target range of cells, and then go to the Home tab and select Conditional Formatting ⇨ Manage Rules.**

   This step opens the Conditional Formatting Rules Manager dialog box shown in Figure 7-19.

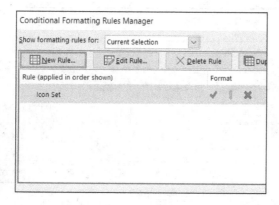

FIGURE 7-19:
Open the
Conditional
Formatting Rules
Manager dialog
box and click
New Rule.

2. **Click the New Rule button to start a new rule.**

   The New Formatting Rule dialog box appears.

3. **Click the Format Only Cells That Contain rule type and then configure the rule so that the format applies only to cell values greater than the average (see Figure 7-20).**

4. **Click OK without changing any of the formatting options.**

5. **Back in the Conditional Formatting Rules Manager, click to select the Stop If True check box, as demonstrated on the right side of Figure 7-21.**

6. **Click OK to apply your changes.**

   As you can see in Figure 7-22, only the X icons are now shown. Again, this allows your audience to focus on the exceptions rather than determining which icons are good and bad.

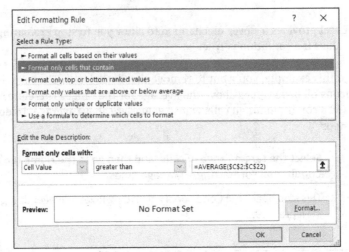

FIGURE 7-20:
This new rule is meant to apply to any cell value that you don't want formatted — in this case, any value that's greater than the average of the range.

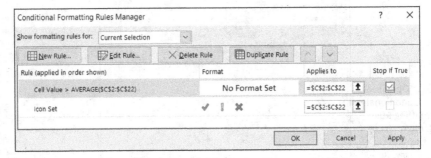

FIGURE 7-21:
Click Stop If True to tell Excel to stop evaluating those cells that meet the first condition.

	A	B		C
1	**REGION**	**MARKET**		**Sales**
2	North	Great Lakes	✖	70,261
3	North	New England		217,858
4	North	New York North	✖	157,774
5	North	New York South	✖	53,670
6	North	North Carolina	✖	124,600
7	North	Ohio	✖	100,512
8	North	Shenandoah Valley	✖	149,742
9	South	Florida	✖	111,606
10	South	Gulf Coast		253,703
11	South	Illinois	✖	129,148
12	South	Indiana	✖	152,471
13	South	Kentucky		224,524
14	South	South Carolina		249,535
15	South	Tennessee		307,490
16	South	Texas		180,167
17	West	California		190,264
18	West	Central	✖	133,628
19	West	Colorado	✖	134,039
20	West	North West	✖	120,143

FIGURE 7-22:
This table is now formatted to show only one icon.

Showing Data Bars and icons outside of cells

Bars and Icon Sets give you a snazzy way to add visualizations to your dashboards; you don't have a lot of say in where they appear within the cell. Take a look at Figure 7-23 to see what I mean.

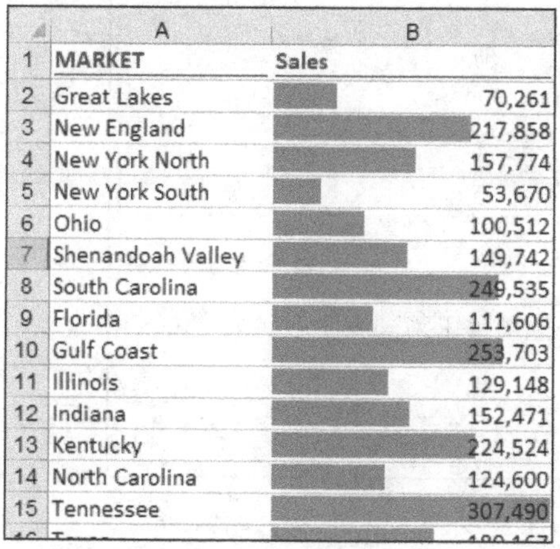

FIGURE 7-23:
Showing Data
Bars inside the
same cell as
values can make
it difficult to
analyze the data.

By default, the Data Bars are placed directly inside each cell, which in this case almost obfuscates the data. From a dashboarding perspective, this is less than ideal, for two reasons:

» The numbers can get lost in the colors of the Data Bars, making them difficult to read — especially when printed in black-and-white.

» It's difficult to see the ends of each bar.

The solution to this problem is to show the Data Bars *outside* the cell that contains the value. Here's how:

1. **To the right of each cell, enter a formula that references the cell containing the data value.**

   For example, if the data is in B2, go to cell C2 and enter **=B2**.

2. **Apply the Data Bar conditional formatting to the formulas you just created.**

3. **Select the formatted range of cells and select Manage Rules under the Conditional Formatting button on the Home tab of the Ribbon.**

4. In the dialog box that opens, click the Edit Rule button.

5. Select the Show Bar Only option, as demonstrated in Figure 7-24.

6. Click OK to apply the change.

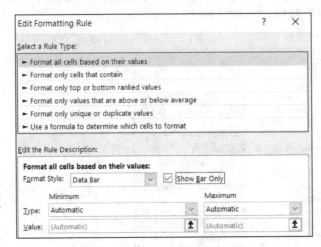

The reward for your efforts is a cleaner view that's much better suited for reporting in a dashboard environment. Figure 7-25 illustrates the improvement gained with this technique.

	A	B	C
1	MARKET	Sales	
2	Great Lakes	70,261	
3	New England	217,858	
4	New York North	157,774	
5	New York South	53,670	
6	Ohio	100,512	
7	Shenandoah Valley	149,742	
8	South Carolina	249,535	
9	Florida	111,606	
10	Gulf Coast	253,703	
11	Illinois	129,148	
12	Indiana	152,471	
13	Kentucky	224,524	
14	North Carolina	124,600	
15	Tennessee	307,490	
16	Texas	180,167	

FIGURE 7-25:
Data Bars, cleanly
placed next to the
data values.

Using the same technique, you can separate Icon Sets from the data — allowing you to position the icons where they best suit your dashboard.

Representing trends with Icon Sets

A dashboard environment may not always have enough space available to add a chart that shows trending. In these cases, Icon Sets are ideal replacements, enabling you to visually represent the overall trending without taking up a lot of space. Figure 7-26 illustrates this concept with a table that provides a nice visual element, allowing for an at-a-glance view of which markets are up, down, or flat over the previous month.

	A	B	C	D	E	
1	REGION	MARKET	Previous Month	Current Month	Variance	
2	North	Great Lakes	70,261	72,505	⬆	3.2%
3	North	New England	217,858	283,324	⬆	30.0%
4	North	New York North	157,774	148,790	⬇	-5.7%
5	North	New York South	53,670	68,009	⬆	26.7%
6	North	Ohio	100,512	98,308	⮕	-2.2%
7	North	Shenandoah Valley	149,742	200,076	⬆	33.6%
8	South	South Carolina	249,535	229,473	⬇	-8.0%
9	South	Florida	111,606	136,104	⬆	22.0%
10	South	Gulf Coast	253,703	245,881	⬇	-3.1%
11	South	Illinois	129,148	131,538	⮕	1.9%
12	South	Indiana	152,471	151,699	⮕	-0.5%
13	South	Kentucky	224,524	225,461	⮕	0.4%
14	North	North Carolina	124,600	130,791	⬆	5.0%
15	South	Tennessee	307,490	268,010	⬇	-12.8%

FIGURE 7-26: Conditional Formatting Icon Sets enable trending visualizations.

You may want to do the same type of thing with your reports. The key is to create a formula that gives you a variance or trending of some sort.

To achieve this type of view, follow these steps:

1. **Select the target range of cells to which you need to apply the conditional formatting.**

   In this case, the target range will be the cells that hold your variance formulas.

2. **Choose Icon Sets from the Conditional Formatting menu on the Home tab and then choose the most appropriate icons for your situation.**

   For this example, choose the set with three arrows shown in Figure 7-27.

   In most cases, you'll adjust the thresholds that define what up, down, and flat mean. Imagine that you need any variance above 3 percent to be tagged with an up arrow, any variance below –3 percent to be tagged with a down arrow, and all others to show flat.

3. **Select the target range of cells and select Manage Rules under the Conditional Formatting button on the Home tab of the Ribbon.**

4. **In the dialog box that opens, click the Edit Rule button.**

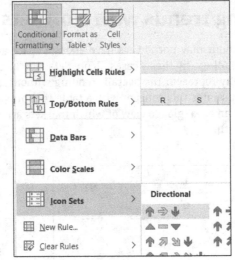

FIGURE 7-27:
The up arrow
indicates an
upward trend;
the down arrow
indicates a
downward trend;
and the right
arrow indicates a
flat trend.

5. **Adjust the properties, as shown in Figure 7-28.**

6. **Click OK to apply the change.**

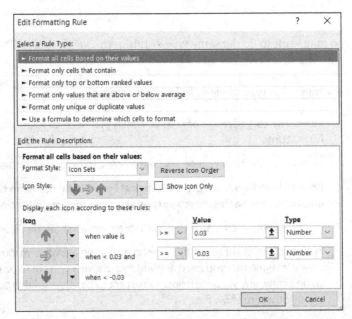

FIGURE 7-28:
You can adjust
the thresholds
that define
what up, down,
and flat mean.

TIP

Notice in Figure 7-28 that the Type property for the formatting rule is set to Number even though the data you're working with (the variances) is percentages. You'll find that working with the Number setting gives you more control and predictability when setting thresholds.

Using Symbols to Enhance Reporting

Symbols are essentially tiny graphics, not unlike those you see when you use Wingdings or Webdings or other fancy fonts. However, symbols are not really fonts. They're Unicode characters. *Unicode characters* are a set of industry standard text elements designed to provide a reliable character set that remains viable on any platform regardless of international font differences.

One example of a commonly used symbol is the copyright symbol (©). This symbol is a Unicode character. You can use it on a Chinese, Turkish, French, or American PC, and it will reliably be available, with no international differences.

In terms of Excel presentations, Unicode characters (or symbols) can be used in places where conditional formatting cannot. For instance, in the chart labels you see in Figure 7-29, the x-axis shows some trending arrows that allow for an extra layer of analysis. This couldn't be done with conditional formatting.

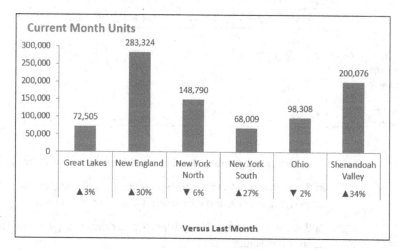

FIGURE 7-29: Use symbols to add an extra layer of analysis to charts.

Let me take some time now to review the steps that led to the chart in Figure 7-29.

Start with the data shown in Figure 7-30. Note that you have a designated cell — C1 in this case — to hold any symbols you're going to use. This cell isn't all that important. It's just a holding cell for the symbols you'll insert.

Now follow these steps:

1. **Click in C1 and then select the Symbol command on the Insert tab.**

   The Symbol dialog box shown in Figure 7-31 opens.

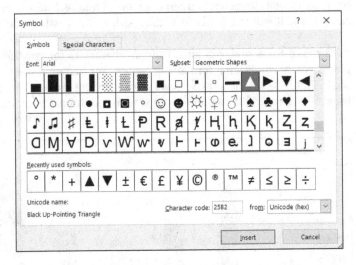

B	C	D
Symbols>>		

vs. Prior Month	Market	Current Month
3%	Great Lakes	72,505
30%	New England	283,324
6%	New York North	148,790
27%	New York South	68,009
2%	Ohio	98,308
34%	Shenandoah Valley	200,076

FIGURE 7-30:
The starting data with a holding cell for symbols.

Symbol ? ✕

Symbols | Special Characters

Font: Arial | Subset: Geometric Shapes

Recently used symbols:

° | * | + | ▲ | ▼ | ± | € | £ | ¥ | © | ® | ™ | ≠ | ≤ | ≥ | ÷

Unicode name:
Black Up-Pointing Triangle

Character code: 2582 | from: Unicode (hex)

Insert | Cancel

FIGURE 7-31:
Use the Symbol dialog box to insert symbols into the holding cell.

2. **Find and select symbols by clicking the Insert button after each symbol.**

   In this scenario, select the down-pointing triangle and click Insert. Then click the up-pointing triangle and click Insert. Close the dialog box when you're done.

   At this point, you have the up-triangle and down-triangle symbols in cell C1, as shown in Figure 7-32.

C1 | ✕ ✓ fₓ | ▲▼

	A	B	C	D
1		Symbols>>	▲▼	
2				
3		vs. Prior Month	Market	Current Month
4		3%	Great Lakes	72,505
5		30%	New England	283,324
6		6%	New York North	148,790
7		27%	New York South	68,009
8		2%	Ohio	98,308
9		34%	Shenandoah Valley	200,076

FIGURE 7-32:
Copy the newly inserted symbols to the Clipboard.

3. Click the C1 cell, go to the Formula bar, and copy the two symbols by highlighting them and pressing Ctrl+C on the keyboard.

4. Go to the data table, right-click the percentages, and then select Format Cells from the menu that appears.

5. In the Format Cells dialog box, create a new custom format by pasting the up- and down-triangle symbols into the appropriate syntax parts (see Figure 7-33).

In this case, any positive percentage will be preceded by the up-triangle symbol, and any negative percentage will be preceded by the down-triangle symbol.

TIP

Not familiar with custom number formatting? Chapter 5 covers the ins and outs of custom number formatting in detail.

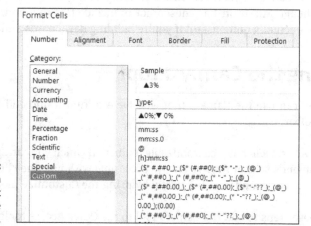

FIGURE 7-33: Create a custom number format using the symbols.

6. Click OK.

The symbols are now part of your number formatting! Figure 7-34 illustrates what the percentages look like. Change any number from positive to negative (or vice versa), and Excel automatically applies the appropriate symbol.

FIGURE 7-34: Your symbols are now part of the number formatting.

	A	B	C	D
1		Symbols>>	▲▼	
2				
3		vs. Prior Month	Market	Current Month
4		▲3%	Great Lakes	72,505
5		▲30%	New England	283,324
6		▼6%	New York North	148,790
7		▲27%	New York South	68,009
8		▼2%	Ohio	98,308
9		▲34%	Shenandoah Valley	200,076

Because charts automatically adopt number formatting, a chart created from this data shows the symbols as part of the labels. Simply use this data as the source for the chart.

This is just one way to use symbols in your reporting. With this basic technique, you can insert symbols to add visual appeal to tables, pivot tables, formulas, or any other object you can think of.

Wielding the Magical Camera Tool

Excel's Camera tool enables you to take a live picture of a range of cells that updates dynamically while the data in that range updates. If you've never heard of it, don't feel bad. This nifty tool has been hidden away in the last few versions of Excel. Although Microsoft has chosen not to include this tool on the mainstream Ribbon, it's actually quite useful if you're building dashboards and reports.

Finding the Camera tool

Before you can use the Camera tool, you have to find it and add it to the Quick Access toolbar.

TIP

The *Quick Access toolbar* is a customizable toolbar on which you can store frequently used commands so that they're always accessible with just one click. You can add virtually any command you find useful by using the Customize menu.

Follow these steps to add the Camera tool to the Quick Access toolbar:

1. **Click the File button.**

2. **Open the Excel Options dialog box by clicking the Options button.**

3. **Click the Quick Access Toolbar button.**

4. **On the Choose Commands From drop-down list, select Commands Not in the Ribbon.**

5. **Scroll down the alphabetical list of commands shown in Figure 7-35 and find Camera; double-click it to add it to the Quick Access toolbar.**

6. **Click OK.**

   After you've taken these steps, you see the Camera tool on the Quick Access toolbar, as shown in Figure 7-36.

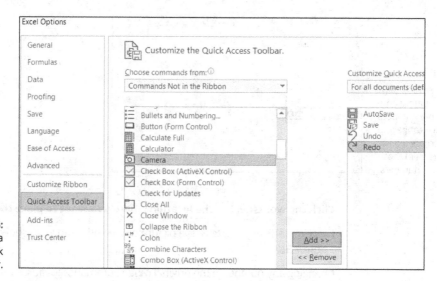

FIGURE 7-35:
Add the Camera
tool to the Quick
Access toolbar.

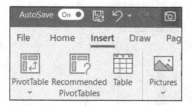

FIGURE 7-36:
Not surprisingly,
the icon for the
Camera tool
looks like a
camera.

Using the Camera tool

To use the Camera tool, you simply highlight a range of cells to then capture everything in that range in a live picture. The cool thing about the Camera tool is that you're not limited to showing a single cell's value, as you are with a linked text box. And because the picture is live, any updates made to the source range automatically change the picture.

Take a moment to walk through this basic demonstration of the Camera tool. In Figure 7-37, you see some simple numbers and a chart based on those numbers. The goal here is to create a live picture of the range that holds both the numbers and the chart.

Follow these steps:

1. **Highlight the range that contains the information you want to capture.**

In this scenario, you select B3:F13 to capture the area with the chart.

2. **Select the Camera tool icon on the Quick Access toolbar.**

You added the Camera tool to the Quick Access toolbar in the preceding section.

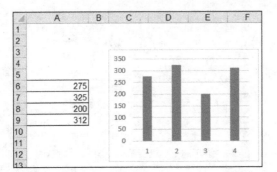

FIGURE 7-37:
Enter some
simple numbers
in a range and
create a basic
chart from those
numbers.

3. **Click the worksheet in the location where you want to place the picture.**

   Excel immediately creates a live picture of the entire range, as shown in
   Figure 7-38.

   Changing any number in the original range automatically causes the picture to
   update.

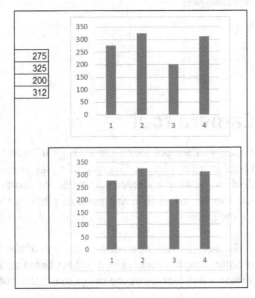

FIGURE 7-38:
A live picture is
created via the
Camera tool.

TIP

By default, the picture that's created has a border around it. To remove the border,
right-click the picture and select Format Picture from the menu that appears. This
opens the Format Picture task pane. On the Colors and Lines tab, you see the Line
Color drop-down list. There, you can select No Color, thereby removing the border. On a similar note, to get a picture without gridlines, simply remove the gridlines from the source range.

Enhancing a dashboard with the Camera tool

Here are a few ways to go beyond the basics and use the Camera tool to enhance your dashboards and reports:

>> **Consolidate disparate ranges into one print area.** Sometimes a data model gets so complex that it's difficult to keep the final data in one printable area. This often forces you to print multiple pages that are inconsistent in layout and size. Given that dashboards are most effective when contained in a compact area that can be printed in a page or two, complex data models prove to be problematic when it comes to layout and design.

You can use the Camera tool in these situations to create live pictures of various ranges that you can place on a single page. Figure 7-39 shows a workbook that contains data from various worksheets. The secret here is that these data ranges are nothing more than linked pictures created by the Camera tool.

As you can see, you can create and manage multiple analyses on different worksheets and then bring together all your presentation pieces into a nicely formatted presentation layer.

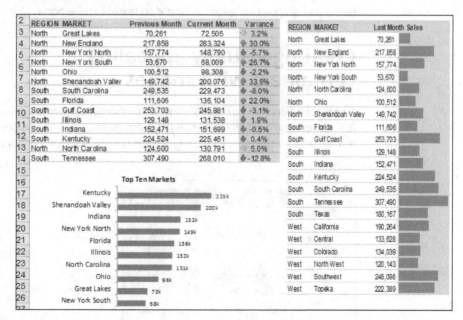

FIGURE 7-39: Use the Camera tool to get multiple source ranges into a compact area.

>> **Rotate objects to save time.** Again, because the Camera tool outputs pictures, you can rotate the pictures in situations in which placing the copied range on its side can help save time. A great example is a chart: Certain charts are relatively easy to create in a vertical orientation but extremely difficult to create in a horizontal orientation.

It's the Camera tool to the rescue! When the live picture of the chart is created, all you have to do is change the alignment of the chart labels and then rotate the picture using the rotate handle to create a horizontal version.

>> **Create small charts.** When you create pictures with the Camera tool, you can resize and move the pictures around freely. This gives you the freedom to test different layouts and chart sizes without the need to work around column widths, hidden rows, or other nonsense.

Enhancing Excel Reports with Shapes

Most people think of Excel shapes as mildly useful objects that can be added to a worksheet if they need to show a square, some arrows, a circle, and so forth. But if you use your imagination, you can leverage Excel shapes to create stylized interfaces that can really enhance your dashboards. Here are a few examples of how Excel shapes can spice up your dashboards and reports.

Creating visually appealing containers with shapes

A peekaboo tab lets you tag a section of your dashboard with a label that looks like it's wrapping around your dashboard components. In Figure 7-40, a peekaboo tab is used to label this group of components as belonging to the North region.

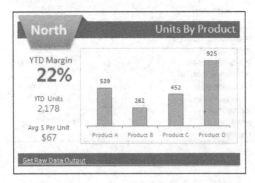

FIGURE 7-40:
A peekaboo tab.

As you can see in Figure 7-41, there's no real magic here. It's just a set of shapes and text boxes that are cleverly arranged to give the impression that a label is wrapping around to show the region name.

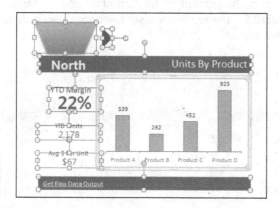

FIGURE 7-41:
A deconstructed view of the peekaboo tab.

Want to draw attention to handful of key metrics? Try wrapping your key metrics with a peekaboo banner. The banner shown in Figure 7-42 goes beyond boring text labels, allowing you to create the feeling that a banner is wrapping around your numbers. Again, this effect is achieved by layering a few Excel shapes so that they fall nicely on top of each other, creating a cohesive effect.

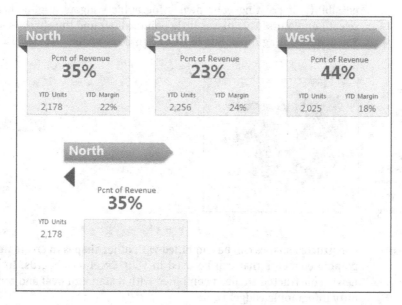

FIGURE 7-42:
A visual banner made with shapes.

Layering shapes to save space

Here's an idea to get the most out of your dashboard real estate. You can layer pie charts with column charts to create a unique set of views (see Figure 7-43). Each pie chart represents the percent of total revenue and a column chart showing some level of detail for the region. Simply layer your pie chart on top of a circle shape and a column chart.

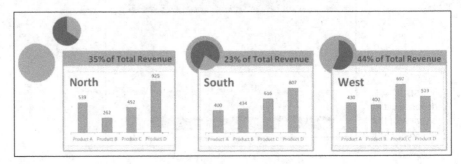

FIGURE 7-43: Combine shapes with a chart to save dashboard real estate.

Constructing your own infographic widgets with shapes

Excel offers a way to alter shapes by editing their anchor points. This opens the possibility of creating your own infographic widgets. Right-click a shape and select Edit Points. This places little points all around the shape (see Figure 7-44). You can then drag the points to reconfigure the shape.

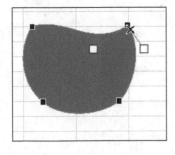

FIGURE 7-44: Use the Edit Points feature to construct your own shape.

Constructed shapes can be combined with other shapes to create interesting infographic elements that can be used in your Excel dashboards. In Figure 7-45, a newly constructed shape is combined with a standard oval and text box to create nifty infographic widgets.

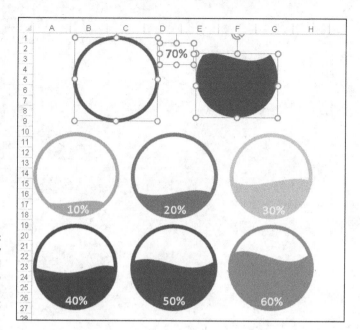

FIGURE 7-45:
Using a newly
constructed
shape to
create custom
infographic
elements.

3

Adding Charts to Your Dashboards

IN THIS PART . . .

Go beyond basic charting with a look at some advanced business techniques that can help create more meaningful visualizations.

Find out how to represent trending across multiple series and distinct time periods.

Uncover techniques that can help you display and measure performance against a target.

Chapter **8**

Charts That Show Trending

No matter what business you're in, you can't escape the tendency to trend. In fact, one of the most common concepts used in dashboards and reports is the concept of trending. A *trend* is a measure of variance over some defined interval — typically, periods such as days, months, or years.

The reason trending is so popular is that trending provides a rational expectation of what might happen in the future. If I know this book has sold 10,000 copies a month over the last 12 months (I wish), I have a reasonable expectation to believe that sales next month will be around 10,000 copies. In short, trending tells you where you've been and where you might be going.

In this chapter, you explore basic trending concepts and some of the advanced techniques you can use to take your trending components beyond simple line charts.

Trending Dos and Don'ts

Building trending components for your dashboards has some dos and don'ts. This section helps you avoid some common trending faux pas.

Using chart types appropriate for trending

It would be nice if you could definitively say which chart type you should use when building trending components. But the truth is, no chart type is the silver bullet for all situations. For effective trending, you want to understand which chart types are most effective in different trending scenarios.

Using line charts

Line charts are the kings of trending. In business presentations, a *line chart* almost always indicates movement across time. Even in areas not related to business, the concept of lines is used to indicate time — consider timelines, family lines, bloodlines, and so on. The benefit of using a line chart for trending is that it's instantly recognized as a trending component, avoiding any delay in information processing.

Line charts are especially effective in presenting trends with many data points — as the top chart in Figure 8-1 shows. You can also use a line chart to present trends for more than one time period, as shown in the bottom chart in Figure 8-1.

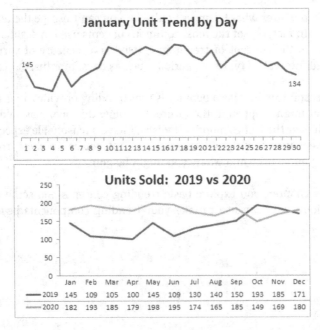

FIGURE 8-1: Line charts are the chart of choice when you need to show trending over time.

Using area charts

An *area chart* is essentially a line chart that's been filled in. So, technically, area charts are appropriate for trending. They're particularly good at highlighting trends over a large time span. For example, the chart in Figure 8-2 spans 120 days of data.

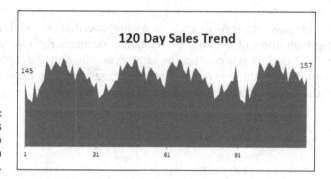

Using column charts

If you're trending a single time series, a line chart is absolutely the way to go. However, if you're comparing two or more periods on the same chart, columns may best bring out the comparisons.

An alternative option is to use a combination chart. A combination of line and column charts is an extremely effective way to show the difference in units sold between two time periods. For instance, Figure 8-3 demonstrates how a combination chart can instantly call attention to the exact months when 2020 sales fell below 2019 sales. (You'll find out more about combination charts later in this chapter.)

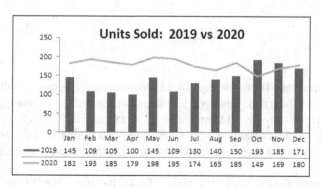

FIGURE 8-3:
Using columns and lines emphasizes the trending differences between two time periods.

Starting the vertical scale at zero

The vertical axis on a trending chart should almost always start at zero. The reason I say *almost* is because you may have trending data that contains negative values or fractions. In those situations, it's generally best to keep Excel's default scaling. However, if you have only non-negative integers, ensure that the vertical axis starts at zero.

This is because the vertical scale of a chart can have a significant impact on the representation of a trend. For instance, compare the two charts shown in Figure 8-4. Both charts contain the same data. The only difference is that in the top chart, I did nothing to fix the vertical scale assigned by Excel (it starts at 96), but in the bottom chart, I fixed the scale to start at zero.

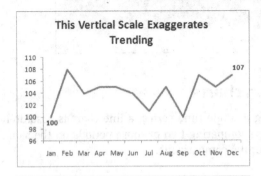

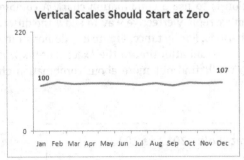

FIGURE 8-4:
Vertical scales should always start at zero.

Now, you may think the top chart is more accurate because it shows the ups and downs of the trend. However, if you look at the numbers closely, you see that the units represented went from 100 to 107 in 12 months. That's not exactly a material change, and it certainly doesn't warrant such a dramatic chart. In truth, the trend is relatively flat, yet the top chart makes it look as though the trend is way up.

The bottom chart more accurately reflects the true nature of the trend. I achieved this effect by locking the Minimum value on the vertical axis to zero.

To adjust the scale of the vertical axis, follow these simple steps:

1. **Right-click the vertical axis and choose Format Axis from the menu that appears.**

   The Format Axis task pane appears (see Figure 8-5).

2. **In the Format Axis task pane, expand the Axis Options section and set the value in the Minimum box to 0.**

3. **(Optional) Set the Major bound value to twice the Maximum value in your data.**

   Setting this value ensures that the trend line gets placed in the middle of the chart.

4. **Click Close to apply your changes.**

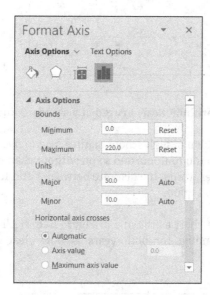

FIGURE 8-5:
Always set the
Minimum value
of the vertical
axis to zero.

TIP

Many would argue that the bottom chart shown in Figure 8-4 hides the small-scale trending that may be important. That is, a 7-unit difference may be significant in some businesses. Well, if that's true, why use a chart at all? If each unit has an impact on the analysis, why use a broad-sweep representation like a chart? A table with conditional formatting would do a better job of highlighting small-scale changes than any chart ever could.

Leveraging Excel's logarithmic scale

In some situations, your trending may start with very small numbers and end with very large numbers. In these cases, you end up with charts that don't accurately represent the true trend. In Figure 8-6, for instance, you see the unit trending for both 2019 and 2020. As you can see in the source data, 2019 started with a modest 50 units. As the months progressed, the monthly unit count increased to 11,100 units through December 2020. Because the two years are on different scales, it's difficult to discern a comparative trending for the two years together.

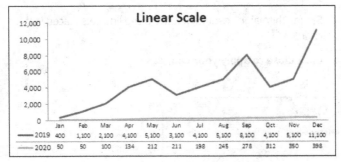

FIGURE 8-6:
A standard linear scale doesn't allow for accurate trending in this chart.

The solution is to use a logarithmic scale instead of a standard linear scale.

Without going into a discussion of high school math, a *logarithmic scale* allows the axis to jump from 1 to 10; to 100 to 1,000; and so on without changing the spacing between axis points. In other words, the distance between 1 and 10 is the same as the distance between 100 and 1,000.

Figure 8-7 shows the same chart as the one in Figure 8-6, but in a logarithmic scale. Notice that the trending for both years is now clear and accurately represented.

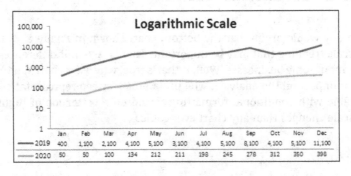

FIGURE 8-7:
Using the logarithmic scale helps bring out trending in charts that contain very small and very large values.

To change the vertical axis of a chart to logarithmic scaling, follow these steps:

1. **Right-click the vertical axis and choose Format Axis from the menu that appears.**

   The Format Axis task pane appears.

2. **Expand the Axis Options section and select the Logarithmic Scale check box, as shown in Figure 8-8.**

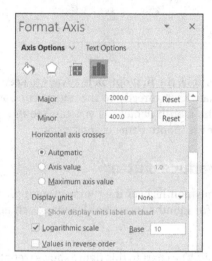

FIGURE 8-8:
Setting the
vertical axis to
logarithmic scale.

REMEMBER

Logarithmic scales work only with positive numbers.

Applying creative label management

As trivial as it may sound, labeling can be one of the sticking points to creating effective trending components. Trending charts tend to hold lots of data points, whose category axis labels take up lots of room. Inundating users with a gaggle of data labels can definitely distract from the main message of the chart. In this section, you find a few tips to help manage the labels in your trending components.

Abbreviating instead of changing alignment

Month names look and feel very long when you place them in a chart — especially when that chart has to fit on a dashboard. However, the solution isn't to change their alignment, as shown in Figure 8-9. Words placed on their sides inherently cause a reader to stop for a moment and read the labels. This isn't ideal when you want them to think about your data and not spend time reading with their heads tilted.

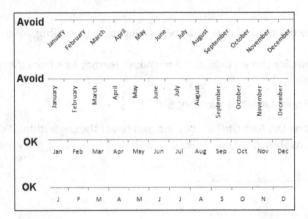

FIGURE 8-9:
Choose to abbreviate category names instead of changing alignment.

Although it's not always possible, the first option is always to keep the labels normally aligned. So rather than jump directly to the alignment option to squeeze them in, try abbreviating the month names. As you can see in Figure 8-9, even using only the first letter of the month name is appropriate.

Implying labels to reduce clutter

When you're listing the same months over the course of multiple years, you may be able to *imply* the labels for months instead of labeling each and every one of them.

Take Figure 8-10, for example. The chart in this figure shows trending through two years. It has so many data points that the labels are forced to be vertically aligned. To reduce clutter, as you can see, only certain months are explicitly labeled. The others are implied by a dot. To achieve this effect, you can simply replace the label in the original source data with a dot (or whatever character you like).

Going vertical when you have too many data points for horizontal

Trending data by day is common, but it does prove to be painful if the trending extends to 30 days or more. In these scenarios, it becomes difficult to keep the chart to a reasonable size and even more difficult to effectively label it.

One solution is to show the trending vertically using a bar chart (see Figure 8-11). On a bar chart, you have room to label the data points and keep the chart to a reasonable size. This isn't something to aspire to, however. Trending vertically isn't as intuitive and may not convey your information in an easy-to-read form. Nevertheless, this solution can be just the work-around you need when the horizontal view is impractical.

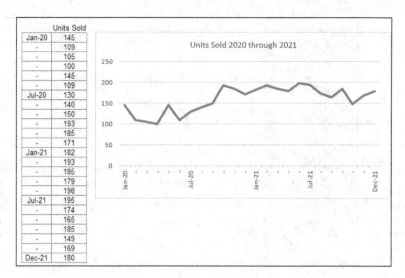

FIGURE 8-10: To save real estate on your dashboard, try labeling only certain data points.

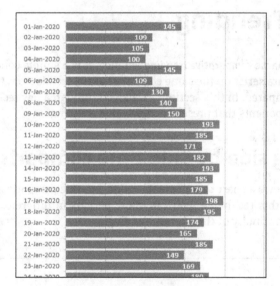

FIGURE 8-11: A bar chart can prove to be effective when trending days extend to 30 or more data points.

Nesting labels for clarity

Often, the data you're trying to chart has multiple time dimensions. In these cases, you can call out these dimensions by nesting your labels. Figure 8-12 demonstrates how including a year column next to the month labels clearly partitions each year's data. You would simply include the year column when identifying the data source for your chart.

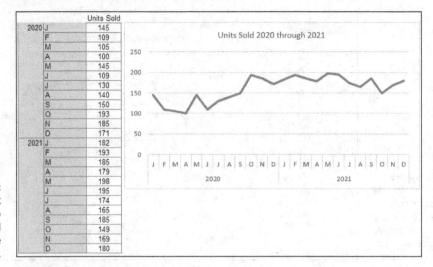

		Units Sold
2020	J	145
	F	109
	M	105
	A	100
	M	145
	J	109
	J	130
	A	140
	S	150
	O	193
	N	185
	D	171
2021	J	182
	F	193
	M	185
	A	179
	M	198
	J	195
	J	174
	A	165
	S	185
	O	149
	N	169
	D	180

FIGURE 8-12: Excel is smart enough to recognize and plot multiple layers of labels.

Comparative Trending

Although the name *comparative trending* is fancy, it is a simple concept: You chart two or more data series on the same chart so that the trends from those series can be visually compared. In this section, I walk you through a few techniques to help you build components that present comparative trending.

Creating side-by-side time comparisons

Figure 8-13 shows a chart that presents a side-by-side comparison of three time periods. With this technique, you can show periods in different colors without breaking the continuity of the overall trending.

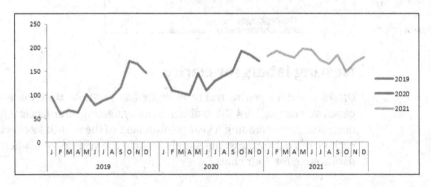

FIGURE 8-13: You can show trends for different time periods side by side.

Here's how to create this type of chart:

1. **Structure your source data similar to the structure shown in Figure 8-14.**

   Note that instead of placing all the data into one column, you're staggering the data into respective years. This tells the chart to create three separate lines, allowing for the three colors.

		2019	2020	2021
2019	J	96		
	F	60		
	M	67		
	A	63		
	M	101		
	J	78		
	J	88		
	A	95		
	S	115		
	O	172		
	N	165		
	D	146		
2020	J		145	
	F		109	
	M		105	
	A		100	
	M		145	
	J		109	
	J		130	
	A		140	
	S		150	
	O		193	
	N		185	
	D		171	
2021	J			182
	F			193
	M			185
	A			179
	M			198
	J			195
	J			174
	A			165
	S			185
	O			149
	N			169
	D			180

FIGURE 8-14: The source data needed to display side-by-side trends.

2. **Select the entire table and create a line chart.**

   This step creates the chart shown earlier, in Figure 8-13.

3. **If you want to get fancy, click the chart to select it, and then right-click and select Change Chart Type from the contextual menu that opens.**

4. **When the Change Chart Type dialog box opens, select Column in the left pane and then select the Stacked Column subtype.**

   As you can see in Figure 8-15, the chart now shows the trending for each year in columns.

Would you like a space between the years? Adding a space in the source data (between each 12-month sequence) adds a space in the chart, as shown in Figure 8-16.

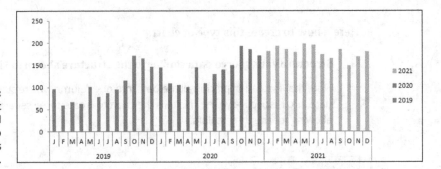

FIGURE 8-15:
Change the chart type to Stacked Column Chart to present columns instead of lines.

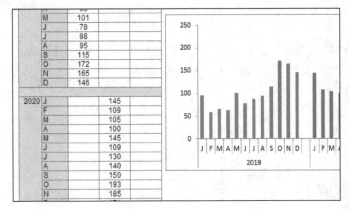

M	101	
J	78	
J	88	
A	95	
S	115	
O	172	
N	165	
D	146	
2020 J		145
F		109
M		105
A		100
M		145
J		109
J		130
A		140
S		150
O		193
N		185

FIGURE 8-16:
If you want to separate each year with a space, simply add a space into the source data.

Creating stacked time comparisons

The stacked time comparison places two series on top of each other instead of side by side. Although this removes the benefit of having an unbroken overall trending, it replaces it with the benefit of an at-a-glance comparison within a compact space. Figure 8-17 illustrates a common stacked time comparison.

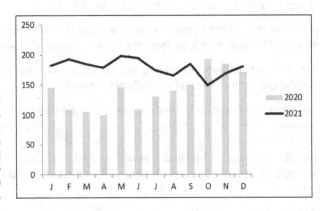

FIGURE 8-17:
A stacked time comparison allows you to view and compare two years of data in a compact space.

To create a stacked time comparison, follow these steps:

1. **Create a new structure and add data to it, like the one shown in Figure 8-18.**

2. **Highlight the entire structure and create a column chart.**

3. **Select and right-click any of the bars for the 2021 data series, and then choose Change Series Chart Type from the menu that appears.**

   The Change Chart Type dialog box appears.

4. **In the Change Chart Type dialog box, select the line type in the Line section.**

FIGURE 8-18:
Start with a structure containing the data for two time periods.

	A	B	C
1		2020	2021
2	J	145	182
3	F	109	193
4	M	105	185
5	A	100	179
6	M	145	198
7	J	109	195
8	J	130	174
9	A	140	165
10	S	150	185
11	O	193	149
12	N	185	169
13	D	171	180

TIP

This technique works well with two time series. You generally want to avoid stacking any more than that. Stacking more than two series often muddies the view and causes users to continually reference the legend to keep track of the series they're evaluating.

Trending with a secondary axis

In some trending components, you have series that trend two different units of measure. For instance, the table in Figure 8-19 shows a trend for People Count and a trend for % Labor Cost.

These are two different units of measure that, when charted, produce the unimpressive chart you see in Figure 8-20. Because Excel builds the vertical axis to accommodate the largest number, the percentage of labor cost trending gets lost at the bottom of the chart. Even a logarithmic scale doesn't help in this scenario.

▲	A	B	C
1		People Count	% Labor Cost
2	J	145	20%
3	F	109	21%
4	M	105	23%
5	A	100	23%
6	M	145	24%
7	J	109	25%
8	J	130	24%
9	A	140	25%
10	S	150	24%
11	O	193	26%
12	N	185	28%
13	D	171	29%

FIGURE 8-19:
You often need to trend two different units of measure, such as counts and percentages.

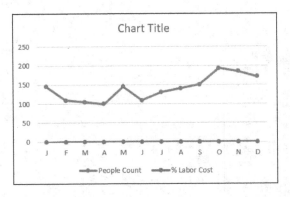

FIGURE 8-20:
The trending for percentage of labor cost gets lost at the bottom of the chart.

Because the default vertical axis (or *primary* axis) doesn't work for both series, the solution is to create another axis to accommodate the series that doesn't fit into the primary axis. This other axis is the *secondary* axis.

To place a data series on the secondary axis, follow these steps:

1. **Right-click the data series and select Format Data Series from the menu that appears.**

   Doing so opens the Format Data Series task pane.

2. **In the Format Data Series task pane, expand the Series Options section (see Figure 8-21) and then click the Secondary Axis radio button.**

   Figure 8-22 illustrates the newly added axis to the right of the chart. Any data series on the secondary axis has its vertical axis labels shown on the right.

Again, changing the chart type of any one of the data series can help in comparing the two trends. In Figure 8-23, the chart type for the People Count trend has been changed to a column. Now you can easily see that although the number of people has gone down in November and December, the percentage of labor cost continues to rise.

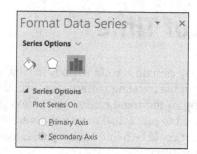

FIGURE 8-21:
Placing a data
series on the
secondary axis.

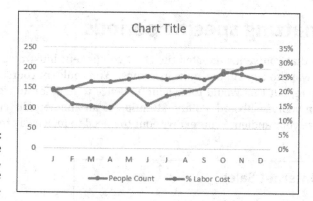

FIGURE 8-22:
Thanks to the
secondary axis,
both trends are
clearly defined.

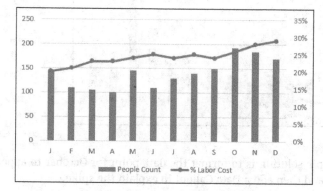

FIGURE 8-23:
Changing the
chart type of one
data series can
underscore
comparisons.

TIP

Technically, it doesn't matter which data series you place on the secondary axis. A general rule is to place the problematic data series on the secondary axis. In this scenario, because the data series for percentage of labor cost seems to be the problem, I place that series on the secondary axis.

Emphasizing Periods of Time

Some trending components may contain certain periods in which a special event occurred, causing an anomaly in the trending pattern. For instance, you may have an unusually large spike or dip in the trend caused by some occurrence in your organization. Or maybe you need to mix actual data with forecasts in your charting component. In such cases, it could be helpful to emphasize specific periods in your trending with special formatting.

Formatting specific periods

Imagine that you've just created the chart component illustrated in Figure 8-24 and you want to explain the spike in October. You could, of course, use a footnote somewhere, but that would force your audience to look for an explanation elsewhere on your dashboard. Calling attention to an anomaly directly on the chart helps give your audience context without the need to look away from the chart.

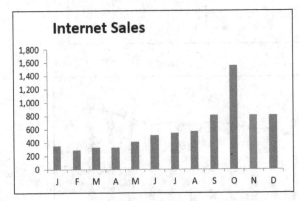

FIGURE 8-24: The spike in October warrants emphasis.

A simple solution is to format the data point for October to appear in a different color and then add a Data Callout to explain the spike.

To format a single data point:

1. **Click the data point once.**

This step places dots on all data points in the series.

2. **Click the data point again to ensure that Excel knows you're formatting only that single data point.**

The dots disappear from all but the target data point.

3. **Right-click to reveal a set of options for the selected data point (see Figure 8-25).**

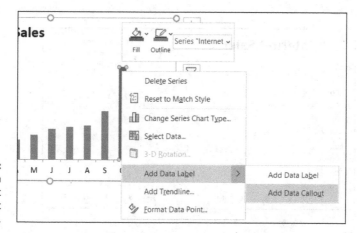

FIGURE 8-25: Right-click a single data point to see a shortcut menu of options.

4. **Use the Fill and Outline drop-downs to change colors.**

5. **Select Add Data Label, then choose the Add Data Callout command.**

A new callout appears for the selected data point. Simply enter the text you want to display directly in the callout. Figure 8-26 illustrates the results of our effort.

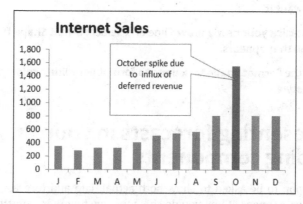

FIGURE 8-26: The chart now draws attention to the spike in October and provides instant context via a text box.

Using dividers to mark significant events

Every now and then a particular event shifts the entire paradigm of your data permanently. A good example is a price increase. The trend shown in Figure 8-27 has been permanently affected by a price increase implemented in October. As you can see, a dividing line (along with some labeling) provides a distinct marker for the price increase, effectively separating the old trend from the new.

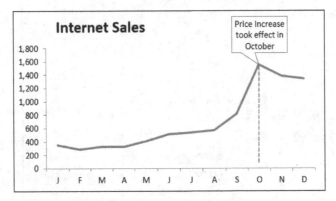

FIGURE 8-27:
Use a simple line to mark particular events along a trend.

Although there are lots of fancy ways to create this effect, you'll rarely need to get any fancier than manually drawing a line yourself. To draw a dividing line inside a chart, take the following steps:

1. Click the chart to select it.

2. Click the Insert tab on the Ribbon and click the Shapes button.

3. Select the line shape you want, go to your chart, and draw the line where you want it.

4. Right-click your newly drawn line and select Format Shape from the menu that appears.

5. Use the Format Shape task pane to format your line's color, thickness, and style.

Representing forecasts in your trending components

It's common to be asked to show both actual data and forecast data as a single trending component. When you do show the two together, you should ensure that your audience can clearly distinguish where actual data ends and where forecasting begins. Take a look at Figure 8-28.

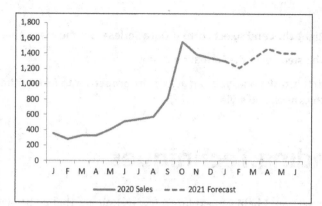

FIGURE 8-28:
You can easily see
where sales
trending ends
and forecast
trending begins.

The best way to achieve this effect is to start with a data structure similar to the one shown in Figure 8-29. As you can see, sales and forecasts are in separate columns so that when charted, you get two distinct data series. Also note the value in cell B14 is actually a formula referencing C14. This value serves to ensure a continuous trend line (with no gaps) when the two data series are charted together.

	A	B	C
1		2020 Sales	2021 Forecast
2	J	355	
3	F	284	
4	M	327	
5	A	326	
6	M	408	
7	J	514	
8	J	541	
9	A	571	
10	S	815	
11	O	1,553	
12	N	1,385	
13	D	1,341	
14	J	1,297	1,297
15	F	↑	1,212
16	M		1,341
17	A		1,469
18	M		1,405
19	J		1,405
20			
21			
22		=C14	

FIGURE 8-29:
Start with a table
that places your
actual data and
your forecasts in
separate
columns.

When you have the appropriately structured data set, you can create a line chart. At this point, you can apply special formatting to the 2021 Forecast data series. Follow these steps:

1. **Click the data series that represents 2021 Forecast.**

   This step places dots on all data points in the series.

2. **Right-click and select Format Data Series from the menu that appears.**

   This step opens the Format Data Series task pane.

3. **In this task pane, you can adjust the properties to format the series color, thickness, and style.**

Other Trending Techniques

In this section, I help you explore a few techniques that go beyond the basic concepts covered in this chapter so far.

Avoiding overload with directional trending

Do you work with a manager who is crazy for data? Are you getting headaches from trying to squeeze three years' worth of monthly data into a single chart? Although it's understandable to want to see a 3-year trend, placing too much information on a single chart can make for a convoluted trending component that tells you almost nothing.

When you're faced with the need to display impossible amounts of data, step back and think about the true purpose of the analysis. When your manager asks for a "three-year sales trend by month," what are they looking for? It could be that they're asking whether current monthly sales are declining versus history. Do you really need to show each and every month, or can you show the directional trend?

A *directional trend* is one that uses simple analysis to imply a relative direction of performance. The key attribute of a directional trend is that the data used is often a set of calculated values as opposed to actual data values. For instance, rather than chart each month's sales for a single year, you could chart the average sales for Q1, Q2, Q3, and Q4. With such a chart, you'd get a directional idea of monthly sales, without the need to look into detailed data.

Take a look at Figure 8-30, which shows two charts. The bottom chart trends each year's monthly data in a single chart. You can see how difficult it is to discern much from this chart. It looks like monthly sales are dropping in all three years. The top chart shows the same data in a directional trend, showing average sales for key periods. The trend jumps at you, showing that sales have flattened out after healthy growth in 2021 and 2022.

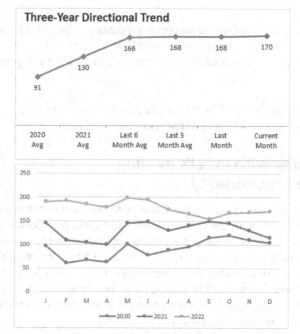

FIGURE 8-30: Directional trending (top) can help you reveal trends that may be hidden in more complex charts.

Smoothing data

Certain lines of business lend themselves to wide fluctuations in data from month to month. For instance, a consulting practice may go months without a steady revenue stream before a big contract comes along and spikes the sales figures for a few months. Some call these ups and downs *seasonality,* or *business cycles.*

Whatever you call them, wild fluctuations in data can prevent you from effectively analyzing and presenting trends. Figure 8-31 demonstrates how highly volatile data can conceal underlying trends.

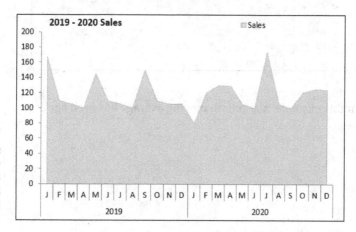

FIGURE 8-31: The volatile nature of this data makes it difficult to see the underlying trend.

This is where the concept of smoothing comes in. *Smoothing* does just what it sounds like — it forces the range between the highest and lowest values in a data set to smooth to a predictable range without disturbing the proportions of the data set.

Now, you can use lots of different techniques to smooth a data set. Take a moment to walk through two of the easier ways to apply smoothing.

Smoothing with Excel's moving average functionality

Excel has a built-in smoothing mechanism, in the form of a moving average trend line — that is, a trend line that calculates and plots the moving average at each data point. A *moving average* is a statistical operation used to track daily, weekly, or monthly patterns. A typical moving average starts calculating the average of a fixed number of data points, and then with each new day's (or week's or month's) numbers, the oldest number is dropped and the newest number is included in the average. This calculation is repeated over the entire data set, creating a trend that represents the average at specific points in time.

Figure 8-32 illustrates how Excel's moving average trend line can help smooth volatile data, highlighting a predictable range.

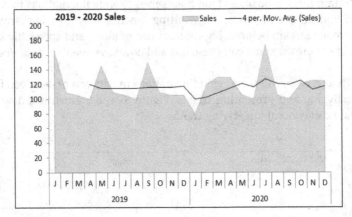

FIGURE 8-32: A four-month moving average trend line has been added to smooth the volatile nature of the original data.

In this example, a 4-month moving average has been applied.

To add a moving average trend line, follow these steps:

1. **Right-click the data series that represents the volatile data and then select Add Trendline from the menu that appears.**

   The Format Trendline task pane appears, shown in Figure 8-33.

2. **In the Format Trendline task pane, select Moving Average and then specify the number of periods.**

   In this case, Excel will average a 4-month moving trend line.

FIGURE 8-33: Applying a 4-month moving average trend line.

Creating your own smoothing calculation

As an alternative to Excel's built-in trend lines, you can create your own smoothing calculation and simply include it as a data series in your chart. In Figure 8-34, a calculated column (appropriately named Smoothing) provides the data points needed to create a smoothed data series.

In this example, the second row of the Smoothing column contains a simple average formula that averages the first data point and the second data point. Note that the reference to the first data point (cell D2) is locked as an absolute value with dollar ($) signs. This ensures that when this formula is copied down, the range grows to include all previous data points.

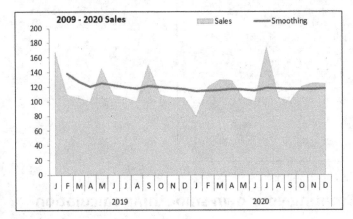

	A	B	C	D	E
1				Sales	Smoothing
2		2019	J	167	
3			F	109	=AVERAGE($D$2:D3)
4			M	105	127
5			A	100	120
6			M	145	125
7			J	109	123
8			J	105	120
9			A	100	118
10			S	150	121
11			O	109	120
12			N	105	119
13			D	105	117
14		2020	J	80	115
15			F	120	115

FIGURE 8-34: A calculated smoothing column feeds a new series to your chart.

After the formula is copied down to fill the entire smoothing column, it can simply be included in the data source for the chart. Figure 8-35 illustrates the smoothed data plotted as a line chart.

FIGURE 8-35: Plotting the smoothed data reveals the underlying trend.

Chapter 9

Grouping and Bucketing Data

t's often helpful to organize your analyses into logical groups of data. Grouping allows you to focus on manageable sets that have key attributes. For example, rather than look at all customers in one giant view, you can analyze customers who buy only one product. Then you can focus attention and resources on those customers who have the potential to buy more products.

The benefit of grouping data is that you can more easily pick out groups that fall outside the norm for your business.

In this chapter, I help you explore some of the techniques you can use to create components that group and bucket data.

Creating Top and Bottom Displays

When you look at the list of Fortune 500 companies, you often look for the top 20 companies. Then perhaps you look at who eked out a spot in the bottom 20 slots. It's unlikely that you would check to see which company came in at number 251. It's not necessarily because you don't care about number 251; it's just that you can't spend the time or energy to process all 500 companies. So you process the top and bottom of the list.

This concept is the same one behind creating top and bottom displays. Your audience has only a certain amount of time and resources to dedicate to solving any issues you can emphasize on your dashboard. Showing them the top and bottom values in your data can help them pinpoint where and how they can have the most impact with the time and resources they possess.

Incorporating top and bottom displays into dashboards

The top and bottom displays you create can be as simple as source data that you incorporate into your dashboard. Typically placed to the right of a dashboard, this data can emphasize details that a manager may use to take action on a metric. For example, the simple dashboard shown in Figure 9-1 shows sales information with top and bottom sales reps.

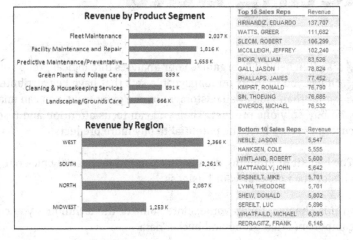

FIGURE 9-1: Top and bottom displays that emphasize certain metrics.

To get a little fancier, you can supplement the top and bottom displays with some ranking information, some in-cell bar charts, or some conditional formatting (see Figure 9-2).

You can create the in-cell bar charts with the Data Bars conditional formatting function, covered in Chapter 7. The arrows are also simple conditional formatting rules that are evaluated against the variance in current and preceding months' ranks.

Top 10 Sales Reps	Sales	Rank	Last Month	vs Last Month
HIRNANDIZ, EDUARDO	$137,707	1	1	⇨ 0
WATTS, GREER	$111,682	2	3	⬆ 1
SLECIM, ROBERT	$106,299	3	5	⬆ 2
MCCILLEIGH, JEFFREY	$102,240	4	2	⬇ -2
BICKIR, WILLIAM	$83,526	5	3	⬇ -2
GALL, JASON	$78,824	6	12	⬆ 6
PHALLAPS, JAMES	$77,452	7	7	⇨ 0
KIMPIRT, RONALD	$76,790	8	9	⬆ 1
SIN, THOEUNG	$76,665	9	8	⬇ -1
IDWERDS, MICHAEL	$76,532	10	4	⬇ -6

Bottom 10 Sales Reps	Sales	Rank	Last Month	vs Last Month
NEBLE, JASON	$5,547	244	244	⇨ 0
CELIMAN, WILLIAM	$9,779	243	241	⬇ -2
KRIZILL, ADAM	$11,454	242	235	⬇ -7
MIDANA, FRANK	$15,044	241	221	⬇ -20
GRANGIR, DAVID	$16,129	240	240	⇨ 0
DALLEARE, ANDRE	$16,265	239	239	⇨ 0
HICKLIBIRRY, JERRY	$16,670	238	225	⬇ -13
VAN HUILE, KENNETH	$18,821	237	242	⬆ 5
RACHERDSEN, KENNETH	$19,675	236	237	⬆ 1
STIGALL, DAVID	$20,092	235	243	⬆ 8

FIGURE 9-2:
You can use conditional formatting to add visual components to your top and bottom displays.

Using pivot tables to get top and bottom views

If you've read Chapter 3, you know that a pivot table is an amazing tool that can help create interactive reporting. Take a moment now to look over an example of how pivot tables can help you build interactive top and bottom displays.

TIP

Open the Chapter 9 Samples.xlsx file, found on this book's companion website, to follow along.

Follow these steps to display Top and Bottom filters with a pivot table:

1. **Start with a pivot table that shows the data you want to display with the top and bottom views.**

   In this case, the pivot table shows Sales Rep and Sales_Amount (see Figure 9-3).

2. **Right-click the field you want to use to determine the top values — in this example, use the Sales Rep field — and then choose Filter ⇨ Top 10 from the menu that appears, as shown in Figure 9-4.**

   The Top 10 Filter (Sales Rep) dialog box appears, as shown in Figure 9-5.

3. **In the Top 10 Filter (Sales Rep) dialog box, define the view you're looking for.**

   In this example, you want the Top 10 Items (Sales Reps) as defined by the Sales_Amount field.

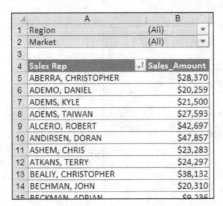

FIGURE 9-3:
Start with a pivot table that contains the data you want to filter.

	A	B
1	Region	(All)
2	Market	(All)
3		
4	Sales Rep	Sales_Amount
5	ABERRA, CHRISTOPHER	$28,370
6	ADEMO, DANIEL	$20,259
7	ADEMS, KYLE	$21,500
8	ADEMS, TAIWAN	$27,593
9	ALCERO, ROBERT	$42,697
10	ANDIRSEN, DORAN	$47,857
11	ASHEM, CHRIS	$23,283
12	ATKANS, TERRY	$24,297
13	BEALIY, CHRISTOPHER	$38,132
14	BECHMAN, JOHN	$20,310
15	BECKMAN, ADRIAN	$9,236

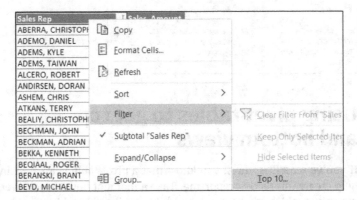

FIGURE 9-4:
Select the Top 10 filter option.

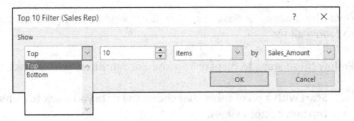

FIGURE 9-5:
Specify the filter you want to apply.

4. **Click OK to apply the filter.**

   At this point, the pivot table is filtered to show the top ten sales reps for the selected region and market. You can change the Market filter to Charlotte and get the top ten sales reps for Charlotte only (see Figure 9-6).

5. **To view the bottom ten Sales Rep list, copy the entire pivot table and paste it next to the existing one.**

	A	B
1	Region	(All)
2	Market	CHARLOTTE
3		
4	**Sales Rep**	**Sales_Amount**
5	MCCILLEIGH, JEFFREY	$98,090
6	CERDWILL, TIMOTHY	$54,883
7	BRADFERD, JAMES	$49,435
8	DIDLIY, CHARLES	$47,220
9	SWANGIR, ADAM	$46,608
10	SKILTEN, JAMES	$43,569
11	PIORSEN, HEYWARD	$41,005
12	CRIOMIR, TIMOTHY	$34,169
13	PERSENS, GREGORY	$33,026
14	BIOCH, RONALD	$30,168
15	**Grand Total**	**$478,172**

FIGURE 9-6: You can interactively filter the pivot table report to instantly show the top ten sales reps for any region and market.

6. **Repeat Steps 2 through 4 in the newly copied pivot table — except this time, choose to filter the bottom ten items as defined by the Sales_ Amount field.**

If all goes well, you now have two pivot tables similar to those in Figure 9-7: one that shows the top ten sales reps and one that shows the bottom ten. You can link back to these two pivot tables in the analysis layer of your data model using formulas. This way, when you update the data, the top and bottom values display the new information.

	A	B	C	D	E
1	Region	(All)		Region	(All)
2	Market	CHARLOTTE		Market	CHARLOTTE
3					
4	**Sales Rep**	**Sales_Amount**		**Sales Rep**	**Sales_Amount**
5	MCCILLEIGH, JEFFREY	$98,090		MEERE, TERRY	$27,149
6	CERDWILL, TIMOTHY	$54,883		BRAGHT, THOMAS	$25,005
7	BRADFERD, JAMES	$49,435		CRAVIY, ANTHONY	$22,761
8	DIDLIY, CHARLES	$47,220		WALLAEMS, SHAUN	$15,477
9	SWANGIR, ADAM	$46,608		HERVIY, CHRISTOPHER	$15,260
10	SKILTEN, JAMES	$43,569		HELT, CHRISTOPHER	$15,147
11	PIORSEN, HEYWARD	$41,005		REBIRTS, ADAMS	$13,237
12	CRIOMIR, TIMOTHY	$34,169		BECKMAN, ADRIAN	$9,236
13	PERSENS, GREGORY	$33,026		GERRUIS, ROBERT	$7,786
14	BIOCH, RONALD	$30,168		MEERE, RUSSELL	$6,635
15	**Grand Total**	**$478,172**		**Grand Total**	**$157,693**

FIGURE 9-7: You now have two pivot tables that show top and bottom displays.

REMEMBER

If there's a tie for any rank in the top or bottom values, Excel shows you all tied records, so you may get more than the number you filtered for. If you filtered for the top 10 sales reps and there's a tie for the number 5 rank, Excel shows you 11 sales reps. (Both reps ranked at number 5 are shown.)

Top Values in Charts

Sometimes a chart is indeed the best way to display a set of data, but you still want to call attention to the top values in that chart. In these cases, you can use a technique that highlights the top values in your charts. That is to say, you can use Excel to figure out which values in your data series are in the top nth value and then apply special formatting to them. Figure 9-8 illustrates an example in which the top five quarters are highlighted and given a label.

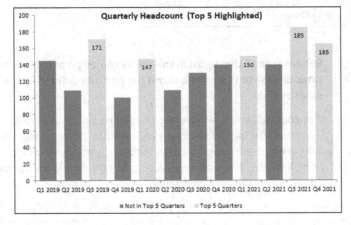

FIGURE 9-8: This chart highlights the top five quarters with different font and labeling.

The secret to this technique is Excel's obscure LARGE function. The LARGE function returns the nth largest number from a data set. In other words, you tell it where to look and the number rank you want.

To find the largest number in the data set, you enter the formula LARGE(Data_Range, 1). To find the fifth largest number in the data set, use LARGE(Data_Range, 5). Figure 9-9 illustrates how the LARGE function works.

The idea is fairly simple: To identify the top five values in a data set, you first need to identify the fifth largest number (LARGE function to the rescue) and then test each value in the data set to see whether it's bigger than the fifth largest number. Here's what you do:

1. **Build a chart feeder that consists of formulas that link back to your raw data.**

   The feeder should have two columns: one to hold data that isn't in the top five and one to hold data that is in the top five (see Figure 9-10).

	A	B	C	D	E
1			People Count		
2		J	145		
3		F	109		
4		M	171		
5		A	100		
6		M	147		
7		J	109		
8		J	130		
9		A	140		
10		S	150		
11		O	140		
12		N	185		
13		D	165		
14					
15		Largest Value	185	◄──	=LARGE(C2:C13,1)
16					
17		5th Largest Value	147	◄──	=LARGE(C2:C13,5)
18					

FIGURE 9-9:
Using the LARGE function returns the *n*th largest number from a data set.

2. **In the first row of the chart feeder, enter the formulas shown in Figure 9-10.**

The formula for the first column (F4) checks to see whether the value in cell C4 is less than the number returned by the LARGE formula (the fifth largest value). If it is, the value in cell C4 is returned. Otherwise, NA is used. The formula for the second column works in the same way, except the IF statement is reversed: If the value in cell C4 is less than the value returned by the LARGE formula, NA is used; otherwise, the value in C4 is returned.

=IF(C4<LARGE($C$4:$C$15,5),"NA",C4)

=IF(C4<LARGE($C$4:$C$15,5),C4,"NA")

	A	B	C	D	E	F	G
1							
2							
3			Head Count			Not in Top 5 Quarters	Top 5 Quarters
4		Q1 2019	145		Q1 2019	145	NA
5		Q2 2019	109		Q2 2019		
6		Q3 2019	171		Q3 2019		
7		Q4 2019	100		Q4 2019		
8		Q1 2020	147		Q1 2020		
9		Q2 2020	109		Q2 2020		

FIGURE 9-10:
Build a new chart feeder that consists of formulas that plot values into one of two columns.

3. **Copy down the formulas to fill the table.**

4. **Use the chart feeder table to plot the data into a stacked column chart.**

You immediately see a chart that displays two data series: one for data points not in the top five and one for data points in the top five (see Figure 9-11).

Notice that the chart in Figure 9-11 shows some rogue zeros. You can complete the next few steps to fix the chart so that the zeros don't appear.

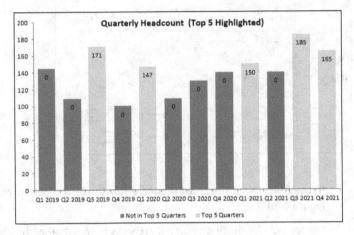

FIGURE 9-11:
After you add data labels to the top five data series and do a bit of formatting, your chart should look similar to the one shown here.

5. **Right-click any of the data labels for the "not in top 5" series and choose Format Data Labels from the menu that appears.**

   The Format Data Labels task pane appears.

6. **In this task pane, expand the Number section and select Custom in the Category list.**

7. **Enter #,##0;; as the custom number format, as shown in Figure 9-12.**

8. **Click Add and then click Close.**

FIGURE 9-12:
Entering **#,##0;;** as the custom format for a data label hides all zeros in that data series.

When you go back to the chart, you see that the rogue zeros are now hidden and the chart is ready for colors, labels, and other formatting you want to apply.

You can apply the same technique to highlight the bottom five values in your data set. The only difference is that instead of using the LARGE function, you use the SMALL function. Whereas the LARGE function returns the largest *n*th value from a range, the SMALL function returns the smallest *n*th value.

Figure 9-13 illustrates the formulas you use to apply the same technique outlined here for the bottom five values.

=IF(C22>SMALL($C$22:$C$33,5),"NA",C22)

=IF(C22>SMALL($C$22:$C$33,5),C22,"NA")

B	C	D	E	F	G
	Head Count			Not in Bottom 5 Quarters	Bottom 5 Quarters
Q1 2019	145		Q1 2019	145	NA
Q2 2019	109		Q2 2019		
Q3 2019	171		Q3 2019		
Q4 2019	100		Q4 2019		
Q1 2020	147		Q1 2020		
Q2 2020	109		Q2 2020		
Q3 2020	130		Q3 2020		
Q4 2020	140		Q4 2020		
Q1 2021	150		Q1 2021		
Q2 2021	132		Q2 2021		
Q3 2021	185		Q3 2021		
Q4 2021	165		Q4 2021		

FIGURE 9-13: Use the SMALL function to highlight the bottom values in a chart.

The formula for the first column (F22) checks to see whether the value in cell C22 is greater than the number returned by the SMALL formula (the fifth smallest value). If it is, the value in cell C22 is returned. Otherwise, NA is used. The formula for the second column works in the same way except the IF statement is reversed: If the value in cell C22 is greater than the number returned by the SMALL formula, NA is used; otherwise, the value is returned.

Using Histograms to Track Relationships and Frequency

A *histogram* is a graph that plots frequency distribution. A *frequency distribution* shows how often an event or category of data occurs. With a histogram, you can visually see the general distribution of a certain attribute.

Take a look at the histogram shown in Figure 9-14. This histogram represents the distribution of units sold in one month among your sales reps. As you can see, most reps sell somewhere between 5 and 25 units per month. As a manager, you want the hump in the chart to move to the right — more people selling a higher number of units per month. So you set a goal for a majority of the sales reps to sell between 15 and 25 units within the next three months. With this histogram, you can visually track the progress toward that goal.

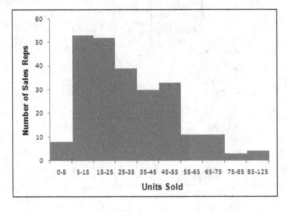

FIGURE 9-14:
A histogram showing the distribution of units sold per month among the sales force.

This section discusses how to create a histogram using various methods available to you. These techniques allow for a level of automation and interactivity, which comes in handy when updating dashboards each month.

See how to develop a data model in Chapter 2.

REMEMBER

Using Excel's Histogram statistical chart

Statistical charts help calculate and visualize common statistical analyses without the need to engage in brain-busting calculations. This chart type lets you essentially point and click your way into a histogram chart, leaving all the mathematical heavy lifting to Excel.

To create a histogram chart with the new statistical chart type, follow these steps:

1. Start with a data set that contains values for a unique group you want to bucket and count.

2. Select your data, click the Statistical Charts icon found on the Insert tab and then select the Histogram chart (see Figure 9-15).

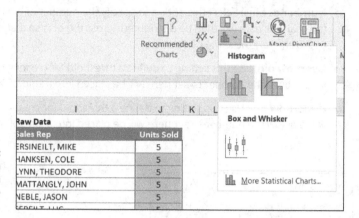

FIGURE 9-15:
Select your data then choose a Histogram as the chart type.

Excel outputs a histogram chart based on the values in your source data set. As you can see in Figure 9-16, Excel attempts to derive the best configuration of bins based on your data.

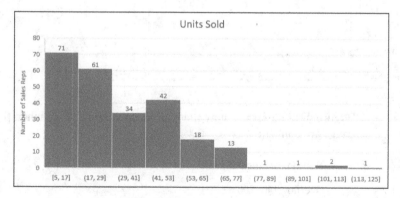

FIGURE 9-16:
Excel's initial attempt at creating a histogram.

You can always change the configuration of the bins if you're not happy with what Excel has come up with. Simply right-click the x-axis and select Format Axis from the menu that appears. In the Axis Options section of the Format Axis task pane (see Figure 9-17), you see a few settings that allow you to override Excel's automatic bins:

>> **Bin width:** Select this option to specify how big the range of each bin should be. For instance, if you were to set the bin width to 12, each bin would represent a range of 12 numbers. Excel would then plot as many 12-number bins as it needs to account for all the values in your source data.

>> **Number of bins:** Select this option to specify the number of bins to show in the chart. All data will then be distributed across the bins so that each bin has approximately the same population.

>> **Overflow bin:** Use this setting to define a threshold for creating bins. Any value above the number to set here will be placed into a kind of "all other" bin.

>> **Underflow bin:** Use this setting to define a threshold for creating bins. Any value below the number to set here will be placed into a kind of "all other" bin.

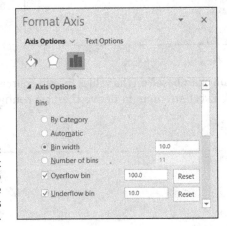

FIGURE 9-17:
Use the Format Axis task pane to adjust how the chart groups data into bins.

Figure 9-18 illustrates how the histogram would change when the following settings are applied:

Number of bins: 10

Overflow bin: 100

Underflow bin: 10

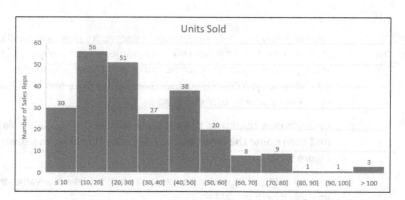

FIGURE 9-18:
A cleaner
histogram after
making a few
adjustments to
the bins.

Creating a formula-driven histogram

If you want a bit more involvement in creating your histogram charts, you can create a formula-driven histogram. This technique fits nicely in data models in which you separate data, analysis, and presentation information.

Follow these steps to create a formula-driven histogram:

1. **Before you create the histogram, you need a table that contains your raw data, and you need to create a bin table (see Figure 9-19).**

   The raw data should ideally consist of records that represent unique counts for the data you want to group. For instance, the raw data table in Figure 9-19 contains unique sales reps and the number of units each has sold.

   The bin table dictates the grouping parameters used to break your raw data into the frequency groups. The bin table tells Excel to cluster all sales reps selling fewer than 5 units into the first frequency group, any sales reps selling 5 to 14 units in the second frequency group, and so on.

FIGURE 9-19:
Start with your
raw data table
and a bin table.

	A	B	C	D
1	**Raw Data**			
2	**Sales Rep**	**Units Sold**		**Bins**
3	ERSINEILT, MIKE	5		0
4	HANKSEN, COLE	5		5
5	LYNN, THEODORE	5		15
6	MATTANGLY, JOHN	5		25
7	NEBLE, JASON	5		35
8	SEREILT, LUC	5		45
9	SHEW, DONALD	5		55
10	WINTLAND, ROBERT	5		65
11	BLANCHIT, DANNY	6		75
12	BLEKE JR, SAMUEL	6		85
13	ETEVAC, ROBERT	6		125

You can freely set your own grouping parameters when you build the bin table. However, you should generally keep parameters as equally spaced as possible. You typically want to end your bin tables with the largest number in the data set. This gives you clean groupings that end in a finite number — not in an open-ended greater-than designation.

2. **Create a new column in the bin table to hold the** FREQUENCY **formulas, and then name the new column** Frequency Formulas, **as shown in Figure 9-20.**

   Excel's FREQUENCY function counts how often values occur within the ranges you specify in a bin table.

3. **Select the cells in the newly created column.**

4. **Type the** FREQUENCY **formula you see in Figure 9-20 and then Enter on the keyboard.**

The FREQUENCY function has a quirk that often confuses first-time users. The FREQUENCY function is an *array* formula — a formula that returns many values at one time. If you're using Office 365, you can simply enter the formula just as you would any other. If you're using Excel 2019 or earlier, you'll need to press Ctrl+Shift+Enter on the keyboard after typing the formula. If you press only the Enter key, you don't get the results you need.

At this point, you should have a table that shows the number of sales reps that fall into each of your bins. You could chart this table, but the data labels would come out wonky. For the best results, build a simple chart feeder table that creates appropriate labels for each bin. You do this in the next step.

FIGURE 9-20:
Type the
FREQUENCY
formula you see
here and then be
sure to hold
down the
Ctrl+Shift+Enter
keys on your
keyboard.

	A	B	C	D	E
1	Raw Data			Frequency Formulas	
2	Sales Rep	Units Sold		Bins	Frequency Formulas
3	ERSINEILT, MIKE	5		0	=FREQUENCY(B3:B246,D3:D13)
4	HANKSEN, COLE	5		5	8
5	LYNN, THEODORE	5		15	53
6	MATTANGLY, JOHN	5		25	52
7	NEBLE, JASON	5		35	39
8	SEREILT, LUC	5		45	30
9	SHEW, DONALD	5		55	33
10	WINTLAND, ROBERT	5		65	11
11	BLANCHIT, DANNY	6		75	11
12	BLEKE JR, SAMUEL	6		85	3
13	ETEVAC, ROBERT	6		125	4

5. **Create a new table that feeds the charts a bit more cleanly (see Figure 9-21).**

   Use a simple formula that concatenates bins into appropriate labels. Use another formula to bring in the results of your FREQUENCY calculations.

In Figure 9-21, the formulas in the first record of the chart feeder table are visible. These formulas are essentially copied down to create a table that's appropriate for charting.

	C	D	E	F	G	H
1		**Frequency Formulas**			**Chart Feeder**	
2		Bins	Frequency Formulas		Units Sold	Count of Sales Reps
3		0	0		=D3& "-" &D4	=E4
4		5	8		5-15	53
5		15	53		15-25	52
6		25	52		25-35	39
7		35	39		35-45	30
8		45	30		45-55	33
9		55	33		55-65	11
10		65	11		65-75	11
11		75	11		75-85	3
12		85	3		85-125	4
13		125	4			

FIGURE 9-21: Build a simple chart feeder table that creates appropriate labels for each bin.

6. **Use the newly created chart feeder table to plot the data into a column chart.**

Figure 9-22 illustrates the resulting chart. You can very well use the initial column chart as your histogram.

If you like your histograms to have spaces between the data points, you're done. If you like the continuous, blocked look you get with no gaps between the data points, follow the next few steps.

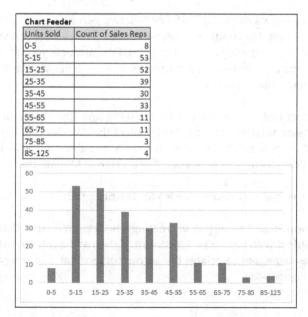

FIGURE 9-22: Plot your histogram data into a column chart.

7. **Right-click any of the columns in the chart and choose Format Data Series from the menu that appears.**

   The Format Data Series task pane appears.

8. **Adjust the Gap Width property to 0%, as shown in Figure 9-23.**

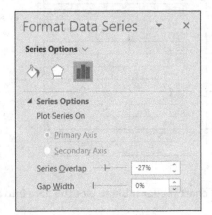

FIGURE 9-23:
To eliminate the spaces between columns, set the Gap Width to 0%.

Adding a cumulative percent

A nice feature to add to your histograms is a cumulative percent series. With a cumulative percent series, you can show the percent distribution of the data points to the left of the point of interest.

Figure 9-24 shows an example of a cumulative percent series. At each data point in the histogram, the cumulative percent series tells you the percent of the population that fills all the bins up to that point. For instance, you can see that 25% of the sales reps represented sold 15 units or less. In other words, 75% of the sales reps sold more than 15 units.

Take another look at the chart in Figure 9-24 and find the point where you see 75% on the cumulative series. At 75%, look at the label for that bin range (you see 35–45). The 75% mark tells you that 75% of sales reps sold between 0 and 45 units. This means that only 25% of sales reps sold more than 45 units.

To create a cumulative percent series for the histogram, follow these steps:

1. **Perform Steps 1 through 5 of creating a histogram (in the "Creating a formula-driven histogram" section) and then add a column to your chart feeder table that calculates the percent of total sales reps for the first bin (see Figure 9-25).**

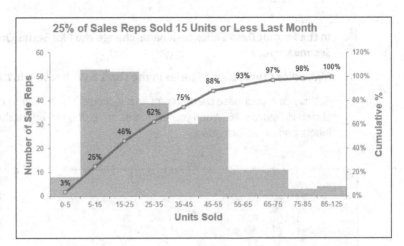

FIGURE 9-24:
The cumulative
percent series
shows the
percent of the
population that
fills all the bins up
to each point in
the histogram.

FIGURE 9-25:
In a new column,
create a formula
that calculates
the percent of
total sales reps
for the first bin.

	F	G	H	I
1		**Chart Feeder**		
2		Units Sold	Count of Sales Reps	Cumulative %
3		0-5	8	=SUM($H$3:H3)/SUM($H$3:$H$12)
4		5-15	53	25%
5		15-25	52	46%
6		25-35	39	62%
7		35-45	30	75%
8		45-55	33	88%
9		55-65	11	93%
10		65-75	11	97%
11		75-85	3	98%
12		85-125	4	100%

Note the dollar symbols ($) used in the formula to lock the references while
you copy down the formula.

2. **Copy down the formula for all bins in the table.**

3. **Use the chart feeder table to plot the data into a line chart.**

The resulting chart needs some additional formatting.

4. **Right-click the series that makes up your histogram (Count of Sales Reps),
select Change Chart Type from the menu that appears, and then change
the chart type to a column chart.**

5. **Right-click any of the columns in the chart and choose Format Data
Series.**

6. **Adjust the Gap Width property to 0%, as demonstrated earlier, in
Figure 9-22.**

7. **Right-click Cumulative % series in the chart and choose Format Data
Series.**

8. **In the Format Data Series task pane, change the Plot Series On option to Secondary Axis.**

9. **Right-click Cumulative % series in the chart and choose Add Data Labels.**

At this point, your base chart is complete. It should look similar to the one shown in Figure 9-26. When you get to this point, you can adjust the colors, labels, and other formatting.

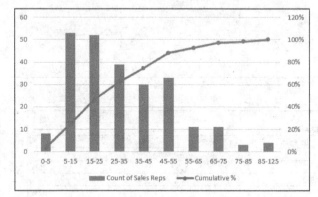

FIGURE 9-26: The initial chart will need some formatting to make it look like a histogram.

Using a pivot table to create a histogram

Did you know you can use a pivot table as the source for a histogram? That's right. With a little-known trick, you can create a histogram that's as interactive as a pivot table!

As in the formula-driven histogram, the first step in creating a histogram with a pivot table is to create a frequency distribution. Just follow these steps:

1. **Create a pivot table and plot the data values in the row area (not the data area).**

As you can see in Figure 9-27, the SumOfSales_Amount field is placed in the Rows drop zone. Place the Sales Rep field in the Values drop zone.

2. **Right-click any value in the Rows area and choose Group from the menu that appears.**

The Grouping dialog box appears, as shown in Figure 9-28.

3. **In this dialog box, set the Starting At and Ending At values and then set the interval.**

This step creates the frequency distribution. In Figure 9-28, the distribution is set to start at 5,000 and to create groups in increments of 1,000 until it ends at 100,000.

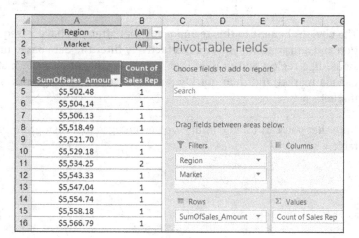

FIGURE 9-27:
Place your data
values in the
Rows drop zone
and the Sales
Rep field in the
Values drop zone
as a Count.

	A	B
1	Region	(All)
2	Market	(All)
4	SumOfSales_Amoun	Count of Sales Rep
5	$5,502.48	1
6	$5,504.14	1
7	$5,506.13	1
8	$5,518.49	1
9	$5,521.70	1
10	$5,529.18	1
11	$5,534.25	2
12	$5,543.33	1
13	$5,547.04	1
14	$5,554.74	1
15	$5,558.18	1
16	$5,566.79	1

FIGURE 9-28:
The Grouping
dialog box.

Grouping

Auto

Starting at: 5000

Ending at: 100000

By: 10000

OK   Cancel

4. Click OK to confirm your settings.

The pivot table calculates the number of sales reps for each defined increment, just as in a frequency distribution (see Figure 9-29). You can now leverage this result to create a histogram!

FIGURE 9-29:
The result of
grouping the
values in the row
area is a
frequency
distribution that
can be charted
into a histogram.

	A	B
1	Region	(All)
2	Market	(All)
4	SumOfSales_Amoun	Count of Sales Rep
5	5000-6000	69
6	6000-7000	78
7	7000-8000	58
8	8000-9000	66
9	9000-10000	41
10	10000-11000	45
11	11000-12000	39
12	12000-13000	33
13	13000-14000	25
14	14000-15000	25
15	15000-16000	22
16	16000-17000	18

The obvious benefit to this technique is that after you have a frequency distribution and a histogram, you can interactively filter the data based on other dimensions, like region and market. For instance, you can see the histogram for the Canada market and then quickly switch to see the histogram for the California market.

TIP

Note that you can't add cumulative percentages to a histogram based on a pivot table.

Chapter **10**

Displaying Performance against a Target

Hopefully, this is an easy one to grasp. Someone sets a target, and someone else tries to reach that target. The target can be anything from a certain amount of revenue to a number of boxes shipped or to phone calls made. The business world is full of targets and goals. Your job is to find effective ways to represent performance against those targets.

What do I mean by performance against a target? Imagine that your goal is to break the land speed record, which is now 763 miles per hour. That makes the target 764 miles per hour, which will break the record. After you jump into your car and go as fast as you can, you will have a final speed. That number is your performance against the target.

In this chapter, I explore some new and interesting ways to create components that show performance against a target.

Showing Performance with Variances

The standard way to display performance against a target is to plot the target and then plot the performance. This is usually done with a line chart or a combination chart, such as the one shown in Figure 10-1.

FIGURE 10-1:
A typical chart showing performance against a target.

Although this chart allows you to visually pick the points where performance exceeded or fell below targets, it gives you a rather one-dimensional view and provides minimal information. Even if this chart offered labels that showed the actual percent of sales revenue versus target, you'd still get only a mildly informative view.

A more effective and informative way to display performance against a target is to plot the variances between the target and the performance. Figure 10-2 shows the same performance data you see in Figure 10-1 but includes the variances (sales revenue minus target) under the month label. This way, you see where performance exceeded or fell below targets, but you also get an extra layer of information showing the dollar impact of each rise and fall.

FIGURE 10-2:
Consider using variances to plot performance against a target.

Showing Performance against Organizational Trends

The target you use to measure performance doesn't necessarily have to be set by management or organizational policy. In fact, some of the things you measure may never have a formal target or goal set for them. In situations in which you don't have a target to measure against, it's often helpful to measure performance against some organizational statistic.

For example, the component in Figure 10-3 measures the sales performance for each division against the median sales for all the divisions. You can see that divisions 1, 3, and 6 fall well below the median for the group.

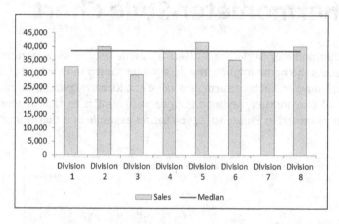

FIGURE 10-3: Measuring data when there's no target for a measure.

Here's how you'd create a median line similar to the one you see in Figure 10-3:

1. **Start a new column next to your data and type the simple MEDIAN formula, as shown in Figure 10-4.**

   Note that this formula can be any mathematical or statistical operation that works for the data you're representing. Just make sure that the values returned are the same for the entire column. This gives you a straight line.

2. **Copy the formula down to fill the table.**

   Again, all numbers in the newly created column should be the same.

3. **Plot the table into a column chart.**

4. **Right-click the Median data series and choose Change Series Chart Type from the menu that appears.**

5. **Change the chart type to a line chart.**

	A	B	C
1		Sales	Median
2	Division 1	32,526	=MEDIAN($B$2:$B$9)
3	Division 2	39,939	38,291
4	Division 3	29,542	38,291
5	Division 4	38,312	38,291
6	Division 5	41,595	38,291
7	Division 6	35,089	38,291
8	Division 7	38,270	38,291
9	Division 8	40,022	38,291

FIGURE 10-4:
Start a new column and enter a formula.

Using a Thermometer-Style Chart

A thermometer-style chart offers a unique way to view performance against a goal. As the name implies, the data points shown in this type of chart resemble a thermometer. Each performance value and its corresponding target are stacked on top of one another, giving an appearance similar to that of mercury rising in a thermometer. In Figure 10-5, you see an example of a thermometer-style chart.

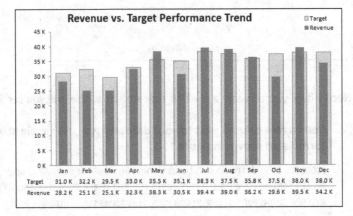

FIGURE 10-5:
Thermometer-style charts offer a unique way to show performance against a goal.

To create this type of chart, follow these steps:

1. **Starting with a table that contains revenue and target data, plot the data into a new column chart.**

2. **Right-click the Revenue data series and choose Format Data Series from the menu that appears.**

3. **In the Format Data Series task pane, select Secondary Axis.**

4. **Go back to the chart and delete the new vertical axis that was added.**

   It's the vertical axis to the right of the chart.

5. **Right-click the Target series and choose Format Data Series.**

6. **In the task pane, adjust the Gap Width property so that the Target series is slightly wider than the Revenue series — between 45% and 55% is typically fine.**

Using a Bullet Graph

A *bullet graph* is a type of column/bar graph developed by visualization expert Stephen Few to serve as a replacement for dashboard gauges and meters. He developed bullet graphs to allow you to clearly display multiple layers of information without occupying a lot of space on a dashboard. A bullet graph, as shown in Figure 10-6, contains a single performance measure (such as YTD [year-to-date] revenue), compares that measure with a target, and displays it in the context of qualitative ranges, such as Poor, Fair, Good, and Very Good.

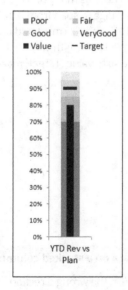

FIGURE 10-6:
Bullet graphs display multiple perspectives in an incredibly compact space.

Figure 10-7 breaks down the three main parts of a bullet graph. The single bar represents the performance measure. The horizontal marker represents the comparative measure. The background color banding represents the qualitative ranges.

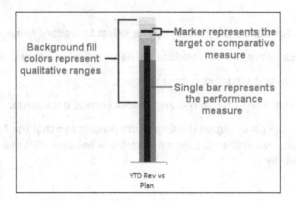

FIGURE 10-7:
The parts of a
bullet graph.

Creating a bullet graph

Creating a bullet graph in Excel involves quite a few steps, but the process isn't necessarily difficult. Follow these steps to create your first bullet graph:

1. **Start with a data table that gives you all the data points you need to create the three main parts of the bullet graph.**

   Figure 10-8 illustrates what that data table looks like. The first four values in the data set (Poor, Fair, Good, and Very Good) make up the qualitative range. You don't have to have four values — you can have as many or as few as you need. In this scenario, you want the qualitative range to span from 0 to 100%. Therefore, the percentages (70%, 15%, 10%, and 5%) must add up to 100%. Again, this can be adjusted to suit your needs. The fifth value in Figure 10-8 (Value) creates the performance bar. The sixth value (Target) makes the target marker.

FIGURE 10-8:
Start with data
that contains the
main data points
of the bullet
graph.

	A	B
1		YTD Rev vs Plan
2	Poor	70%
3	Fair	15%
4	Good	10%
5	VeryGood	5%
6	Value	80%
7	Target	90%

2. **Select the entire table and plot the data on a stacked column chart.**

   The chart that's created is initially plotted in the wrong direction.

3. **To fix the direction, click the chart and select the Switch Row/Column button on the Chart Design tab of the Ribbon, as shown in Figure 10-9.**

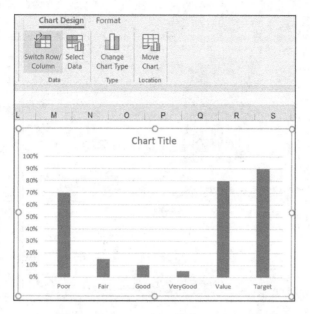

FIGURE 10-9:
Switch the
orientation of the
chart to read
from columns.

4. **Right-click the Target series and choose Change Series Chart Type from the menu that appears.**

   Doing so calls up the Change Chart Type dialog box.

5. **Use the Change Chart Type dialog box to change the Target series to Line with Markers and to place it on the secondary axis (see Figure 10-10).**

   After your change is confirmed, the Target series appears on the chart as a single dot.

6. **Right-click the Target series again and choose Format Data Series to open that task pane.**

7. **Click Marker to expand the Marker options and then adjust the marker to look like a dash, as shown in Figure 10-11.**

8. **Still in the Format Data Series task pane, expand the Fill section, and in the Solid Fill property, set the color of the marker to a noticeable color such as red.**

9. **Still in the Format Data Series task pane, expand the Border section and set the Border to No Line.**

10. **Go back to your chart and delete the new secondary axis that was added to the right of your chart (see Figure 10-12).**

    This is an important step to ensure that the scale of the chart is correct for all data points.

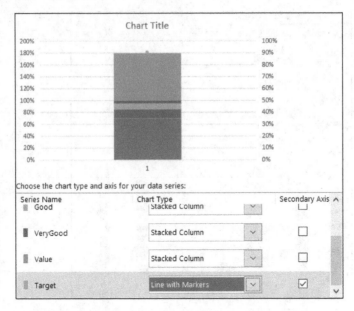

FIGURE 10-10:
Use the Change
Chart Type
dialog box to
change the Target
series to Line with
Markers and
place it on the
secondary axis.

Choose the chart type and axis for your data series:

Series Name	Chart Type	Secondary Axis
Good	Stacked Column	☐
VeryGood	Stacked Column	☐
Value	Stacked Column	☐
Target	Line with Markers	☑

FIGURE 10-11:
Adjust the marker
to a dash.

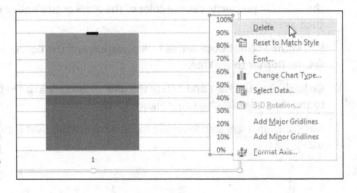

FIGURE 10-12:
Be sure to delete
the newly created
secondary
vertical axis.

11. Right-click the Value series and choose Format Data Series from the menu that appears.

12. In the Format Data Series task pane, click Secondary Axis.

13. Still in the Format Data Series task pane, under Series Options, adjust the Gap Width property so that the Value series is slightly narrower than the other columns in the chart — between 205% and 225% is typically okay.

14. Still in the Format Data Series task pane, click the Fill icon (the paint bucket), expand the Fill section, and then select the Solid Fill option to set the color of the Value series to black.

15. All that's left to do is change the color for each qualitative range to incrementally lighter hues.

At this point, your bullet graph is essentially done! You can apply minor formatting adjustments to the size and shape of the chart to make it look the way you want. Figure 10-13 shows your newly created bullet graph formatted with a legend and horizontal labels.

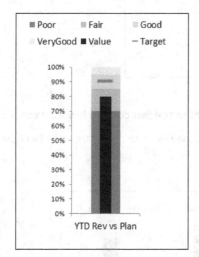

FIGURE 10-13:
Your formatted bullet graph.

Adding data to your bullet graph

After you've built your chart for the first performance measure, you can use the same chart for any additional measures. Take a look at Figure 10-14.

As you can see in Figure 10-14, you've already created this bullet graph with the first performance measure. Imagine that you add two more measures and want to graph those. Here's how to do it:

1. Click the chart so that the blue outline appears around the original source data.

2. Hover the mouse pointer over the blue dot in the lower-right corner of the blue box (see Figure 10-14).

The cursor turns into an arrow.

	A	B	C	D
1		YTD Rev vs Plan	% to Code	% On Time
2	Poor	70%	65%	75%
3	Fair	15%	20%	10%
4	Good	10%	10%	10%
5	VeryGood	5%	5%	5%
6	Value	80%	105%	92%
7	Target	90%	95%	95%

FIGURE 10-14: To add more data to your chart, manually expand the chart's data source range.

3. Click and drag the blue dot to the last column in your expanded data set.

Figure 10-15 illustrates how the new data points are added without one ounce of extra work!

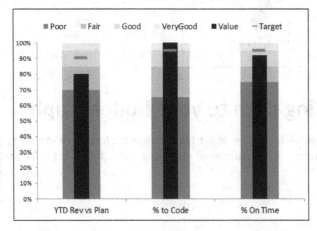

FIGURE 10-15: Expanding the data source automatically creates new bullet graphs.

Final thoughts on formatting bullet graphs

Before wrapping up this introduction to bullet graphs, I discuss two final thoughts on formatting:

» Creating qualitative bands

» Creating horizontal bullet graphs

Creating qualitative bands

First, if the qualitative ranges are the same for all performance measures in your bullet graphs, you can format the qualitative range series to have no gaps between them. For instance, Figure 10-16 shows a set of bullet graphs in which the qualitative ranges have been set to 0% Gap Width. This creates the clever effect of qualitative bands.

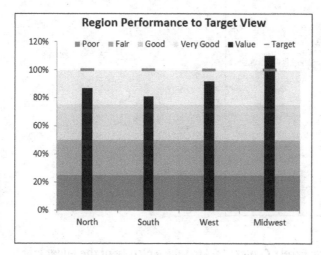

FIGURE 10-16: Try setting gap widths to zero to create clean-looking qualitative bands.

Here's how to do it:

1. **Right-click any one of the qualitative series and choose Format Data Series from the menu that appears.**

2. **In the Format Series task pane, adjust the Gap Width property to 0%.**

Creating horizontal bullet graphs

For those of you waiting on the section about horizontal bullet graphs, I have good news and bad news. The bad news is that creating a horizontal bullet graph from scratch in Excel is a much more complex endeavor than creating a vertical bullet graph — one that doesn't warrant the time and effort it takes to create them.

The good news is that there is a clever way to get a horizontal bullet graph from a vertical one — and in three steps, no less. Here's how you do it:

1. **Create a vertical bullet graph.**

   For how to do this, see the "Creating a bullet graph" section, earlier in this chapter.

2. **To change the alignment for the axis and other labels on the bullet graph so that they're rotated 270 degrees, right-click the axis labels, select Format Axis, go to the Alignment settings, and then adjust the Text Direction property to rotate the axis labels as shown in Figure 10-17.**

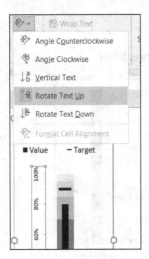

FIGURE 10-17:
Rotate all labels so that they're on their sides.

3. **Use Excel's Camera tool to take a picture of the bullet graph.**

   After you have a picture, you can rotate it to be horizontal. Figure 10-18 illustrates a horizontal bullet graph.

   The nifty thing about this trick is that because the picture is taken with the Camera tool, the picture automatically updates when the source table changes.

Check out Chapter 7 to discover how to find and use the Camera tool.

TIP

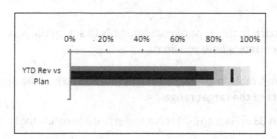

FIGURE 10-18:
A horizontal bullet graph.

Showing Performance against a Target Range

In some businesses, a target isn't one value — it's a range of values. That is to say, the goal is to stay within a defined target range. Imagine that you manage a small business selling boxes of meat. Part of your job is to keep the inventory stocked between 25 and 35 boxes in a month. If you have too many boxes of meat, the meat will go bad. If you have too few boxes, you'll lose money.

To track how well you do at keeping the inventory of meat between 25 and 35 boxes, you need a performance component that displays on-hand boxes against a target range. Figure 10-19 illustrates a component you can build to track performance against a target range. The gray band represents the target range you must stay within each month. The line represents the trend of on-hand meat.

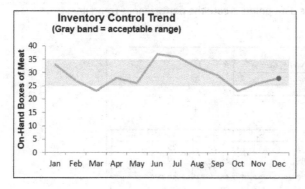

FIGURE 10-19:
You can create a component that plots performance against a target range.

Obviously, the trick to this type of component is to set up the band that represents the target range. Here's how you do it:

1. **Set up a limit table in which you can define and adjust the upper and lower limits of the target range.**

Cells B2 and B3 in Figure 10-20 serve as the place to define the limits for the range.

2. **Build a chart feeder that's used to plot the data points for the target range.**

This feeder consists of the formulas revealed in cells B8 and B9 in Figure 10-20. The idea is to copy these formulas across all data. The values you see in the Feb, Mar, and Apr columns are the results of these formulas.

	A	B	C	D	E
1	Limit Table				
2	Lower Limit	25			
3	Upper Limit	35			
4					
5					
6					
7		Jan	Feb	Mar	Apr
8	Lower Limit	=$B$2	25	25	25
9	Upper Limit	=$B$3-$B$2	10	10	10

FIGURE 10-20: Create a chart feeder that contains formulas that define the data points for the target range.

3. **Add a row for the actual performance values, as shown in Figure 10-21.**

These data points create the performance trend line.

	A	B	C	D	E
1	Limit Table				
2	Lower Limit	25			
3	Upper Limit	35			
4					
5					
6					
7		Jan	Feb	Mar	Apr
8	Lower Limit	25	25	25	25
9	Upper Limit	10	10	10	10
10	Values	33	27	23	28

FIGURE 10-21: Add a row for the performance values.

4. **Select the entire chart feeder table and plot the data on a stacked area chart.**

5. **Right-click the Values series and choose Change Series Chart Type from the menu that appears.**

Doing so calls up the Change Chart Type dialog box.

6. Using the Change Chart Type dialog box, change the Values series to a line chart and place it on the secondary axis, as shown in Figure 10-22.

After your change is confirmed, the Values series appears on the chart as a line.

FIGURE 10-22: Use the Change Chart Type dialog box to change the Values series to a line chart and place it on the secondary axis.

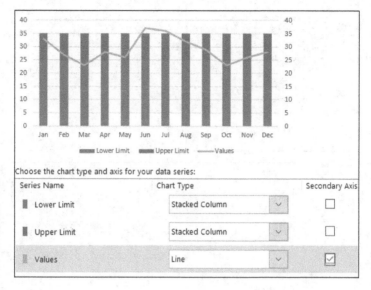

7. Go back to your chart and delete the new vertical axis that was added.

It's the vertical axis to the right of the chart.

8. Right-click the Lower Limit data series and choose Format Data Series from the menu that appears.

9. In the Format Data Series task pane, click the Fill icon and then choose the No Fill option under Fill and the No Line option under Border (see Figure 10-23).

10. Right-click the Upper Limit series and select Format Data Series.

11. In the Format Data Series task pane, adjust the Gap Width property to 0%.

That's it. All that's left to do is apply the minor adjustments to colors, labels, and other formatting.

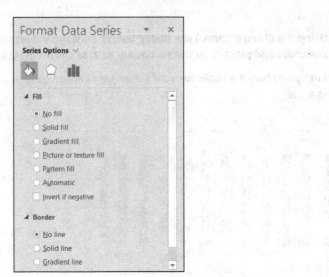

FIGURE 10-23:
Format the Lower
Limit series so
that it's hidden.

4

Advanced Reporting Techniques

IN THIS PART . . .

Take an in-depth look at how you can leverage macros to automate your reporting systems.

Discover how interactive controls can provide your clients with simple interfaces, allowing them to easily navigate through, and interact with, your dashboard or report.

Explore the various methods for protecting your dashboards and reports before distributing.

IN THIS CHAPTER

» **Introducing macros**

» **Recording macros**

» **Adding macros to your dashboards and reports**

» **Introducing Form controls**

» **Using Form controls to dynamically filter your report views**

Chapter **11**

Giving Users an Interactive Interface

oday, business professionals increasingly want to be empowered to switch from one view of data to another with a simple list of choices. For those who build dashboards and reports, this empowerment comes with a whole new set of issues. The overarching question is — how do you handle a user who wants to see multiple views for multiple regions or markets?

Fortunately, Excel offers a handful of tools that enable you to add interactivity into your reporting. With these tools and a bit of creative data modeling, you can accomplish these goals with relative ease. In this chapter, you discover how to incorporate various controls, such as buttons, check boxes, and scroll bars, into your dashboards and reports. Also, I present you with several solutions that you can implement.

Introducing Macros

A *macro* is essentially a set of instructions or code that you create to tell Excel to execute any number of actions. In Excel, macros can be written or recorded. The keyword here is *recorded*.

Recording a macro is like programming a phone number into your cellphone. You first manually dial and save a number. Then when you want, you can redial those numbers with the touch of a button. Just as on a cellphone, you can record your actions in Excel while you perform them. While you record, Excel gets busy in the background, translating your keystrokes and mouse clicks to written code, also known as Visual Basic for Applications (VBA). After you record a macro, you can play back those actions anytime you want.

Why use a macro?

The first step in using macros is admitting you have a problem. Actually, you may have several problems:

>> **Repetitive tasks:** As each new month rolls around, you have to make the doughnuts — that is, crank out those reports. You have to import that data, you have to update those pivot tables, you have to delete those columns, and so on. Wouldn't it be nice if you could fire up a macro and have those more redundant parts of your dashboard processes done automatically?

>> **Mistakes:** When you enter into hand-to-hand combat with Excel, you're bound to make mistakes. When you're repeatedly applying formulas, sorting, and moving things around manually, you always run the risk of catastrophe. Add to that the looming deadlines and endless change requests, and your error rate goes up. Why not calmly record a macro, ensure that everything is running correctly, and then forget it? The macro is sure to perform every action the same way every time you run it, reducing the chance of errors.

>> **Awkward navigation:** Remember that you're creating these dashboards and reports for an audience that probably has a limited knowledge of Excel. If your reports are a bit too difficult to use and navigate, you'll find that you slowly lose support for your cause. It's always helpful to make your dashboard more user-friendly.

Here are some ideas for macros that make things easier for everyone:

>> A macro that formats and prints a worksheet or range of worksheets at the touch of a button

>> Macros that navigate a multisheet workbook with a navigation page or with a go-to button for each sheet in a workbook

>> A macro that saves the open document in a specified location and then closes the application at the touch of a button

Obviously, you can perform each of these examples in Excel without the aid of a macro. However, your audience will appreciate these little touches that help make perusal of your dashboard a bit more pleasant.

Recording your first macro

If you're a beginner to dashboard automation, you're unlikely to be able to write the VBA code by hand. Without full knowledge of Excel's object model and syntax, writing the needed code would be impossible for most beginning users. This is where recording a macro comes in handy. The idea is that you record an action and then run the macro every time you want that action performed.

REMEMBER

To get started in creating your first macro, open the `Chapter 11 Macro Samples.xlsx` file found on this book's companion website. After the file is open, select the Recording Your First Macro tab.

To begin, you need to unhide the Developer tab. You can find the full macro toolset in Excel on the Developer tab, which is initially hidden. You have to explicitly tell Excel to make it visible. To enable the Developer tab, follow these steps:

1. Go to the Ribbon and click the File button.

2. Click the Options button.

The Excel Options dialog box opens.

3. Click the Customize Ribbon button.

In the list box on the right, you see all available tabs.

4. Select the Developer tab, as shown in Figure 11-1.

5. Click OK.

Now that you have the Developer tab visible on the Ribbon, select it and click the Record Macro command. This opens the Record Macro dialog box, as shown in Figure 11-2.

Here are the four fields in the Record Macro dialog box:

>> **Macro Name:** Excel gives a default name to your macro, such as Macro1, but it's best practice to give your macro a name more descriptive of what it actually does. For example, you might name a macro that formats a generic table as AddDataBars.

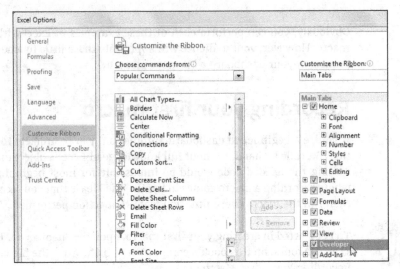

FIGURE 11-1:
Enabling the
Developer tab.

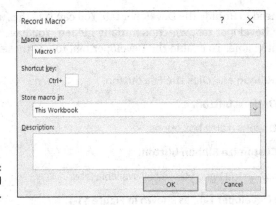

FIGURE 11-2:
The Record
Macro dialog box.

>> **Shortcut Key:** This field is optional. Every macro needs an event, or something to happen, for it to run. This event can be a button click, a workbook opening, or in this case, a keystroke combination. When you assign a shortcut key to your macro, entering that combination of keys triggers the macro to run. You don't need to enter a shortcut key to run the macro.

>> **Store Macro In:** This Workbook is the default option. Storing your macro in this workbook simply means that the macro is stored along with the active Excel file. The next time you open that particular workbook, the macro will be available to run. Similarly, if you send the workbook to another user, that user can run the macro as well, as long as the macro security is properly set by your user — but more on that later.

>> **Description:** This field is optional, but it's useful if you have numerous macros in a spreadsheet or if you need to give a user a more detailed description about what the macro does.

In this first example, enter AddDataBars into the Macro Name field and select This Workbook from the Store Macro In drop-down menu (see Figure 11-3). Click OK.

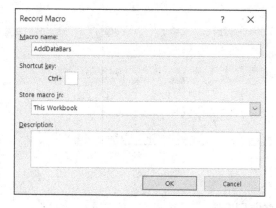

FIGURE 11-3:
Start recording a
new macro called
AddDataBars.

Excel is now recording your actions. While Excel is recording, you can perform any actions you want. In this scenario, you record a macro to add Data Bars to a column of numbers.

Follow along using these steps:

1. **Highlight cells C1:C21.**

2. **Select the Home tab and select Conditional Formatting ⇨ New Rule.**

3. **In the New Formatting Rule dialog box, select Data Bar from the Format Style drop-down menu.**

4. **In the new dialog box that appears, select the Show Bar Only check box.**

5. **Click OK to apply your change.**

6. **Select the Developer tab and click the Stop Recording command.**

   At this point, Excel stops recording. You now have a macro that replaces the data in C1:C21 with Data Bars. Now you record a new macro to remove the Data Bars.

7. **Go to the Developer tab and click the Record Macro command.**

8. **Enter** RemoveDataBars **into the Macro Name field and select the This Workbook option from the Store Macro In drop-down menu (see Figure 11-4).**

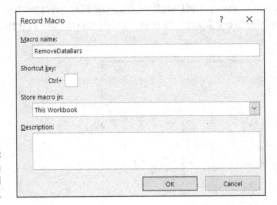

FIGURE 11-4:
Start recording a new macro called RemoveDataBars.

9. **Click OK.**

10. **Highlight cells C1:C21.**

11. **Select the Home tab and select Conditional Formatting ⇨ Clear Rules ⇨ Clear Rules from Selected Cells.**

12. **Select the Developer tab and click the Stop Recording command.**

Again, Excel stops recording. You now have a new macro that removes conditional formatting rules from cells C1:C21.

Running your macros

To see your macros in action, select the Macros command from the Developer tab. The dialog box in Figure 11-5 appears, allowing you to select the macro you want to run. Select the AddDataBars macro and click the Run button.

If all goes well, the macro plays back your actions to a T and applies the Data Bars as designed (see Figure 11-6).

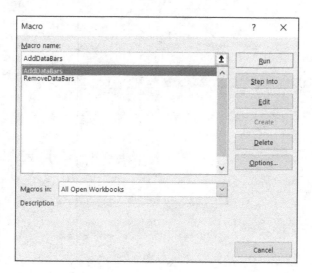

FIGURE 11-5:
Use the Macro
dialog box to
select a macro
and run it.

	A	B	C
1	Customer	Revenue	vs Prior Month
2	ANATUD Corp.	39,943	
3	ANIVUS Corp.	31,566	
4	CALTRA Corp.	71,684	
5	CATYOF Corp.	87,382	
6	DEALYN Corp.	25,795	
7	DEAMLU Corp.	43,461	
8	FUSDMT Corp.	33,689	
9	GMNOOF Corp.	23,788	
10	LOSVUG Corp.	26,002	
11	MACHUL Corp.	30,443	
12	NATAUN Corp.	29,241	
13	NYCTRA Corp.	74,152	
14	OMUSAC Corp.	73,373	
15	PRUCAS Corp.	25,015	
16	SANFRA Corp.	48,997	
17	SAOUSA Corp.	28,818	

FIGURE 11-6:
Your macro
applies Data Bars
automatically!

You can now call up the Macro dialog box again and test the RemoveDataBars macro shown in Figure 11-7.

When you create macros, you want to give your audience a clear and easy way to run each macro. A button, used directly on the dashboard or report, can provide a simple but effective user interface.

Excel Form controls enable you to create user interfaces directly on your worksheets, simplifying work for your users. Form controls range from buttons (the most commonly used control) to scroll bars and check boxes.

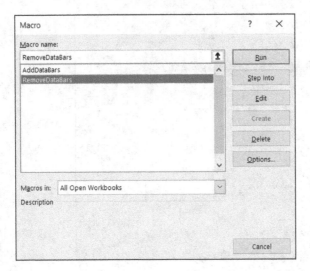

FIGURE 11-7:
The RemoveDa-
taBars macro
removes the
applied Data
Bars.

To run a macro you've recorded, you can place a Form control on a worksheet and then assign the macro to the control. When a macro is assigned to the control, that macro is executed, or played, every time the control is clicked.

Take a moment to create buttons for the two macros (AddDataBars and Remove-DataBars) that you create earlier in this chapter. Here's how:

1. **Click the Insert drop-down list on the Developer tab.**

2. **Select the Button Form control, as shown in Figure 11-8.**

FIGURE 11-8:
You can find the
Form Controls
menu on the
Developer tab.

3. **Click the location where you want to place your button.**

   When you drop the Button control into the worksheet, the Assign Macro dialog box, shown in Figure 11-9, opens and asks you to assign a macro to this button.

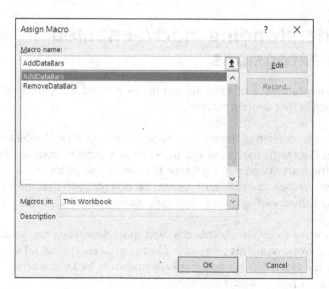

4. **Select the macro that you want to assign.**

   In this case, select the AddDataBars macro and click OK.

5. **Repeat Steps 1 through 4 for the RemoveDataBars macro.**

TIP

The buttons you create come with a default name, such as Button3. To rename a button, right-click the button and then click the existing name. Then you can delete the existing name and replace it with a name of your choosing.

Keep in mind that all controls on the Form Controls menu work in the same way as the command button, in that you can assign a macro to run when the control is selected.

REMEMBER

Notice the Form Controls and ActiveX Controls shown earlier (refer to Figure 11-8). Although they look similar, they're quite different. Form controls are designed specifically for use on a worksheet, and ActiveX controls are typically used on VBA-driven UserForms. As a general rule, you should always use Form controls when working on a worksheet. Why? Form controls need less overhead, so they perform better, and configuring Form controls is far easier than configuring their ActiveX counterparts.

Enabling and trusting macros

With the release of Office 2007, Microsoft introduced significant changes to its Office security model. One of the most significant changes is the concept of trusted documents. Without getting into the technical minutia, a *trusted document* is essentially a workbook you've deemed safe by enabling macros.

Understanding macro-enabled file extensions

It's important to note that Microsoft has created a separate file extension for workbooks that contain macros.

Workbooks created in Excel 2010 and later versions have the default file extension .xlsx. Files with the .xlsx extension cannot contain macros. If your workbook contains macros and you then save that workbook as an .xlsx file, your macros are removed automatically. Of course, Excel warns you that macro content will be disabled when saving a workbook with macros as an .xlsx file.

If you want to retain the macros, you must save your file as an Excel macro-enabled workbook. This gives your file an .xlsm extension. All workbooks with an .xlsx file extension are automatically known to be safe, whereas you can recognize .xlsm files as a potential threat.

Enabling macro content

When you open a workbook that contains macros in Excel, you get a message in the form of a yellow bar under the Ribbon stating that macros (active content) have in effect been disabled.

If you click Enable Content, it automatically becomes a trusted document. You're then no longer prompted to enable the content as long as you open that file on your computer. If you told Excel that you trust a particular workbook by enabling macros, it's highly likely that you'll enable macros every time you open it. Thus, Excel remembers that you've enabled macros before and inhibits any further messages about macros for that workbook.

This is great news for you and your clients. After enabling your macros just one time, they won't be annoyed at the constant messages about macros, and you won't have to worry that your macro-enabled dashboard will fall flat because macros have been disabled.

Setting up trusted locations

If the thought of any macro message coming up (even one time) unnerves you, you can set up a trusted location for your files. A *trusted location* is a directory deemed a safe zone where only trusted workbooks are placed. A trusted location allows you and your clients to run a macro-enabled workbook with no security restrictions as long as the workbook is in that location.

To set up a trusted location, follow these steps:

1. **Select the Macro Security button on the Developer tab.**

2. **Click the Trusted Locations button.**

    This step opens the Trusted Locations pane, shown in Figure 11-10. There, you see all the directories that Excel considers trusted.

3. **Click the Add New Location button.**

4. **Click Browse to find and specify the directory that will be considered a trusted location.**

    After you specify a trusted location, any Excel file that's opened from this location will have macros automatically enabled. Have your clients specify a trusted location and use your Excel files from there.

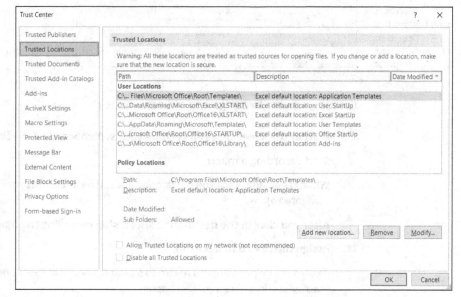

FIGURE 11-10:
The Trusted
Locations menu
allows you to add
directories that
are considered
trusted.

Examining some macro examples

Covering the fundamentals of building and using macros is one thing. Coming up with good ways to incorporate them into your reporting processes is another. Take a moment to review a few examples of how you can implement macros in your dashboards and reports.

Open the `Chapter 11 Macro Samples.xslm` file found on this book's companion website to follow along in the next section.

Building navigation buttons

The most common use of macros is navigation. Workbooks that have many worksheets or tabs can be frustrating to navigate. To help your audience, you can create some sort of a switchboard, like the one shown in Figure 11-11. When users click the `Example 1` button, they're taken to the Example 1 sheet.

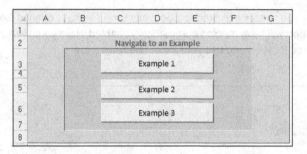

FIGURE 11-11:
Use macros to build buttons that help users navigate your reports.

Creating a macro to navigate to a sheet is quite simple:

1. **Start at the sheet that will become your switchboard or starting point.**

2. **Start recording a macro.**

3. **While recording, click the *destination sheet* (the sheet this macro will navigate to).**

4. **After you click in the destination sheet, stop recording the macro.**

5. **Assign the macro to a button.**

   If you need help assigning a macro to a button, check out the "Running your macros" section, earlier in this chapter.

TIP

Excel has a built-in hyperlink feature, allowing you to convert the contents of a cell into a hyperlink that links to another location. That location can be a separate Excel workbook, a website, or even another tab in the current workbook. Although using a hyperlink may be easier than setting up a macro, you can't apply a hyperlink to Form controls (like buttons). Instead of a button, you use text to let users know where they'll go when they click the link.

Dynamically rearranging pivot table data

In Figure 11-12, macros allow a user to change the perspective of the chart simply by selecting any one of the buttons shown.

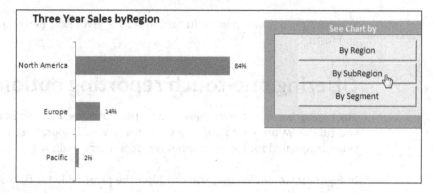

FIGURE 11-12: This report allows users to choose their perspective.

Figure 11-13 reveals that the chart is actually a pivot chart tied to a pivot table. The recorded macros assigned to each button are doing nothing more than rearranging the pivot table to slice the data using various pivot fields.

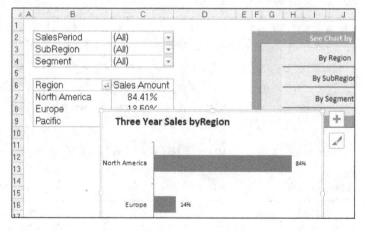

FIGURE 11-13: The macros behind these buttons rearrange the data fields in a pivot table.

Here are the high-level steps needed to create this type of setup:

1. **Create the pivot table and then add a pivot chart by clicking inside the pivot table and selecting Insert ⇨ Charts ⇨ Bar.**

2. **Start recording a macro.**

3. While recording, move a pivot field from one area of the pivot table to the other. When you're done, stop recording the macro.

4. Record another macro to move the data field back to its original position.

5. After both macros are set up, assign each one to a separate button.

You can fire your new macros in turn to see the pivot field dynamically move back and forth.

Offering one-touch reporting options

The two earlier macro examples demonstrate that you can record any action that you find of value. That is, if you think users would appreciate a certain feature being automated for them, why not record a macro to do so?

In Figure 11-14, notice that you can filter the pivot table for the top or bottom 20 customers. Because the steps to filter a pivot table for the top and bottom 20 have been recorded, anyone can get the benefit of this functionality without knowing how to do it themselves. Also, recording specific actions allows you to manage risk a bit. That is to say, you'll know that your users will interact with your reports in a method that has been developed and tested by you.

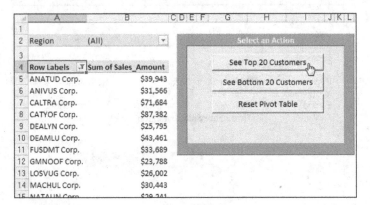

FIGURE 11-14: Macros can offer your users prerecorded views.

This not only saves them time and effort but also allows users who don't know how to take these actions to benefit from them.

Figure 11-15 demonstrates how you can give your audience a quick and easy way to see the same data on different charts. Don't laugh too quickly at the uselessness of this example. It's not uncommon to be asked to see the same data different ways. Rather than take up real estate, just record a macro that changes the chart type. Your clients can switch views to their hearts' content.

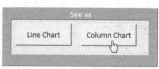

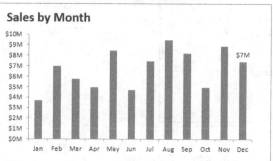

Getting Started with Form Controls

Excel offers a set of controls called Form controls, designed specifically for adding user interface elements directly onto a worksheet. After you place a Form control on a worksheet, you can then configure it to perform a specific task. Later in this chapter, I demonstrate how to apply the most useful controls to a presentation.

Finding Form controls

Select the Developer tab and choose the Insert command, as shown in Figure 11-16. Here, you find two sets of controls: Form controls and ActiveX controls. Form controls are designed specifically for use on a worksheet, whereas ActiveX controls are typically used on Excel UserForms. Because Form controls can be configured far more easily than their ActiveX counterparts, you generally should use Form controls.

Here are the nine Form controls that you can add directly to a worksheet, as shown in Figure 11-17:

» **Button:** Executes an assigned macro when a user clicks the button.

» **Combo Box:** Gives a user an expandable list of options from which to choose.

» **Check Box:** Provides a mechanism for a select/deselect scenario. When selected, it returns a value of True. Otherwise, it returns False.

» **Spin Button:** Enables a user to easily increase or decrease a value by clicking the up and down arrows.

FIGURE 11-16:
Form controls
and ActiveX
controls.

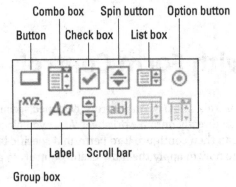

FIGURE 11-17:
Nine labeled
Form controls
that you can add
to your
worksheet.

>> **List Box:** Gives a user a list of options from which to choose.

>> **Option Button:** Enables a user to toggle through two or more options, one at a time. Selecting one option automatically deselects the others.

>> **Scroll Bar:** Enables a user to scroll to a value or position using a sliding scale that can be moved by clicking and dragging the mouse.

>> **Label:** Allows you to add text labels to your worksheet. You can also assign a macro to the label, effectively using it as a button of sorts.

>> **Group Box:** Typically used for cosmetic purposes, this control serves as a container for groups of other controls.

Adding a control to a worksheet

To add a control to a worksheet, simply click the control that you require and click the approximate location where you want to place the control. You can easily move and resize the control later, just as you would a chart or shape.

After you add a control, you configure it to define its look, behavior, and utility. Each control has its own set of configuration options that allow you to customize it for your purposes. To get to these options, right-click the control and select Format Control from the menu that appears. This opens the Format Control dialog box, illustrated in Figure 11-18, with all the configuration options for that control.

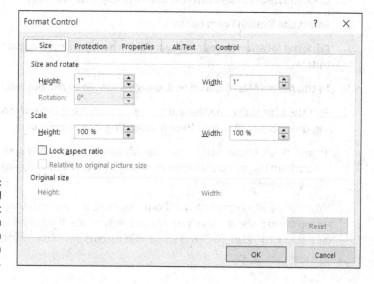

FIGURE 11-18:
Right-click and
select Format
Control to open a
dialog box with
the configuration
options.

Each control has its own set of tabs that allow you to customize everything from formatting to security to configuration arguments. You see different tabs based on which control you're using, but most Form controls have the Control tab, where the meat of the configuration lies. There, you find the variables and settings that need to be defined for the control to function.

REMEMBER

The Button and Label controls don't have the Control tab. They have no need for one. The button simply fires whichever macro you assign it. As for the label, it's not designed to run macro events.

Throughout the rest of this chapter, you walk through a few exercises that demonstrate how to use the most useful controls in a reporting environment. At the end of this chapter, you'll have a solid understanding of Form controls and how they can enhance your dashboards and reports.

Using the Button Control

The Button control gives your audience a clear and easy way to execute the macros you've recorded. To insert and configure a Button control, follow these steps:

1. Click the Insert drop-down list under the Developer tab.

2. Select the Button Form control.

3. Click the location in your spreadsheet where you want to place the button.

4. In the Assign Macro dialog box, assign a macro to the button.

5. Edit the text shown on the button by right-clicking the button, highlighting the existing text, and then overwriting it with your own.

TIP

To assign a different macro to the button, simply right-click and select Assign Macro from the menu that appears in order to reactivate the Assign Macro dialog box (refer to Figure 11-9).

When you add macros to a workbook, you have to save that workbook as an .xlsm file in order to share your macros with others. If you save the workbook as a standard .xlsx file, Excel strips your macros out of the workbook.

Using the Check Box Control

The Check Box control provides a mechanism for selecting and deselecting options. When a check box is selected, it returns a value of True. When it isn't selected, False is returned. To add and configure a Check Box control, follow these steps:

1. Click the Insert drop-down list on the Developer tab.

2. Select the Check Box Form control.

3. Click the location in your spreadsheet where you want to place the check box.

4. After you drop the Check Box control onto your spreadsheet, right-click the control and select Format Control from the menu that appears.

5. Click the Control tab to see the configuration options shown in Figure 11-19.

FIGURE 11-19:
Formatting the
Check Box
control.

6. **Select the state in which the check box should open.**

   The default selection (Unchecked) typically works for most scenarios, so it's rare that you'd have to change this selection.

7. **In the Cell Link box, enter the cell to which you want the check box to output its value.**

   By default, a Check Box control outputs either True or False, depending on whether it's checked. Notice in Figure 11-19 that this particular check box outputs to cell A5.

8. **(Optional) You can select the 3-D Shading check box if you want the control to have a three-dimensional appearance.**

9. **Click OK to apply your changes.**

TIP

To rename the Check Box control, right-click the control, select Edit Text from the menu that appears, and then overwrite the existing text with your own.

As Figure 11-20 illustrates, the check box outputs its value to the specified cell. If the check box is selected, a value of True is output. If the check box isn't selected, a value of False is output.

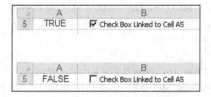

FIGURE 11-20:
The two states of
the check box.

If you're having a hard time figuring out how this could be useful, take a stab at the exercise in the following section, which illustrates how you can use a check box to toggle a chart series on and off.

Toggling a Chart Series On and Off

Figure 11-21 shows the same chart twice. Notice that the bottom chart contains only one series, with a check box offering to show 2020 trend data. The top chart shows the same chart with the check box selected. The on/off nature of the Check Box control is ideal for interactivity that calls for a visible/not visible state.

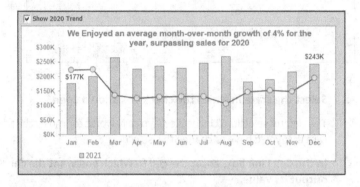

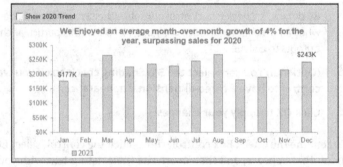

FIGURE 11-21:
A check box can help create the disappearing data series effect.

REMEMBER

To download the `Chapter 11 Form Control Samples.xlsx` file, go to this book's companion website.

You start with the raw data (in `Chapter 11 Form Control Samples.xlsx`) that contains both 2020 and 2021 data (see Figure 11-22). The first column has a cell in which the Check Box control will output its value (cell A12 in this example). This cell will contain either `True` or `False`.

Next, create the analysis layer (staging table) that consists of all formulas, as shown in Figure 11-23. The chart actually reads from this data, not the raw data. This way, you can control what the chart sees.

As you can see in Figure 11-23, the formulas for the 2021 row simply reference the cells in the raw data for each respective month. You do that because you want the 2021 data to appear at all times.

FIGURE 11-22:
Start with raw
data and a cell in
which a Check
Box control can
output its value.

	A	B	C	D	E	F	G
10			Raw Data				
11	Toggle for 2020 Data		Jan	Feb	Mar	Apr	May
12	TRUE	2020	$222,389	$224,524	$136,104	$125,260	$130,791
13		2021	$176,648	$201,000	$265,720	$225,461	$235,494

FIGURE 11-23:
Create a staging
table that will
feed the chart.
The values of
this data are
all formulas.

	A	B	C	D	E
4					
5			Jan	Feb	Mar
6		2020	=IF($A12=TRUE,C12,NA())	=IF($A12=TRUE,D12,NA())	=IF($A12=TRUE,E12,NA())
7		2021	=C13	=D13	=E13
8					
9					
10			Raw Data		
11	Toggle for 2020 Data		Jan	Feb	Mar
12	TRUE	2020	222389	224524	136104
13		2021	176648	201000	265720

For the 2020 row, test the value of cell A12 (the cell that contains the output from the check box). If A12 reads True, you reference the respective 2020 cell in the raw data. If A12 doesn't read True, the formula uses Excel's NA() function to return an #N/A error. Excel charts can't read a cell with the #N/A error. Therefore, they simply don't show the data series for any cell that contains #N/A. This is ideal when you don't want a data series to be shown at all.

TIP

Notice that the formula shown in Figure 11-23 uses an absolute reference with cell A12 — that is, the reference to cell A12 in the formula is prefixed with a $ sign ($A12). This ensures that the column references in the formulas don't shift when they're copied across.

Figure 11-24 illustrates the two scenarios in action in the staging tables. In the scenario shown at the bottom of Figure 11-24, cell A12 is True, so the staging table actually brings in 2011 data. In the scenario shown at the top of Figure 11-24, cell A12 is False, so the staging table returns #N/A for 2020.

Finally, create the chart that you saw earlier in this section (refer to Figure 11-21) using the staging table. Keep in mind that you can scale this to as many series as you like.

You can apply this technique to as many check boxes as you need. For instance, Figure 11-25 illustrates a chart that has multiple series whose visibility is controlled by Check Box controls. This allows you to make all but two series invisible so that you can compare those two series unhindered. Then you can make another two visible, comparing those.

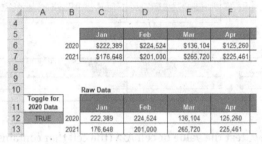

▲	A	B	C	D	E	F
4						
5			Jan	Feb	Mar	Apr
6		2020	#N/A	#N/A	#N/A	#N/A
7		2021	$176,648	$201,000	$265,720	$225,461
8						
9						
10			Raw Data			
11	Toggle for 2020 Data		Jan	Feb	Mar	Apr
12	FALSE	2020	222,389	224,524	136,104	125,260
13		2021	176,648	201,000	265,720	225,461
14						

▲	A	B	C	D	E	F
4						
5			Jan	Feb	Mar	Apr
6		2020	$222,389	$224,524	$136,104	$125,260
7		2021	$176,648	$201,000	$265,720	$225,461
8						
9						
10			Raw Data			
11	Toggle for 2020 Data		Jan	Feb	Mar	Apr
12	TRUE	2020	222,389	224,524	136,104	125,260
13		2021	176,648	201,000	265,720	225,461

FIGURE 11-24: When cell A12 reads `True`, 2020 data is displayed; when it reads `False`, the 2020 row shows only #N/A errors.

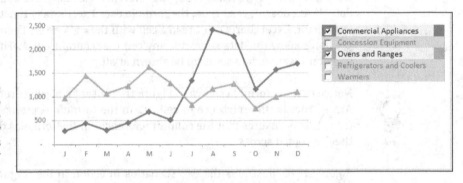

FIGURE 11-25: You can use check boxes to control how much data is shown in your chart at one time.

Using the Option Button Control

Option buttons allow users to toggle through several options one at a time. The idea is to have two or more option buttons in a group. Then selecting one option button automatically deselects the others. To add option buttons to your worksheet, follow these steps:

1. Click the Insert drop-down list under the Developer tab.

2. Select the Option Button Form control.

3. Click the location in your spreadsheet where you want to place the option button.

4. After you drop the control onto your spreadsheet, right-click the control and select Format Control from the menu that appears.

5. Click the Control tab to see the configuration options shown in Figure 11-26.

6. Select the state in which the option button should open.

The default selection (Unchecked) typically works for most scenarios, so it's rare that you'd have to change this selection.

7. In the Cell Link box, enter the cell to which you want the option button to output its value.

By default, an Option Button control outputs a number that corresponds to the order it was put on the worksheet. For instance, the first option button you place on the worksheet outputs a number 1, the second outputs a number 2, the third outputs a number 3, and so on. Notice in Figure 11-26 that this particular control outputs to cell A5.

8. (Optional) You can select the 3-D Shading check box if you want the control to have a three-dimensional appearance.

9. Click OK to apply these changes.

10. To add another option button, simply copy the button you created and paste as many option buttons as you need.

The nice thing about copying and pasting is that all the configurations you made to the original persist in all copies.

TIP

To give your option button a meaningful label, right-click the control, select Edit Text from the menu that appears, and then overwrite the existing text with your own.

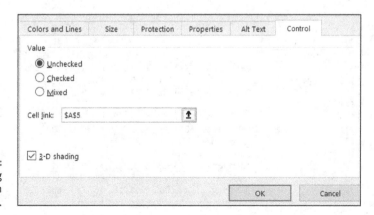

FIGURE 11-26:
Formatting
the Option
Button control.

Showing Many Views through One Chart

One of the ways you can use option buttons is to feed a single chart with different data, based on the option selected. Figure 11-27 illustrates an example. When each category is selected, the single chart is updated to show the data for that selection.

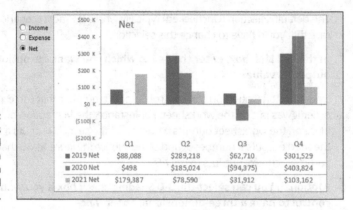

FIGURE 11-27:
This chart is dynamically fed different data based on the selected option button.

Now, you could create three separate charts and show them all on your dashboard at the same time. However, using option buttons as an alternative saves valuable real estate by not having to show three separate charts. Plus it's much easier to troubleshoot, format, and maintain one chart than three.

To create this example, start with three raw data sets — as shown in Figure 11-28 — that contain three categories of data; Income, Expense, and Net. Near the raw data, reserve a cell where the option buttons output their values (cell A8, in this example). This cell contains the ID of the option selected: 1, 2, or 3.

	A	B	C	D	E	F
7	Option Button Trigger					
8	1		Q1	Q2	Q3	Q4
9		2021 Income	$399,354	$573,662	$244,661	$790,906
10		2020 Income	$219,967	$495,072	$212,749	$687,744
11		2019 Income	$159,832	$289,825	$181,961	$456,016
12						
13		2021 Expense	$219,967	$495,072	$212,749	$687,744
14		2020 Expense	$219,468	$310,048	$307,124	$283,920
15		2019 Expense	$71,744	$607	$119,251	$154,487
16						
17		2021 Net	$179,387	$78,590	$31,912	$103,162
18		2020 Net	$498	$185,024	-$94,375	$403,824
19		2019 Net	$88,088	$289,218	$62,710	$301,529

FIGURE 11-28:
Start with the raw data sets and a cell where the option buttons can output their values.

You then create the analysis layer (the staging table) that consists of all formulas, as shown in Figure 11-29. The chart reads from this staging table, allowing you to control what the chart sees. The first cell of the staging table contains the following formula:

```
=IF($A$8=1,B9,IF($A$8=2,B13,B17))
```

	A	B
3		=IF($A$8=1,B9,IF($A$8=2,B13,B17))
4		
5		
6		
7	Option Button Trigger	
8	1	
9		2021 Income
10		2020 Income
11		2019 Income
12		
13		2021 Expense
14		2020 Expense
15		2019 Expense
16		
17		2021 Net
18		2020 Net

FIGURE 11-29: Create a staging table and enter this formula in the first cell.

This formula tells Excel to check the value of cell A8 (the cell where the option buttons output their values). If the value of cell A8 is 1, which represents the value of the Income option, the formula returns the value in the Income data set (cell B9). If the value of cell A8 is 2, which represents the value of the Expense option, the formula returns the value in the Expense data set (cell B13). If the value of cell A8 is not 1 or 2, the Net value (cell B17) is returned.

TIP

Notice that the formula shown in Figure 11-29 uses absolute references with cell A8. That is, the reference to cell A8 in the formula is prefixed with dollar ($) signs ($A$8). This ensures that the cell references in the formulas don't shift when they're copied down and across.

To test that the formula is working fine, you could change the value of cell A8 manually, from 1 to 3. When the formula works, you simply copy the formula across and down to fill the rest of the staging table.

When the setup is created, all that's left to do is create the chart using the staging table. Again, the major benefits you get from this type of setup are that you can

» Make any formatting changes to one chart and then easily add another data set by adding another option button.

» Edit your formulas easily.

Using the Combo Box Control

The Combo Box control allows users to select from a drop-down list of predefined options. When an item from the Combo Box control is selected, an action is taken with that selection. To add a combo box to your worksheet, follow these steps:

1. **Click the Insert drop-down list under the Developer tab.**

2. **Select the Combo Box Form control.**

3. **Click the location in your spreadsheet where you want to place the combo box.**

4. **After you drop the control onto your spreadsheet, right-click the control and select Format Control from the menu that appears.**

5. **Click the Control tab to see the configuration options shown in Figure 11-30.**

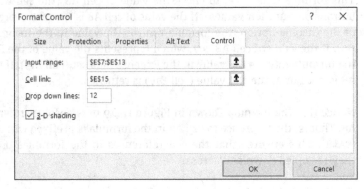

FIGURE 11-30:
Formatting
the Combo
Box control.

6. **In the Input Range setting, identify the range that holds the predefined items you want to present as choices in the combo box.**

7. **In the Cell Link box, enter the cell to which you want the combo box to output its value.**

   A Combo Box control outputs the index number of the selected item. This means that if the second item on the list is selected, the number 2 will be output. If the fifth item on the list is selected, the number 5 will be output. Notice in Figure 11-30 that this particular control outputs to cell E15.

8. **In the Drop Down Lines box, enter the number of items you want shown at one time.**

   You see in Figure 11-30 that this control is formatted to show 12 items at one time. When users expand the combo box, they'll see 12 items.

9. **(Optional) You can select the 3-D Shading check box if you want the control to have a three-dimensional appearance.**

10. **Click OK to apply your changes.**

Changing Chart Data with a Drop-Down Selector

You can use Combo Box controls to give your users an intuitive way to select data via a drop-down selector. Figure 11-31 shows a thermometer chart that's controlled by the combo box above it. When a user selects the Southwest region, the chart responds by plotting the data for the selected region.

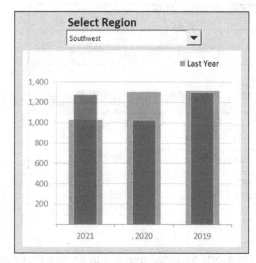

FIGURE 11-31:
Use combo boxes to give your users an intuitive drop-down selector.

To create this example, start with the raw data set shown in Figure 11-32. This data set contains the data for each region. Near the raw data, reserve a cell where the combo box will output its value (cell M7, in this example). This cell will catch the index number of the combo box entry selected.

FIGURE 11-32:
Start with the raw data set and a cell where the combo box can output its value.

	M	N	O	P	Q	R	S
5			Raw Data				
6	Trigger						
7	7		Market	2021	2020	2019	2018
7			Canada	730	854	1911	1608
8			Midwest	952	1389	1113	1603
9			North	443	543	541	386
10			Northeast	1536	1760	1088	1737
11			South	1500	1600	1588	1000
12			Southeast	1257	1280	1734	1007
13			Southwest	1275	1024	1298	1312
14			West	1402	1045	1759	1075

You then create the analysis layer (the staging table) that consists of all formulas, as shown in Figure 11-33. The chart reads from this staging table, allowing you to control what the chart sees. The first cell of the staging table contains the following INDEX formula:

```
=INDEX(P7:P14,$M$7)
```

FIGURE 11-33:
Create a staging table that uses the INDEX function to extract the appropriate data from the raw data set.

	M	N	O	P	Q
1				2021	2020
2			Current Year	=@INDEX(P7:P14,$M$7)	=@INDEX(Q7:Q14,$M$7)
3			Last Year	=Q2	=R2
4					
5			Raw Data		
6	Trigger		Market	2021	2020
7	7		Canada	730	854
8			Midwest	952	1389
9			North	443	543
10			Northeast	1536	1760
11			South	1500	1600
12			Southeast	1257	1280
13			Southwest	1275	1024
14			West	1402	1045

The INDEX function converts an index number to a value that can be recognized. An INDEX function requires two arguments to work properly. The first argument is the range of the list you're working with. The second argument is the index number.

In this example, you're using the index number from the combo box (in cell M7) and extracting the value from the appropriate range (2021 data in P7:P14). Again, notice the use of the absolute dollar signs ($). This ensures that the cell references in the formulas don't shift when they're copied down and across.

Take another look at Figure 11-33 to see what's happening. The INDEX formula in cell P2 points to the range that contains the 2021 data. It then captures the index number in cell M7 (which traps the output value of the combo box). The index number happens to be 7. So the formula in cell P2 will extract the seventh value from the 2021 data range (in this case, Southwest).

When you copy the formula across, Excel adjusts the formula to extract the seventh value from each year's data range.

After your INDEX formulas are in place, you have a clean staging table that you can use to create your chart (see Figure 11-34).

	M	N	O	P	Q	R	S
1				2021	2020	2019	2018
2			Current Year	1,275	1,024	1,298	1,312
3			Last Year	1,024	1,298	1,312	
4							
5			Raw Data				
6	Trigger		Market	2021	2020	2019	2018
7	7		Canada	730	854	1911	1608
8			Midwest	952	1389	1113	1603
9			North	443	543	541	386
10			Northeast	1536	1760	1088	1737
11			South	1500	1600	1588	1000
12			Southeast	1257	1280	1734	1007
13			Southwest	1275	1024	1298	1312
14			West	1402	1045	1759	1075

FIGURE 11-34: Create a chart using this clean staging table.

Using the List Box Control

The List Box control allows users to select from a list of predefined choices. When an item from the List Box control is selected, an action is taken with that selection. To add a list box to your worksheet, follow these steps:

1. Select the Insert drop-down list under the Developer tab.

2. Select the List Box Form control.

3. Click the location in your spreadsheet where you want to place the list box.

4. After you drop the control onto your worksheet, right-click the control and select Format Control from the menu that appears.

5. Click the Control tab to see the configuration options shown in Figure 11-35.

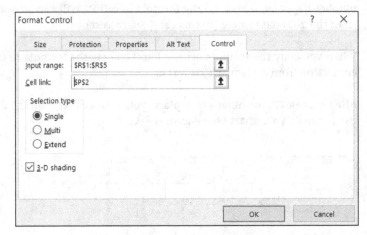

FIGURE 11-35:
Formatting the
List Box control.

6. In the Input Range setting, identify the range that holds the predefined items you want to present as choices in the list box.

As you can see in Figure 11-22, this list box is filled with region selections.

7. In the Cell Link box, enter the cell where you want the list box to output its value.

By default, a List Box control outputs the index number of the selected item. This means that if the second item on the list is selected, the number 2 will be output. If the fifth item on the list is selected, the number 5 will be output. Notice in Figure 11-35 that this particular control outputs to cell P2. The Selection Type setting allows users to choose more than one selection in the list box. The choices here are Single, Multi, and Extend.

Always leave this setting on Single because Multi and Extend work only in the VBA environment.

REMEMBER

8. (Optional) You can select the 3-D Shading check box if you want the control to have a three-dimensional appearance.

9. Click OK to apply your changes.

Controlling Multiple Charts with One Selector

One of the more useful ways to use a list box is to control multiple charts with one selector. Figure 11-36 illustrates an example of this. As a region selection is made in the list box, all three charts are fed the data for that region, adjusting the charts to correspond with the selection made. Happily, all this is done without VBA code; all it takes is a handful of formulas and a list box.

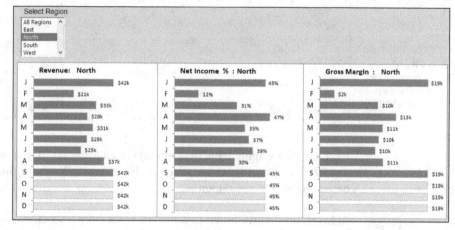

FIGURE 11-36: This list box feeds the region selection to multiple charts, changing each chart to correspond with the selection made.

To create this example, start with three raw data sets — as shown in Figure 11-37 — that contain three categories of data: Revenues, Net Income %, and Gross Margin. Each data set contains a separate line for each region, including one for All Regions.

	A	B	C	D	E	F	G	H	I	J	K	L	M
5													
6	Revenues	Jan	Feb	Mar	Apr	May	Jun	Jul	Aug	Sep	Oct	Nov	Dec
7	All Regions	98,741	54,621	96,555	109,625	87,936	84,637	81,339	97,281	98,741	98,741	98,741	98,741
8	East	27,474	22,674	35,472	36,292	31,491	27,672	23,853	25,284	27,474	27,474	27,474	27,474
9	North	41,767	20,806	32,633	28,023	31,090	27,873	24,656	36,984	41,767	41,767	41,767	41,767
10	South	18,911	1,125	17,020	34,196	12,989	18,368	23,747	22,087	18,911	18,911	18,911	18,911
11	West	10,590	10,016	11,430	11,115	12,367	10,724	9,082	12,926	10,590	10,590	10,590	10,590
12													
13	Net Income %	Jan	Feb	Mar	Apr	May	Jun	Jul	Aug	Sep	Oct	Nov	Dec
14	All Regions	49.9%	50.6%	48.7%	47.8%	41.4%	47%	52.8%	48.7%	49.9%	49.9%	49.9%	49.9%
15	East	63.1%	53.6%	55.8%	47.4%	41.5%	42%	42.5%	31.7%	63.1%	63.1%	63.1%	63.1%
16	North	45.3%	11.8%	31.0%	47.5%	35.2%	37%	39.1%	29.8%	45.3%	45.3%	45.3%	45.3%
17	South	31.2%	61.7%	41.8%	30.9%	9.0%	33%	56.9%	71.5%	31.2%	31.2%	31.2%	31.2%
18	West	60.1%	75.4%	66.1%	65.2%	79.8%	76%	72.7%	61.9%	60.1%	60.1%	60.1%	60.1%
19													
20	Gross Margin	Jan	Feb	Mar	Apr	May	Jun	Jul	Aug	Sep	Oct	Nov	Dec
21	All Regions	48,508	22,850	44,586	48,340	35,056	37,469	39,881	42,849	48,508	48,508	48,508	48,508
22	East	17,326	12,154	19,799	17,206	13,079	11,605	10,131	8,020	17,326	17,326	17,326	17,326
23	North	18,914	2,455	10,115	13,299	10,938	10,290	9,641	11,019	18,914	18,914	18,914	18,914
24	South	5,904	694	7,115	10,582	1,171	7,339	13,506	15,803	5,904	5,904	5,904	5,904
25	West	6,364	7,547	7,557	7,253	9,867	8,235	6,604	8,005	6,364	6,364	6,364	6,364

FIGURE 11-37: Start with the raw data sets that contain one line per region.

You then add a list box that outputs the index number of the selected item to cell P2 (see Figure 11-38).

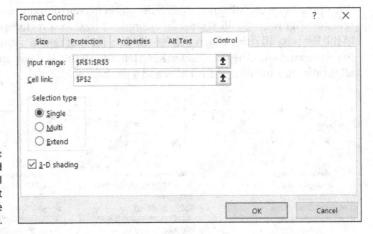

Next, create a staging table that consists of all formulas. In this staging table, you use Excel's CHOOSE function to select the correct value from the raw data tables based on the selected region.

TIP

In Excel, the CHOOSE function returns a value from a specified list of values based on a specified position number. For instance, the formula CHOOSE(3,"Red", "Yellow", "Green", "Blue") returns Green because Green is the third item in the list of values. The formula CHOOSE(1, "Red", "Yellow", "Green", "Blue") returns Red. See Chapter 2 to get a detailed look at the CHOOSE function.

As you can see in Figure 11-39, the CHOOSE formula retrieves the target position number from cell P2 (the cell where the list box outputs the index number of the selected item) and then matches that position number to the list of cell references given. The cell references come directly from the raw data table.

FIGURE 11-39:
Use the CHOOSE function to capture the correct data corresponding to the selected region.

	A	B	O	P
1		J		List Output
2	Revenues	=CHOOSE($P$2,B7,B8,B9,B10,B11)		3
3	Net Income %			
4	Gross Margin			=INDEX(R1:R5,P2)
5				
6	Revenues	Jan		
7	All Regions	98741.4		
8	East	27473.82		
9	North	41767.27		
10	South	18910.81		
11	West	10589.5		

In the example shown in Figure 11-39, the data that will be returned with this CHOOSE formula is 41767. Why? Because cell P2 contains the number 3, and the third cell reference within the CHOOSE formula is cell B9 — the cell containing January revenues for the North region.

You enter the same type of CHOOSE formula into the Jan column and then copy it across (see Figure 11-40).

	A	B	C
1		J	F
2	Revenues	=CHOOSE($P$2,B7,B8,B9,B10,B11)	=CHOOSE($P$2,C7,C8,C9,C10,C11)
3	Net Income %	=CHOOSE($P$2,B14,B15,B16,B17,B18)	=CHOOSE($P$2,C14,C15,C16,C17,C18)
4	Gross Margin	=CHOOSE($P$2,B21,B22,B23,B24,B25)	=CHOOSE($P$2,C21,C22,C23,C24,C25)

To test that your formulas are working, change the value of cell P2 manually by entering 1, 2, 3, 4, or 5. When the formulas work, all that's left to do is create the charts using the staging table.

REMEMBER

If Excel functions such as CHOOSE or INDEX are a bit intimidating for you, don't worry. You can use various combinations of Form controls and Excel functions in literally hundreds of ways to achieve interactive reporting. The examples I give in this chapter are designed to give you a sense of how you can incorporate Form controls into your dashboards and reports. There are no set rules on which Form controls or Excel functions you need to use in your model.

Start with basic improvements to your dashboard, using controls and formulas you're comfortable with. Then gradually try to introduce some of the more complex controls and functions. With a little imagination and creativity, you can take the basics in this chapter and customize your own dynamic dashboards.

Chapter **12**

Adding Interactivity with Pivot Slicers

S licers allow you to filter your pivot table in a way that's similar to the way Filter fields filter a pivot table. The difference is that slicers offer a user-friendly interface, enabling you to better manage the filter state of your pivot table reports. Happily, Microsoft has added another dimension to slicers with the introduction of Timeline slicers. Timeline slicers are designed to work specifically with date-based filtering.

In this chapter, you explore slicers and their potential to add an attractive *and interactive* user interface to your dashboards and reports.

Understanding Slicers

If you've worked your way through Chapter 3, you know that pivot tables allow for interactive filtering using Filter fields. *Filter fields* are the drop-down lists you can include at the top of a pivot table, allowing users to interactively filter for specific data items. As useful as Filter fields are, they have always had a couple of drawbacks.

First of all, Filter fields are not cascading filters — the filters don't work together to limit selections when needed. Take, for example, Figure 12-1. You can see that the Region filter is set to the North region. However, the Market filter still allows you to select markets that are clearly not in the North region (California, for example). Because the Market filter is not in any way limited based on the Region Filter field, you have the annoying possibility of selecting a market that could yield no data because it's not in the North region.

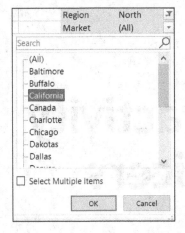

FIGURE 12-1:
Default pivot table Filter fields do not work together to limit filter selections.

Another drawback is that Filter fields don't provide an easy way to tell what exactly is being filtered when you select multiple items. In Figure 12-2, you can see an example of this. The Region filter has been limited to three regions: Midwest, North, and Northeast. However, notice that the Region filter value shows (Multiple Items). By default, Filter fields show (Multiple Items) when you select more than one item. The only way to tell what has been selected is to click the drop-down menu. You can imagine the confusion on a printed version of this report, in which you can't click down to see which data items make up the numbers on the page.

By contrast, slicers don't have these issues. Slicers respond to one another. As you can see in Figure 12-3, the Market slicer visibly highlights the relevant markets when the North region is selected. The rest of the markets are muted, signaling that they are not part of the North region.

When selecting multiple items in a slicer, you can easily see that multiple items have been chosen. In Figure 12-4, you can see that the pivot table is being filtered by the Midwest and North regions. No more (Multiple Items).

| Region | (Multiple Items) |
| Market | (All) |

Ship Date	Revenue
Jan	431,794
Feb	1,142,718
Mar	697,451
Apr	510,333
May	1,405,497
Jun	586,846
Jul	477,691
Aug	1,527,340
Sep	1,116,476
Oct	511,945
Nov	1,311,642
Dec	1,250,069
Grand Total	10,969,803

FIGURE 12-2: Filter fields show the text (Multiple Items) when multiple selections are made.

Ship Date	Revenue
Jan	61,111
Feb	69,617
Mar	265,264
Apr	86,056
May	67,749
Jun	177,452
Jul	78,398
Aug	64,156
Sep	157,804
Oct	75,625
Nov	81,356
Dec	250,086
Grand Total	1,434,675

Region

Canada	Midwest
North	Northeast
South	Southeast
Southwest	West

Market

Dakotas	Great Lakes
Baltimore	Buffalo
California	Canada
Charlotte	Chicago

FIGURE 12-3: Slicers work together to show you relevant data items based on your selection.

Ship Date	Revenue
Jan	198,050
Feb	558,317
Mar	488,533
Apr	405,731
May	713,176
Jun	468,928
Jul	302,474
Aug	586,697
Sep	771,006
Oct	322,154
Nov	557,011
Dec	807,154
Grand Total	6,179,231

Region

Canada	Midwest
North	Northeast
South	Southeast
Southwest	West

Market

Chicago	Dakotas
Great Lakes	Kansas City
Omaha	Tulsa
Baltimore	Buffalo

FIGURE 12-4: Slicers do a better job of displaying multiple item selections.

Creating a Standard Slicer

Enough talk. It's time to create your first slicer. Just follow these steps:

1. **Place the cursor anywhere inside the pivot table.**

   Doing so activates the PivotTable Analyze contextual tabs on the Ribbon.

2. **Select the PivotTable Analyze tab and then click the Insert Slicer command.**

   This step activates the Insert Slicers dialog box, shown in Figure 12-5.

3. **Using the Insert Slicers dialog box, select the dimensions you want to filter.**

   In this example, the Region and Market slicers are created.

4. **After the slicers are created, simply click the filter values to filter the pivot table.**

   As you can see in Figure 12-6, not only does clicking Midwest in the Region slicer filter your pivot table, but the Market slicer also responds by highlighting the markets that belong to the Midwest region.

   You can also select multiple values by holding down the Ctrl key on the keyboard while selecting the needed filters. In Figure 12-7, I held down the Ctrl key while selecting Baltimore, California, Charlotte, and Chicago. This highlights not only the selected markets in the Market slicer, but also their associated regions in the Region slicer.

TIP

   To clear the filtering on a slicer, simply click the Clear Filter icon (see Figure 12-8) on the target slicer.

FIGURE 12-5:
Select the dimensions for which you want slicers created.

FIGURE 12-6:
Select the dimensions you want filtered using slicers.

Ship Date	Revenue
Jan	136,939
Feb	488,700
Mar	223,268
Apr	319,675
May	645,427
Jun	291,476
Jul	224,076
Aug	522,541
Sep	613,202
Oct	246,529
Nov	475,655
Dec	557,068
Grand Total	**4,744,556**

Region: Canada, Midwest, North, Northeast, South, Southeast, Southwest, West

Market: Chicago, Kansas City, Omaha, Tulsa, Baltimore, Buffalo, California, Canada, Charlotte, Dakotas

FIGURE 12-7:
The fact that you can see the current filter state gives slicers a unique advantage over Filter fields.

Ship Date	Revenue
Jan	767,777
Feb	1,181,050
Mar	1,443,527
Apr	1,207,014
May	1,536,345
Jun	1,520,544
Jul	1,905,681
Aug	2,579,320
Sep	2,817,887
Oct	1,518,105
Nov	2,115,237
Dec	2,562,649
Grand Total	**21,155,134**

Region: Midwest, Northeast, Southeast, West, Canada, North, South, Southwest

Market: Baltimore, Buffalo, California, Canada, Charlotte, Chicago, Dakotas, Dallas, Denver, Florida

FIGURE 12-8:
Click the Clear Filter icon to reset the slicer.

Market: Baltimore, Buffalo, California, Canada, Charlotte, Chicago, Dakotas, Dallas, Denver, Florida

Getting Fancy with Slicer Customizations

If you're going to use slicers on a dashboard, you should do a bit of formatting to have your slicers match the theme and layout of your dashboard. The following sections cover a few formatting adjustments you can make to your slicers.

Size and placement

A slicer behaves like a standard Excel shape object in that you can move it around and adjust its size by clicking it and dragging its position points (see Figure 12-9). You can expose these position points by clicking anywhere on the slicer (other than one of the slicer buttons).

FIGURE 12-9:
Adjust the slicer size and placement by dragging the circular position points.

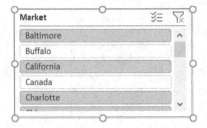

You can also right-click the slicer and select Size and Properties from the shortcut menu that appears. This brings up the Format Slicer pane, illustrated in Figure 12-10, allowing you to adjust the size of the slicer, how the slicer should behave when cells are shifted, and whether the slicer should appear on a printed copy of your dashboard.

Data item columns

By default, all slicers are created with one column of data items. You can change this by right-clicking the slicer and selecting Size and Properties from the menu that appears. This brings up the Format Slicer pane. Under the Position and Layout section, you can specify the number of columns in the slicer. Adjusting the number to 2, as demonstrated in Figure 12-11, forces the data items to be displayed in two columns, adjusting the number to 3 forces the data items to be displayed in three columns, and so on.

FIGURE 12-10: The Format Slicer pane offers more control over how the slicer behaves in relation to the worksheet it's on.

FIGURE 12-11: Adjust the Number of Columns property to display the slicer data items in more than one column.

Other slicer settings

Right-clicking your slicer and selecting Slicer Settings from the shortcut menu that appears activates the Slicer Settings dialog box, shown in Figure 12-12. With this dialog box, you can control the look of the slicer's header, how the items in your slicer are sorted, and how filtered items are handled.

Creating your own slicer style

The default slicer styles are, let's face it, a bit of a drag. Oftentimes, the look and feel of slicers don't match the aesthetic of your dashboard. Luckily, Excel provides a way for you to customize your slicers to fit into any reporting theme. With minimal effort, your slicers can be integrated nicely into your dashboard layout.

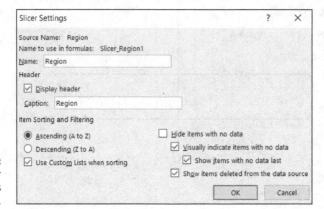

FIGURE 12-12:
The Slicer
Settings
dialog box.

Figure 12-13 illustrates a few examples of how slicers can be customized to almost any style you can think of.

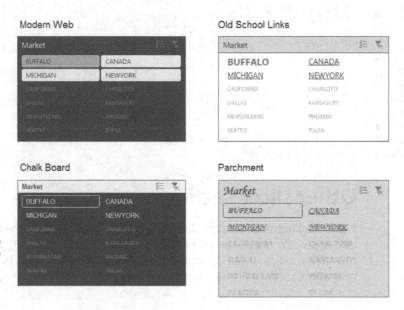

FIGURE 12-13:
Examples of how
drastically
different you can
make your
slicers look.

To change the look and feel of your slicer, you have to get into some style customizations. The following steps show you how:

1. **Click the slicer to reveal the Slicer tab on the Ribbon and then expand the tab's Slicer Styles gallery.**

2. **Click the New Slicer Style button at the bottom of the gallery (see Figure 12-14).**

   Doing so brings up the New Slicer Style dialog box, shown in Figure 12-15.

3. **Using the New Slicer Style dialog box, customize any (or all) of the following slicer elements:**

   - Whole Slicer
   - Header
   - Selected Item with Data
   - Selected Item with no Data
   - Unselected Item with Data
   - Unselected Item with no Data
   - Hovered Selected Item with Data
   - Hovered Selected Item with no Data
   - Hovered Unselected Item with Data
   - Hovered Unselected Item with no Data

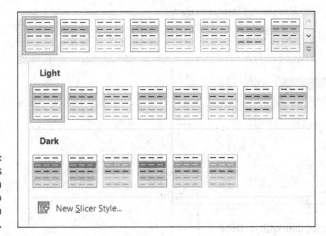

FIGURE 12-14:
The Slicer Styles gallery has an option for you to create your own new style.

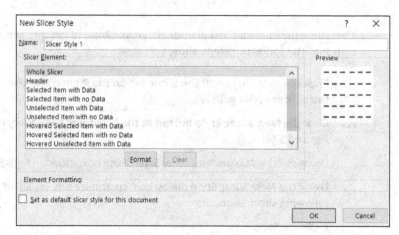

The idea here is to select each slicer element and then format that element by clicking the Format button. Sound easy enough, but it can be a bit difficult to know exactly which part of the slicer you are formatting.

Whole Slicer and Header are fairly self-explanatory, but what does the other junk mean?

Well, the other options refer to the values within the slicer. Some values have data associated with them, and others do not. The elements that are listed let you define what each value (values "with Data" and values "with no Data") looks like when selected, unselected, and hovered over. Figure 12-16 offers a visual map to help understand how each kind of value is typically represented in the slicer.

FIGURE 12-16:
Slicers allow
you to format
each element
separately.

After you finish making the needed customizations to all the elements, you can apply your newly created style by clicking the slicer and then selecting your custom style in the Slicer Styles Gallery.

You can also right-click on your custom style to modify, duplicate, and delete it (see Figure 12-17), using the contextual menu that appears.

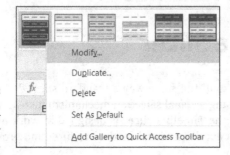

FIGURE 12-17:
You can modify,
duplicate, or
delete any of your
custom styles.

REMEMBER

Custom styles are saved at the workbook level, so your custom style is saved and travels with your workbook. However, other workbooks will not have your styles included.

Controlling Multiple Pivot Tables with One Slicer

Another advantage you gain with slicers is that each slicer can be tied to more than one pivot table; that is to say, any filter you apply to your slicer can be applied to multiple pivot tables.

To connect your slicer to more than one pivot table, simply right-click the slicer and select Report Connections from the menu that appears. This activates the Report Connections dialog box, shown in Figure 12-18. Place a check next to any pivot table that you want to filter using the current slicer.

At this point, any filter you apply to your slicer will be applied to all connected pivot tables. Controlling the filter state of multiple pivot tables is a powerful feature, especially in dashboards that run on multiple pivot tables.

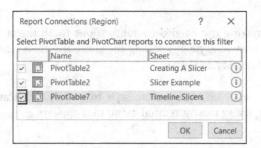

Creating a Timeline Slicer

The Timeline slicer works in the same way a standard slicer does, in that it lets you filter a pivot table using a visual selection mechanism instead of the old Filter fields. The difference is the Timeline slicer is designed to work exclusively with date fields, providing an excellent visual method to filter and group the dates in your pivot table.

To create a Timeline slicer, your pivot table must contain a field where *all* data is formatted as a date. It's not enough to have a column of data that contains a few dates. All values in the date field must be a valid date and formatted as such.

To create a Timeline slicer, follow these steps:

1. **Place the cursor anywhere inside the pivot table and then select the PivotTable Analyze tab on the Ribbon.**

2. **Click the Insert Timeline command.**

   The Insert Timelines dialog box shown in Figure 12-19 appears, showing you all available date fields in the chosen pivot table.

3. **In the Insert Timelines dialog box, select the date fields for which you want to create the timeline.**

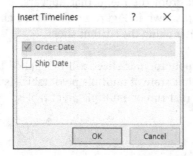

After your Timeline slicer is created, you can filter the data in the pivot table and pivot chart using this dynamic data selection mechanism. Figure 12-20 demonstrates how selecting Mar, Apr, and May in the Timeline slicer automatically filters the pivot chart.

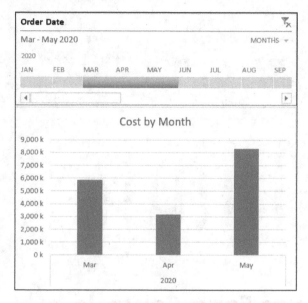

FIGURE 12-20: Click a date selection to filter your pivot table or pivot chart.

Figure 12-21 illustrates how you can expand the slicer range with the mouse to include a wider range of dates in your filtered numbers.

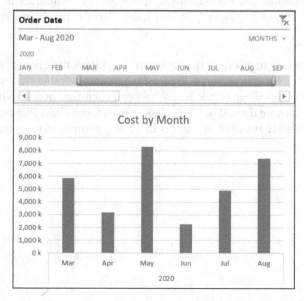

FIGURE 12-21: You can expand the range on the Timeline slicer to include more data in the filtered numbers.

Want to quickly filter your pivot table by quarters? Well, that's easy with a Timeline slicer. Simply click the time period drop-down menu and select Quarters. As you can see in Figure 12-22, you can also switch to Years or Days, if needed.

FIGURE 12-22:
Quickly switch
among quarters,
years, months,
and days.

Using Slicers as Form Controls

In Chapter 11, you explore how to add interactivity to a dashboard using data modeling techniques and Form controls. Although the techniques in that chapter are powerful, the one drawback is that Excel Form controls are starting to look a bit dated.

One clever way to alleviate this problem is to hijack the Slicer feature for use as a proxy Form control of sorts. Figure 12-23 demonstrates this with a chart that responds to the slicer on the left. When you click the Income selection, the chart fills with income data. When you click Expense, the chart fills with expense data. Keep in mind that the chart itself is in no way connected to a pivot table.

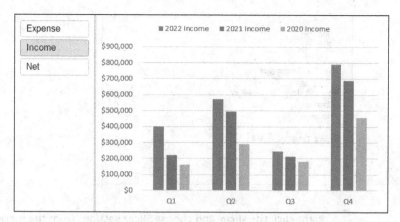

FIGURE 12-23:
You can hijack
pivot slicers and
use them as more
attractive Form
controls for
models not built
on pivot tables.

To build this basic model, follow these steps:

1. **Create a simple table that holds the names you want for your controls, along with some index numbering.**

   In this case, the table should contain three rows under a field called Metric. Each row should contain a metric name and an index number for each metric (Income, Expense, and Net).

2. **Create a pivot table using that simple table, as illustrated in Figure 12-24.**

FIGURE 12-24:
Create a simple
table that holds
the names you
want for your
controls, along
with some index
numbering. After
you have that,
create a pivot
table from it.

Metric	Key
Income	1
Expense	2
Net	3

Row Labels	Sum of Key
Expense	2
Income	1
Net	3
Grand Total	**6**

3. **Place the cursor anywhere inside your newly created pivot table, click the PivotTable Analyze tab, and then click the Insert Slicer command.**

4. **In the Insert Slicers dialog box that appears, create a slicer for the Metric field (see Figure 12-25).**

   At this point, you have a slicer with the three metric names.

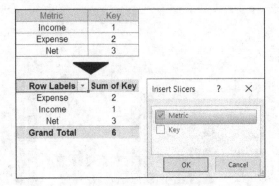

FIGURE 12-25:
Create a slicer for the Metric field.

5. **Right-click the slicer and choose Slicer Settings from the menu that appears, in order to activate the Slicer Settings dialog box.**

6. **In the Slicer Settings dialog box, deselect the Display Header check box, shown in Figure 12-26.**

   Each time you click the Metric slicer, the associated pivot table is filtered to show only the selected metric. Figure 12-27 demonstrates that this also filters the index number for that metric. The filtered index number will always show up in the same cell (N8, in this case). So this cell can now be used as a trigger cell for VLOOKUP formulas, INDEX formulas, IF statements, and so on.

7. **Use the slicer-fed trigger cell (N8) to drive the formulas in your staging area, as demonstrated in Figure 12-28.**

   This formula tells Excel to check the value of cell N8. If the value of cell N8 is 1, which represents the value of the Income option, the formula returns the value in the Income data set (cell G9). If the value of cell N8 is 2, which represents the value of the Expense option, the formula returns the value in the Expense data set (cell G13). If the value of cell N8 is not 1 or 2, the Net value (cell G17) is returned.

8. **Copy the formula down and across to build out the full staging table (see Figure 12-29).**

9. **The final step is to simply create a chart using the staging table as the source.**

   With this simple technique, you can provide your customers with an attractive interactive menu that more effectively adheres to the look and feel of their dashboards.

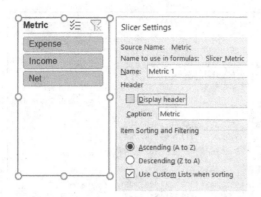

FIGURE 12-26:
Use the Slicer
Settings dialog
to uncheck
the Display
Header setting.

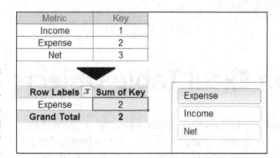

FIGURE 12-27:
Clicking an item
in the slicer
filters out the
correct index
number for the
selected metric.

	G	H	I	J	K	L	M	N
1							Metric	Key
2		Q1	Q2	Q3	Q4		Income	1
3	=IF($N$8=1,G9,IF($N$8=2,G13,G17))						Expense	2
4							Net	3
5								
6							▼	
7							Row Labels ▼	Sum of Key
8		Q1	Q2	Q3	Q4		Expense	2
9	2022 Income	$399,354	$573,662	$244,661	$790,906		Grand Total	2
10	2021 Income	$219,967	$495,072	$212,749	$687,744			
11	2020 Income	$159,832	$289,825	$181,961	$456,016			
12								
13	2022 Expense	$219,967	$495,072	$212,749	$687,744			
14	2021 Expense	$219,468	$310,048	$307,124	$283,920			
15	2020 Expense	$71,744	$607	$119,251	$154,487			
16								
17	2022 Net	$179,387	$78,590	$31,912	$103,162			
18	2021 Net	$498	$185,024	-$94,375	$403,824			
19	2020 Net	$88,088	$289,218	$62,710	$301,529			

FIGURE 12-28:
Use the filtered
trigger cell to
drive the
formulas in the
staging area.

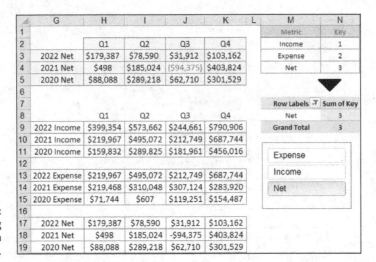

FIGURE 12-29:
The final staging
table fed via
the slicer.

Using Slicers on Excel Table Objects

You can leverage all the benefits of slicers without the need to create a pivot table first. Figure 12-30 demonstrates how slicers can be used to filter a Table object to give your customers an intuitive way to quickly filter data.

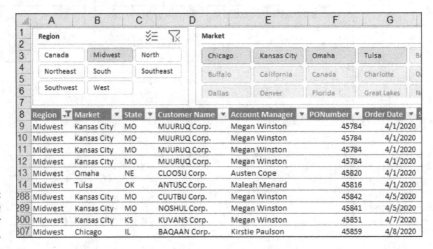

FIGURE 12-30:
You can use
slicers to filter
Table objects.

The key to this interaction is to convert your normal range of data into an Excel Table object first. Follow these steps to build this reporting model:

1. **Select your entire range of data, and then press Ctrl+T.**

   The Create Table dialog box opens.

2. **Click the OK button to convert your selected range to a Table object.**

3. **Select the Insert tab on the Excel Ribbon, and then select the Slicer command.**

   The Insert Slicers dialog box opens.

4. **Choose the fields for which you want to created slicers.**

At this point, you need only to format and position your slicers how you'd like.

Chapter 13

Sharing Your Workbook with the Outside World

L et's face it: You're not making these dashboards and reports for your health. At some point, you'll want to share your handiwork with others. The focus of this chapter is on preparing your dashboards for life outside your PC. Here, I help you explore the various methods of protecting your work from accidental and intentional meddling and show how you can distribute your dashboards via PowerPoint, PDF, and the web.

Protecting Your Dashboards and Reports

You've put in a ton of hours getting your dashboard and reports to work the way you want them to. The last thing you need is to have a clumsy client or an over-zealous power user botching up your Excel file.

Before distributing any Excel-based work, you should always consider protecting your file using the protection capabilities native to Excel. Although none of Excel's protection methods are hacker-proof, they do serve to prevent accidental corruption and to protect sensitive information from unauthorized users.

Securing access to the entire workbook

Perhaps the best way to protect your Excel file is to use Excel's protection options for file sharing. These options enable you to apply security at the workbook level, requiring a password to view or make changes to the file. This method is by far the easiest to apply and manage because there's no need to protect each worksheet one at a time. You can apply blanket protection to guard against unauthorized access and edits. Take a moment to review the file-sharing options, listed here:

>> Set read-only access to a file until a password is given.

>> Require a password to open an Excel file.

>> Remove workbook-level protection.

The next few sections discuss these options in detail.

Permitting read-only access unless a password is given

You can set your workbook to read-only mode until the user types the password. This way, you can keep your file safe from unauthorized changes yet still allow authorized users to edit the file.

Here are the steps to force read-only mode:

1. **With your file open, click the File button.**

2. **Press F12 on your keyboard to open the Save As dialog box.**

3. **In the Save As dialog box, click the Tools button and select General Options, as shown in Figure 13-1.**

    The General Options dialog box appears.

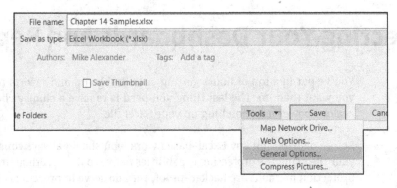

FIGURE 13-1:
The file-sharing options are hidden away in the Save As dialog box under General Options.

4. **Type an appropriate password in the Password to Modify input box, shown in Figure 13-2, and click OK.**

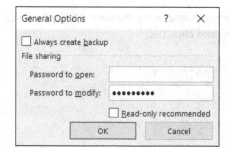

5. **Excel asks you to reenter your password, so reenter your chosen password.**

6. **Save the file with a new name.**

   At this point, the file is password-protected from unauthorized changes. If you were to open it, you'd see something similar to Figure 13-3. Failing to type the correct password causes the file to go into read-only mode.

TIP

   Note that Excel passwords are case-sensitive, so make sure Caps Lock on the keyboard is turned off when entering your password.

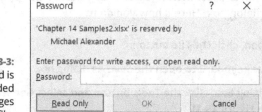

Requiring a password to open an Excel file

You may have instances in which your Excel dashboards are so sensitive that only certain users are authorized to see them. In these cases, you can require users to enter a password to open the workbook. Here are the steps to set up a password for the file:

1. **With the file open, click the File button.**

2. **Press F12 on your keyboard to open the Save As dialog box.**

3. **In the Save As dialog box, click the Tools button and select General Options (refer to Figure 13-1).**

   The General Options dialog box opens.

4. **Type an appropriate password in the Password to Open text box, as shown in Figure 13-4, and click OK.**

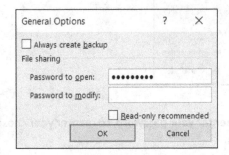

5. **Excel asks you to reenter your password.**

6. **Save your file to a new name.**

   At this point, your file is password-protected from unauthorized viewing.

Removing workbook-level protection

Removing workbook-level protection is as easy as clearing the passwords from the General Options dialog box. Here's how you do it:

1. **With your file open, click the File button.**

2. **Press F12 on your keyboard to open the Save As dialog box.**

3. **In the Save As dialog box, click the Tools button and select General Options (refer to Figure 13-1).**

   The General Options dialog box opens.

4. **Clear the Password to Open input box as well as the Password to Modify input box and then click OK.**

5. **Save your file.**

TIP

When you select the Read-Only Recommended check box in the General Options dialog box (refer to Figure 13-4), you get a cute but useless message recommending read-only access upon opening the file. This message is only a recommendation and doesn't prevent anyone from opening the file as read/write.

Limiting access to specific worksheet ranges

You may find that you need to lock specific worksheet ranges, preventing users from taking certain actions. For example, you may not want users to break your data model by inserting or deleting columns and rows. You can prevent this by locking those columns and rows.

Unlocking editable ranges

By default, all cells in a worksheet are set to be locked when you apply worksheet-level protection. The cells on that worksheet can't be altered in any way. That being said, you may find you need certain cells or ranges to be editable even in a locked state, like the example shown in Figure 13-5.

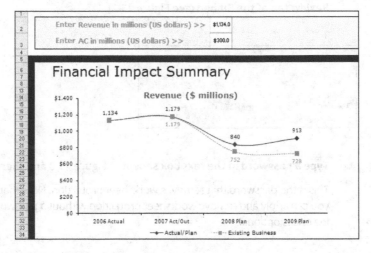

FIGURE 13-5: Though this sheet is protected, users can enter their data into the input cells provided.

Before you protect your worksheet, you can unlock the cell or range of cells that you want users to be able to edit. (The next section shows you how to protect your entire worksheet.) Here's how to do it:

1. **Select the cells you need to unlock.**

2. **Right-click and select Format Cells.**

3. **On the Protection tab, as shown in Figure 13-6, deselect the Locked check box.**

4. **Click OK to apply the change.**

Applying worksheet protection

After you've selectively unlocked the necessary cells, you can begin to apply worksheet protection. Just follow these steps:

1. **To open the Protect Sheet dialog box, click the Protect Sheet icon on the Review tab of the Ribbon (see Figure 13-7).**

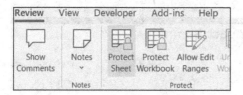

2. **Type a password in the text box shown in Figure 13-8 and then click OK.**

   This is the password that removes worksheet protection. Note that because you can apply and remove worksheet protection without a password, specifying one is optional.

3. **In the list box shown in Figure 13-8, select which elements users can change after you protect the worksheet.**

   When a check box is cleared for a particular action, Excel prevents users from taking that action.

4. **Click OK to apply the worksheet protection.**

5. **If you provided a password, reenter the password.**

Protecting sheet elements and actions

Take a moment to familiarize yourself with some of the other actions you can limit when protecting a worksheet (refer to Figure 13-8). They are described in this list:

>> **Select Locked Cells:** Allows or prevents the selection of locked cells.

>> **Select Unlocked Cells:** Allows or prevents the selection of unlocked cells.

>> **Format Cells:** Allows or prevents the formatting of cells.

>> **Format Columns:** Allows or prevents the use of column formatting commands, including changing column width or hiding columns.

>> **Format Rows:** Allows or prevents the use of row formatting commands, including changing row height or hiding rows.

>> **Insert Columns:** Allows or prevents the inserting of columns.

>> **Insert Rows:** Allows or prevents the inserting of rows.

>> **Insert Hyperlinks:** Allows or prevents the inserting of hyperlinks.

>> **Delete Columns:** Allows or prevents the deleting of columns. Note that if Delete Columns is protected and Insert Columns is not protected, you can technically insert columns you then can't delete.

>> **Delete Rows:** Allows or prevents the deleting of rows. Note that if Delete Rows is protected and Insert Rows is not protected, you can technically insert rows you then can't delete.

>> **Sort:** Allows or prevents the use of Sort commands. Note that this doesn't apply to locked ranges. Users can't sort ranges that contain locked cells on a protected worksheet, regardless of this setting.

>> **Use AutoFilter:** Allows or prevents the use of Excel's AutoFilter functionality. Users can't create or remove AutoFiltered ranges on a protected worksheet, regardless of this setting.

>> **Use PivotTable Reports:** Allows or prevents the modifying, refreshing, or formatting of pivot tables found on the protected sheet.

» **Edit Objects:** Allows or prevents the formatting and altering of shapes, charts, text boxes, controls, or other graphics objects.

» **Edit Scenarios:** Allows or prevents the viewing of scenarios.

Removing worksheet protection

Just follow these steps to remove any worksheet protection you may have applied to your worksheets:

1. **Click the Unprotect Sheet icon on the Review tab.**

2. **If you specified a password while protecting the worksheet, Excel asks you for that password (see Figure 13-9). Type the password and click OK to immediately remove protection.**

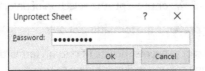

Protecting the workbook structure

If you look under the Review tab on the Ribbon, you see the Protect Workbook icon next to the Protect Sheet icon. *Protecting* the workbook enables you to prevent users from taking any action that affects the structure of the workbook, such as adding or deleting worksheets, hiding or unhiding worksheets, and naming or moving worksheets. Just follow these steps to protect a workbook:

1. **To open the Protect Structure and Windows dialog box, shown in Figure 13-10, click the Protect Workbook icon on the Review tab of the Ribbon.**

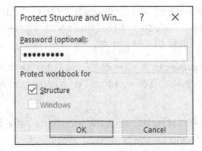

2. **Choose which elements you want to protect: workbook structure, windows, or both. When a check box is cleared for a particular action, Excel prevents users from taking that action.**

Selecting the Structure option prevents users from doing the following:

- Viewing worksheets you've hidden

- Moving, deleting, hiding, or changing the names of worksheets

- Inserting new worksheets or chart sheets

- Moving or copying worksheets to another workbook

- Displaying the source data for a cell in a pivot table Values area or displaying pivot table Filter pages on separate worksheets

- Creating a scenario summary report

- Using an Analysis ToolPak utility that requires results to be placed on a new worksheet

- Recording new macros

You'll notice a disabled option for Windows. This option has been deprecated and only works with versions of Excel before Excel 2013. The Windows option prevented users from changing, moving, or sizing the workbook windows while the workbook was open.

3. **If you provided a password, reenter the password.**

4. **Click OK to apply the worksheet protection.**

Linking Your Excel Dashboards to PowerPoint

You may find that your organization heavily favors PowerPoint presentations for periodic updates. Several methods exist for linking your Excel dashboards to a PowerPoint presentation. For current purposes, I focus on the method that is most conducive to presenting frequently updated dashboards and reports in PowerPoint — creating a dynamic link. A *dynamic link* allows your PowerPoint presentation to automatically pick up changes that you make to data in your Excel workbook.

TIP

This technique of linking Excel charts to PowerPoint is ideal if you aren't proficient at building charts in PowerPoint. Build the chart in Excel and then create a link for the chart in PowerPoint.

Creating a link between Excel and PowerPoint

When you create a link to a range in Excel, PowerPoint stores the location information to the source field and then displays a representation of the linked data. The net effect is that when the data in the source file changes, PowerPoint updates its representation of the data to reflect the changes.

You can find the `Chapter 14Samples.xlsx` file example for this chapter on this book's companion website.

To test this concept of linking to an Excel range, follow these steps:

1. **Open the** `Chapter 14Samples.xlsx` **file.**

2. **Click the chart to select it and press Ctrl+C on the keyboard to copy the chart.**

3. **Open a new PowerPoint presentation and place the cursor at the location that you want to display the linked table.**

4. **On the Home tab in PowerPoint, choose Paste ⇨ Paste Special, as shown in Figure 13-11.**

   The Paste Special dialog box appears, illustrated in Figure 13-12.

FIGURE 13-11:
Select Paste Special from the Home tab in PowerPoint.

5. **Select the Paste Link radio button and choose Microsoft Excel Chart Object from the list of document types.**

6. **Click OK to apply the link.**

   The chart on your PowerPoint presentation now links back to your Excel worksheet (see Figure 13-13).

TIP

If you're copying multiple charts, select the range of cells that contains the charts and press Ctrl+C to copy. This way, you're copying everything in that range of cells — charts and all.

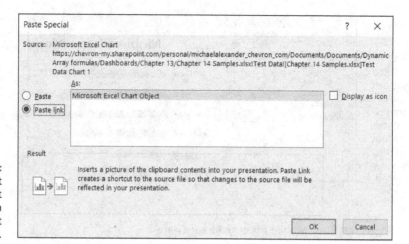

FIGURE 13-12:
Be sure to select
Paste Link and set
the link as an
Excel Chart
Object.

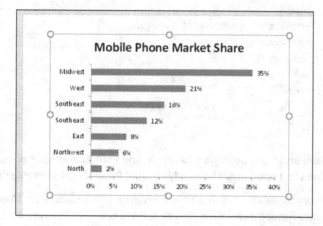

FIGURE 13-13:
Your Excel chart
is now linked into
your new
PowerPoint
presentation.

Manually updating links to capture updates

The nifty thing about dynamic links is that they can be updated, enabling you to capture any new data in your Excel worksheets without re-creating the links. To see how this works, follow these steps:

1. **Go back to your Excel file (from the example in the previous section) and change the values for Southeast and Midwest, as shown in Figure 13-14.**

   Note the chart has changed.

2. **Return to PowerPoint, right-click the chart link in your presentation, and choose Update Link from the menu that appears, as demonstrated in Figure 13-15.**

   You see that your linked chart automatically captures the changes.

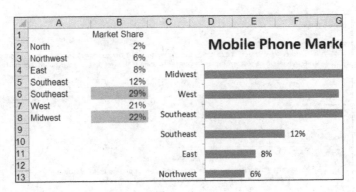

FIGURE 13-14:
With a linked chart, you can make changes to the raw data without worrying about re-exporting the data into PowerPoint.

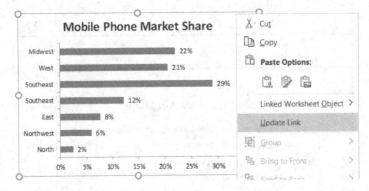

FIGURE 13-15:
You can manually update links.

3. **Save and close both your Excel file and your PowerPoint presentation and then open only the newly created PowerPoint presentation.**

   Now you see the message shown in Figure 13-16. Clicking the Update Links button updates all links in the PowerPoint presentation. Each time you open any PowerPoint presentation with links, it asks you whether you want to update the links.

REMEMBER

   Note the scary language warning you about potential security concerns (see Figure 13-16). This is just a reminder that opening untrusted documents can open the door to malicious viruses. Use your best judgment, and only open documents from trusted sources.

Turning off automatic updating of links

Having PowerPoint ask you whether you want to update the links each and every time you open your presentation quickly gets annoying. You can avoid this message by turning off automatic link updates. Here's how:

FIGURE 13-16:
PowerPoint, by
default, asks
whether you
want to update all
links in the
presentation.

1. **In PowerPoint, click the File button to get to the Backstage View.**

2. **In the Info pane, go to the lower-right corner of the screen and select Edit Links to Files, as shown in Figure 13-17.**

   The Links dialog box opens, as shown in Figure 13-18.

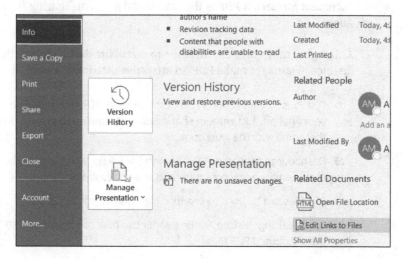

FIGURE 13-17:
Open the dialog
box to manage
your links.

3. **Click each of your links and deselect the Automatic Update check box at the bottom of the dialog box.**

   Your PowerPoint presentation will now open without the message shown in Figure 13-16.

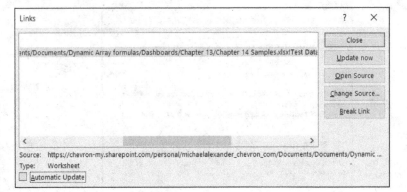

FIGURE 13-18:
Deselect the
Automatic
Update check box
to turn off
automatic link
updates.

TIP

To select multiple links in the Links dialog box, press the Ctrl key on the keyboard while you select your links.

Distributing Your Dashboards via a PDF

Microsoft has made it possible to export an Excel workbook to a PDF (*portable document format*). A PDF is the standard document–sharing format developed by Adobe.

Although it may not seem intuitive to distribute dashboards with PDF files, some distinct advantages make PDF an attractive distribution tool:

>> Distributing your reports and dashboards as PDF files allows you to share your final product without sharing all the formulas and back-end plumbing that come with the workbook.

>> Dashboards appear in PDF files with full *fidelity*, which means that they appear consistently on any computer and screen resolution.

>> PDF files can be used to produce high-quality prints.

>> Anyone using the free Adobe Reader can post comments and sticky notes on the distributed PDF files.

>> Unlike Excel's security, the security in a PDF is generally better, allowing for multiple levels of security, including public-key encryption and certificates.

To export your workbook to a PDF, follow these simple steps:

1. **Click the File button and then choose the Export command.**

2. **In the Export pane, select Create PDF/XPS Document and then click the Create PDF/XPS button, as shown in Figure 13-19.**

   The Publish as PDF or XPS dialog box opens.

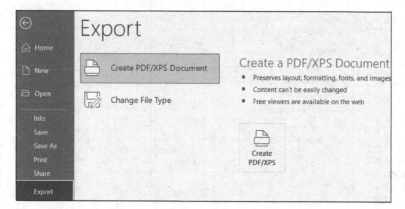

FIGURE 13-19: You can export your Excel workbook to PDF.

3. **Select a location for your PDF and then click the Options button, as shown in Figure 13-20.**

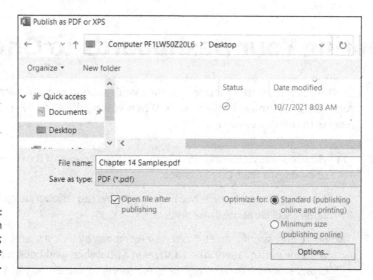

FIGURE 13-20: Select a location for your PDF; then click the Options button.

4. **In the Options dialog box, illustrated in Figure 13-21, you can specify what you want to publish.**

   You have the option of publishing the entire workbook, specific pages, or a range that you've selected.

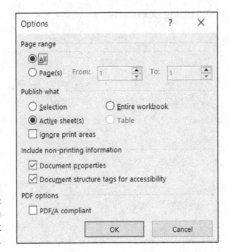

5. **Click OK to confirm your selections.**

6. **Back in the Publish as PDF or XPS dialog box, click Publish.**

Distributing Your Dashboards to OneDrive

OneDrive is Microsoft's platform in the cloud, allowing you to save, view, and edit your Office documents on the web. When you publish your Excel dashboards or reports to OneDrive, you can

» View and edit your workbooks from any browser, even if the computer you're using doesn't have Excel installed.

» Provide a platform where two or more people can collaborate on and edit the same Excel file at the same time.

» Share only specific sheets from your workbook by hiding sheets you don't want the public to see. When a sheet in a published workbook is hidden, the browser doesn't even recognize its existence, so there is no way for the sheet to be unhidden or hacked into.

>> Offer up web-based interactive reports and dashboards that can be sorted and filtered.

To publish a workbook to OneDrive, follow these steps:

1. **Click the File button on the Ribbon, click the Save As command, and choose Add a Place to add your OneDrive account as a save location.**

2. **Select the OneDrive option.**

3. **Sign in to your OneDrive account.**

   At this point, you'll see the OneDrive icon in the Save As screen.

4. **Click the OneDrive icon, then click the More Options hyperlink shown in Figure 13-22.**

   A new Save As dialog box appears.

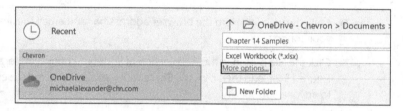

FIGURE 13-22:
Click the More
Options
hyperlink.

5. **Click the Browser View Options button.**

   The Browser View Options dialog box allows you to control what the public is able to see and manipulate in your workbook.

6. **Click the Show tab, illustrated in Figure 13-23.**

   Here, you can select and deselect sheets and other Excel objects. Removing the check next to any sheet or object prevents it from being viewable from the browser. Again, this is a fantastic way to share your dashboard interfaces without exposing the back-end calculations and data models.

7. **After you confirm your Browser View options, save the file.**

   At this point, you can sign in to OneDrive and navigate to your documents to see your newly published file.

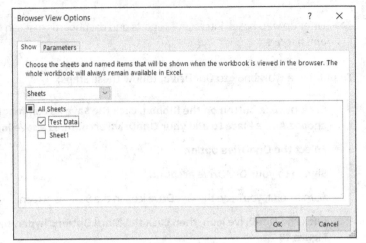

FIGURE 13-23:
You have full control over which sheets and objects are available to the public when publishing to the web.

There are several ways to share your newly published workbook:

» Copy the web link from the browser address bar and email the link to your cohorts.

» Click the File button in the web version of your file, choose Share, as shown in Figure 13-24, and then click the Share with People command to send an email to anyone you specify.

» Use the Embed command on the same Share pane to generate HTML code to embed your workbook in a web page or blog.

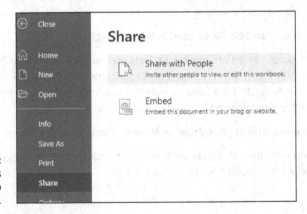

FIGURE 13-24:
Sharing options in an Excel web document.

Limitations When Publishing to the Web

It's important to understand that workbooks that run on the web are running in an Excel Web App that is quite different from the Excel client application you have on your PC. The Excel Web App has limitations on the features it can render in the web browser. Some limitations exist because of security issues, whereas others exist simply because Microsoft hasn't had time to evolve the Excel Web App to include the broad set of features that come with standard Excel.

In any case, the Excel Web App has some limitations:

>> **Data Validation doesn't work on the web.** This feature is simply ignored when you publish your workbook to the web.

>> **No form of VBA, including macros, will run in the Excel Web App.** Your VBA procedures simply will not transfer with the workbook.

>> **Worksheet protection will not work on the web.** Instead, you need to plan for and use the Browser View options demonstrated earlier, in Figure 13-23.

>> **Links to external workbooks will no longer work after publishing to the web.**

>> **Array formulas work on the web, but you can't create array formulas while editing a workbook online.** You need to create array formulas before publishing to the web.

>> **You can use any pivot tables with full fidelity on the web, but you cannot create any new pivot tables while your workbook is on the web.** You need to create pivot tables in the Excel client on your PC before publishing to the web.

>> **You can create simple charts in the Excel Web App, but not all customization and formatting options are available on the web.** Although you have a limited set of chart formatting options on the web, any chart created before publishing will retain all of its original look and feel.

5

The Part of Tens

Take a look at a few chart-building best practices that can help you design more effective charts.

Discover some of the questions you should ask before distributing your dashboards.

Chapter 14

Ten Chart Design Principles

'm the first to admit that I've created my share of poorly designed charts — bar charts with every color known to man, line charts with ten or more lines slapped on top of each other, and pie charts with slices so thin they melded into a blob of black ink. When I look at these early disasters, I feel the shame of a Baby Boomer looking at pictures of himself in white bell-bottom jeans.

Excel makes charting so simple that it's often tempting to accept the charts it creates no matter how bad the default colors or settings are. But I'm here to implore you to turn away from the glitzy lure of the default settings. You can easily avoid charting fiascos by following a few basic design principles.

In this chapter, I share a few of these principles and help you avoid some of the mistakes I've made in the past. (No thanks needed.)

Avoid Fancy Formatting

Excel makes it easy to apply effects that make everything look shiny, glittery, and oh-so-pretty. Now, don't get me wrong; these new graphics are more than acceptable for charts created for sales and marketing presentations. However, when it comes to dashboards, you definitely want to stay away from them.

A *dashboard* is a platform to present your case with data. Why dress up your data with superfluous formatting when the data itself is the thing you want to get across? It's like making a speech in a Roman general's uniform. How well will you get your point across when your audience is thinking "What's the deal with Tiberius?"

Take Figure 14-1, for instance — I created this chart (formatting and all) with just a few clicks. Excel makes it super easy to achieve these types of effects with its Layout and Style features. The problem is that these effects subdue the very data you're trying to present. Furthermore, if you include this chart on a page with five to ten other charts with the same formatting, you create a blinding mess that's difficult to look at, much less read.

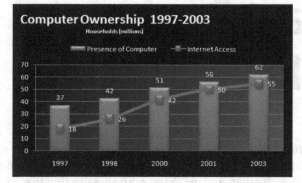

FIGURE 14-1:
Fancy formatting can be overwhelming, subduing the very data you're trying to present.

The key to communicating effectively with charts is to present data as simply as possible. I promise you: Your data is interesting on its own. There's no need to wrap it in eye candy to make it more interesting.

Figure 14-2 shows the same data without the fancy formatting. I think you'll find that not only is the chart easier to read, but you can also process the data more effectively.

Here are some simple "don'ts" to keep you from overdoing the fancy factor:

>> **Don't apply background colors to the Chart area or Plot area.** Colors in general should be reserved for key data points in your chart.

>> **Don't use 3D charts or 3D effects.** No one's going to give you an Oscar for special effects. Nothing 3D belongs on a dashboard.

>> **Don't apply fancy effects such as gradients, pattern fills, shadows, glow, soft edges, and other formatting.** Again, the word of the day is *focus,* as in "Focus on the data and not on the shiny, happy graphics."

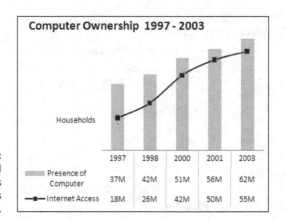

FIGURE 14-2:
Charts should present data as simply as possible.

Computer Ownership 1997 - 2003	1997	1998	2000	2001	2003
Presence of Computer	37M	42M	51M	56M	62M
Internet Access	18M	26M	42M	50M	55M

>> **Don't try to enhance your charts with clip art or pictures.** They do nothing to further data presentation, and they often just look tacky.

Skip the Unnecessary Chart Junk

Data visualization pioneer Edward Tufte introduced the notion of *data-to-ink ratio*. Tufte's basic idea is that a large percentage of the ink on a chart or dashboard should be dedicated to data. Very little ink should be used to present what he calls *chart junk*: borders, gridlines, trend lines, labels, backgrounds, and other elements.

Figure 14-3 illustrates the impact that chart junk can have on your ability to communicate your data. At first glance, the top chart in Figure 14-3 may look exaggerated in its ambition to show many chart elements at one time, but believe me, other charts out there also look like this. Notice how convoluted and cramped the data looks.

The bottom chart presents the same information as the top chart. However, the bottom chart more effectively presents the core message that driver registrations in Texas rose from more than 10 million in 1980 to almost 17 million in 2004 (a message that was diluted in the top chart). You can see from this simple example how a chart can be dramatically improved by simply removing the elements that don't directly contribute to the core message of the chart.

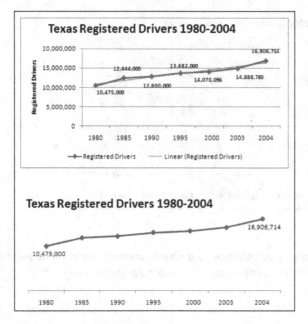

FIGURE 14-3: Charts with too many chart elements can become convoluted and hard to read. Removing the unnecessary elements clarifies the message.

Here are a few ways to avoid chart junk and ensure that your charts clearly present your data:

» **Remove gridlines.** Gridlines (both vertical and horizontal) are almost always unnecessary. The implied reason for gridlines is that they help to visually gauge the value represented by each data point. The truth is, however, that you typically gauge the value of a data point by comparing its position to the other data points in the chart. So gridlines become secondary reference points that simply take up ink.

» **Remove borders.** You'll find that eliminating borders and frames gives your charts a cleaner look and helps avoid the dizzying lines you get when placing many charts with borders on a single dashboard. Instead of borders, use the white space between the charts as implied borders.

» **Skip the trend lines.** Seldom does a trend line provide insight that can't be gained with the already plotted data or a simple label. In fact, trend lines often state the obvious and sometimes confuse readers into thinking that they're another data series. Why place a trend line on a line chart when the line chart is itself a trend line of sorts? Why place a trend line on a bar chart when it's just as easy to look at the top of the bars? In lieu of trend lines, add a simple label that states what you're trying to say about the overall trend of the data.

>> **Avoid data label overload.** Nothing says that you need to show the data label for every value on your chart. It's okay to plot a data point and not display its value. You'll find that your charts have more impact when you show only numbers relevant to your message. For example, the bottom chart in Figure 14-3 shows a trend that includes seven years of data. Although all the years are plotted to show the trend, only values of the first and last plotted years are shown. The first and last plotted years' data is enough to fulfill the purpose of this chart, which is to show the trend and ultimate growth of driver registrations.

>> **Don't show a legend if you don't have to.** When you're plotting one data series, there's no need to display a space-taking chart legend. If you allow the chart title to identify the lone data series in your chart, you can simply delete the legend.

>> **Remove any axis that doesn't provide value.** The purpose of the x- and y-axes are to help a user visually gauge and position the values represented by each data point. However, if the nature and utility of the chart don't require a particular axis, you should remove it. For the bottom chart in Figure 14-3, for example, there's no real need for the y-axis because the two data points I'm trying to draw attention to are labeled already. Again, the goal here isn't to hack away at your chart. The goal is to include only those chart elements that directly contribute to the core message of your chart.

Format Large Numbers Where Possible

It's never fun to count the zeros in a large number, especially when you're staring at 8-point font. When plotting very large numbers on a chart, consider formatting the values so that they're truncated for easy reading.

For instance, in Figure 14-4, I've formatted the values to appear as 10M and 17M instead of the hard-to-read 10,475,000 and 16,906,714.

You can easily format large numbers in Excel by using the Format Cells dialog box. On the Number tab, you can specify a custom number format by selecting Custom in the Category list and entering a number format code in the Type input box. In Figure 14-5, the code 0,, "M" ensures that the numbers are formatted to millions with an M appendage.

TIP

To get to the Format Cells dialog box, highlight the numbers you're formatting, right-click, and then choose Format Cells from the menu that appears.

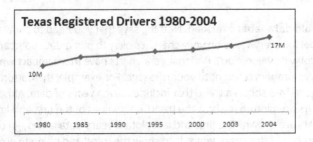

FIGURE 14-4:
Formatting
large numbers
to millions or
thousands
makes for a
clearer chart.

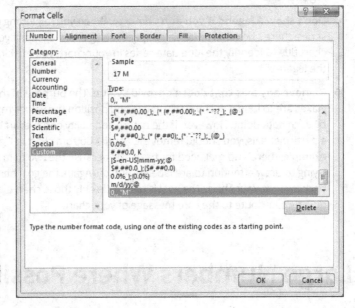

FIGURE 14-5:
Select Custom in
the Category list,
and enter a
number format
code in the Type
input box.

It's generally good practice to format the source data that feeds your chart as opposed to the data labels on your chart. This way, your formatting persists even as you add and remove data labels.

REMEMBER

The table in Chapter 5 lists common format codes and their effect on your numbers.

Use Data Tables Instead of Data Labels

Sometimes it's valuable to show all the data values along with the plotted data points. However, earlier sections in this chapter show how data labels can inundate users with chart junk.

Rather than use data labels, you can attach a data table to your Excel chart. A *data table* allows you to see the data values for each plotted data point, beneath the chart. Figure 14-6 illustrates a data table, showing the data values for two series. As you can see, a lot of information is shown here without overcrowding the chart itself.

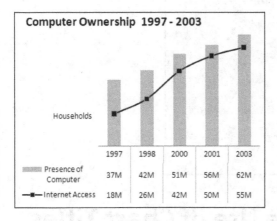

FIGURE 14-6:
Data tables
enable you
to show data
values without
overloading
your chart with
data labels.

Although data tables increase the space that your charts occupy on your dashboard, they respond well to formatting and can be made to meld nicely into your charts. Data tables come in particularly handy if your clients are constantly asking to see the detailed information behind your charts.

To add or remove data tables, select the chart and click the Chart Elements button next to the chart. This action expands a menu of chart elements that you can add to your chart (see Figure 14-7). Place a check next to Data Table to add a data table. Remove the check mark to remove the data table.

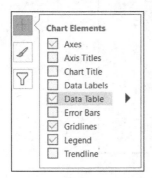

FIGURE 14-7:
Adding a data
table to a chart.

TIP

You can right-click the data table at any time to call up the Format Table task pane and apply additional formatting to the table (see Figure 14-8).

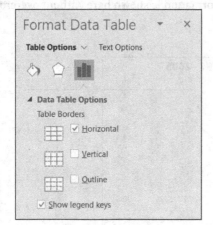

FIGURE 14-8:
The Format Data Table task pane.

Make Effective Use of Chart Titles

A chart title doesn't have to be limited to simple labeling and naming duties. You can use a chart title to add an extra layer of information, presenting analysis derived from the data presented in the chart. Figure 14-9 demonstrates this.

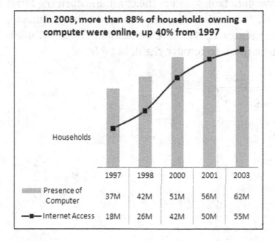

FIGURE 14-9:
Use chart titles to present extra layers of data without taking up extra space on your dashboard.

Sort Your Data before Charting

Unless there's an obvious natural order, such as age or time, it's generally good practice to sort your data when charting. By *sorting*, I mean sort the source data that feeds your chart in ascending or descending order by data value.

As you can see in Figure 14-10, building a chart using a data set sorted by values enhances its readability and somehow gives the chart a professional look and feel.

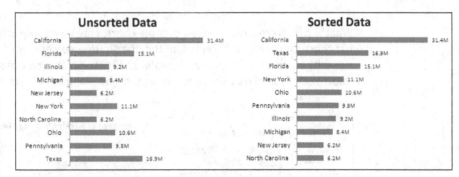

FIGURE 14-10: Using sorted data in a chart improves readability and clarity.

Limit the Use of Pie Charts

Although pie charts have long been considered a viable charting option for business reporting, they often aren't well suited for dashboard reporting. There are a couple of reasons for this.

First, they typically take up more space than their cousins, the line and bar charts. Sure, you can make them small, but pixel for pixel, you get a lot less bang for your data-visualization buck with a pie chart.

Second, pie charts can't clearly represent more than two or three data categories. Figure 14-11 demonstrates this fact.

The pie chart on the left does a good job visually of representing two data categories. You can easily distinguish the two categories and clearly get a sense of distribution for each category. The pie chart on the right is a different story. As you can see, when you go past two or three categories, a pie chart isn't as effective in relaying the proper sense of percent distribution. The slices are too similar in size and shape to visually compare the categories. Plus the legend and data categories are disconnected, causing your eyes to jump back and forth from pie to legend. (Even in color, the legend doesn't help.) Sure, you could add category labels, but that would cause the chart to take up more real estate without adding much value.

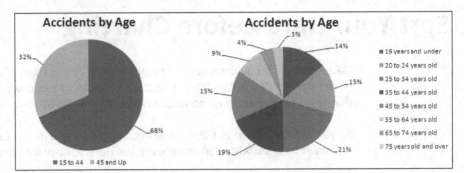

FIGURE 14-11:
Pie charts can't clearly represent more than two or three data categories.

What's the alternative? Instead of a pie chart, consider using a bar chart. With a bar chart, you can clearly represent the distribution percentages for many categories without taking up extra real estate. In Figure 14-12, you can see the dramatic improvement in clarity that you can achieve by using bar charts.

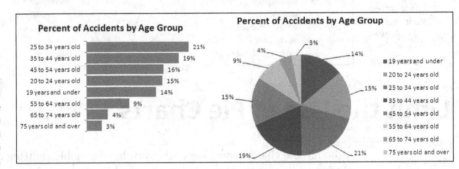

FIGURE 14-12:
Bar charts are an alternative to pie charts when you have more than two or three data categories.

Don't Be Afraid to Parse Data into Separate Charts

Be aware that a single chart can lose its effectiveness if you try to plot too much data into it. Take Figure 14-13, for example.

This chart has a couple of problems. First, the data is split into nine age groups, which forces you to use nine lines. When you start plotting more than three lines on a line chart, your chart begins to look jumbled. Second, the age groups have a wide range of data values. This causes the chart's y-axis scale to be so spread out that each line essentially looks like a straight line.

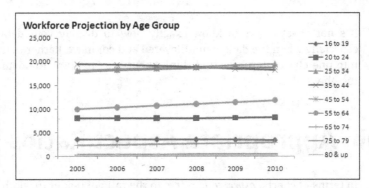

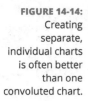
FIGURE 14-13:
Sometimes you
work with so
much data that
your charts no
longer make
sense.

In situations like this, step back and try to boil down what exactly the chart needs
to do. What is the ultimate purpose of the chart? In this case, the ultimate purpose
of this chart is to show the growth or decline of the workforce numbers for each age
group. Now, you obviously can't show every data point on the same chart, so you
have to show each age group in its own chart. That means you want to make sure
that you can see each age group alongside the other for comparison purposes.

Figure 14-14 shows just one of many solutions for this particular example.

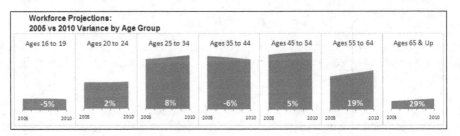

FIGURE 14-14:
Creating
separate,
individual charts
is often better
than one
convoluted chart.

Here, I've created a separate area chart for each age group and then lined them up
side by side. Each chart individually shows a general trend from 2005 to 2010.
Because they're placed together, you can get an idea of the magnitude of each age
group. Also, notice that I merged the last three age groups into one category called
65 & Up. This groups the three smallest categories into one that's worthy of plotting. Finally, I used data labels to quickly show the growth or decline percentage
from 2005 to 2010 for each group.

Again, this isn't the only solution to this problem, but it does do the job of displaying the analysis I chose to present.

It's not always easy to know exactly how to display your data in a chart — especially when the data is multilayered and complex. Rather than jam the world into one chart, step back and think about how to show the data separately but together.

Maintain Appropriate Aspect Ratios

In terms of charts, *aspect ratio* refers to the ratio of height to width. That is to say, charts should maintain an appropriate height-to-width ratio in order for the integrity of the chart to remain intact. Take a look at Figure 14-15 to see what I mean.

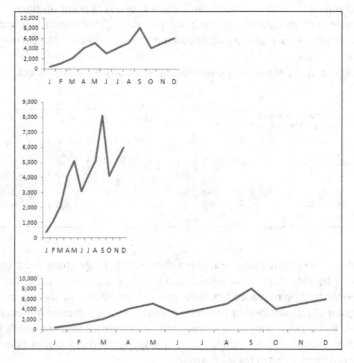

FIGURE 14-15: A skewed aspect ratio can distort your charts.

The chart at the top of Figure 14-15 is at an appropriate aspect ratio that correctly renders the chart. The bottom two charts display the same data, but the aspect ratios of these charts are skewed. The middle chart is too tall, and the bottom chart is too wide. This essentially distorts the visual representation, exaggerating the trend in the chart that's too tall and flattening the trend in the chart that's too wide.

I've seen lots of people contort their charts just to fit them into the empty space on their dashboards. If you want to avoid distorting your charts, you must keep them at an appropriate aspect ratio.

What is that ratio? Generally, the most appropriate aspect ratio for a chart is one in which the width of the chart is about twice as long as the height. For example, 1 inch tall by 2 inches wide is an appropriate ratio. And 1.5 inches tall by 3 inches wide is also appropriate. The actual height and width aren't important. You can make your charts as small or as big as they need to be. What is important is the ratio of height to width.

Don't Be Afraid to Use Something Other Than a Chart

Ask yourself whether a simple table will present the data just fine. If the data you're reporting can be more effectively shared in a table, that's how it should be presented. Remember that the goal of a dashboard is not to present everything in a chart — it's to present key data in *the most effective way* possible.

Chapter **15**

Ten Questions to Ask Before Distributing Your Dashboard

Y ou started this book with two chapters that discuss the design and data modeling principles that make up what could be considered dashboarding best practices. Before you send out your finished product, it's valuable to use the ten questions in this chapter as a checklist to ensure your dashboard follows the best practices covered in this book.

Does My Dashboard Present the Right Information?

Look at the information you're presenting and determine whether it meets the purpose of the dashboard identified during requirements gathering. Don't be timid about clarifying the purpose of the dashboard again with your core users. You want to avoid building the dashboard in a vacuum. Allow a few test users to see iterations as you develop it. This way, communication remains open, and you won't go too far in the wrong direction.

Does Everything on My Dashboard Have a Purpose?

Take an honest look at how much information on your dashboard doesn't support its main purpose. To keep your dashboard as valuable as possible, you don't want to dilute it with nice-to-know data that's interesting but not actionable.

REMEMBER

If the data doesn't support the core purpose of the dashboard, leave it out. Nothing says you have to fill every bit of white space on the page.

Does My Dashboard Prominently Display the Key Message?

Every dashboard has one or more key messages. You want to ensure that these messages are prominently displayed. To test whether the key messages in a dashboard are prominent, stand back and squint while you look at the dashboard. Look away and then look at the dashboard several times. What jumps out at you first? If it's not the key components you want to display, you'll have to change something.

TIP

Here are a few actions you can take to ensure that your key components have prominence:

>> **Place the key components of your dashboard in the upper left or middle left of the page.** Studies show that these areas attract the most attention for longer periods of time.

>> **De-emphasize borders, backgrounds, and other elements that define dashboard areas.** Try to use the natural white space between your components to partition your dashboard. If borders are necessary, format them to lighter hues than your data.

>> **Format labels and other text to lighter hues than your data.** Lightly colored labels give your users the information they need without distracting them from the information displayed.

Can I Maintain This Dashboard?

There is a big difference between updating a dashboard and rebuilding a dashboard. Before you excitedly send out the sweet-looking dashboard you just built, take a moment to think about the maintenance of such a dashboard. Consider the frequency of updates and what processes you'll need to go through every time you update the data. If it's a one-time reporting event, set that expectation with your users. If you know it'll become a recurring report, negotiate development time, refresh intervals, and phasing before agreeing to any timetable.

Does My Dashboard Clearly Display Its Scope and Shelf Life?

A dashboard should clearly specify its scope and shelf life. That is to say, anyone should be able to look at your dashboard and know the period it's relevant to and the scope of the information on the dashboard.

TIP

You can do a few simple things to effectively label your dashboards and reports.

>> **Always include a timestamp on your dashboard.** This minimizes confusion when distributing the same dashboard or report in monthly or weekly installments.

>> **Always include some text indicating when the data for the measures was retrieved.** In many cases, timing of the data is a critical piece of information when analyzing a measure.

>> **Use descriptive titles for each component on your dashboard.** Be sure to avoid cryptic titles with lots of acronyms and symbols.

Is My Dashboard Well Documented?

It's important to document your dashboard and the data model behind it. Anyone who has ever inherited an Excel worksheet knows how difficult it can be to translate the various analytical gyrations that go into a report. If you're lucky, the data model will be small enough to piece together in a week or so. If you're not so lucky, you'll have to ditch the entire model and start from scratch.

By the way, that troublesome Excel data model doesn't even have to be someone else's. I've actually gone back to a model that I built, and after six or so months I had forgotten what I had done. Without documentation, it took me a few days to remember and decipher my own work!

TIP

The documentation doesn't even have to be hifalutin fancy stuff. A few simple things can help in documenting your dashboard:

>> **Add a Model Map tab to your data model.** The Model Map tab is a separate sheet you can use to summarize the key ranges in the data model and spell out how each range interacts with the reporting components in the final presentation layer.

>> **Use notes and labels liberally.** It's amazing how a few explanatory notes and labels can help clarify your data model even after you've been away from it for a long time.

>> **Use colors to identify the ranges in your data model.** Using colors in your data model enables you to quickly look at a range of cells and get a basic indication of what that range does. Each color can represent a range type. For example, yellow could represent staging tables, gray could represent formulas, and purple could represent reference tables.

Is My Dashboard Overwhelmed with Formatting and Graphics?

TIP

When it comes to formatting dashboards and reports, less is more. Eye candy doesn't make your data more interesting. If you're not convinced, try creating a version of your dashboard without the fancy formatting:

>> **Remove distracting colors and background fills.** If you must have colors in charts, use colors commonly found in nature: soft grays, browns, blues, and greens.

>> **De-emphasize borders by formatting them to hues lighter than the ones you've used for your data.** Light grays are typically ideal for borders. The idea is to indicate sections without distracting from the information displayed.

>> **Remove all fancy graphical effects such as gradients, pattern fills, shadows, glows, soft edges, and other formatting.**

>> **Remove clip art and other pictures.**

When you compare the two versions, you'll find that the toned-down version does a better job of highlighting the actual data.

Does My Dashboard Overuse Charts When Tables Will Do?

Just because you're building a dashboard doesn't mean everything on it has to be a chart. In some analyses, a simple table will present the data just fine. You typically use a chart when there's some benefit to visually seeing trends, relationships, or comparisons. Ask yourself if there's a benefit to seeing your data in chart form. If the data is relayed better in a table, that's how it should be presented.

Figure 15-1 illustrates a simple example. The chart on the left and the table on the right show the exact same data. The table does a fine job at presenting the key message of the analysis — revenue is at 95 percent of plan. Why use the chart that requires more real estate, not to mention more work and maintenance?

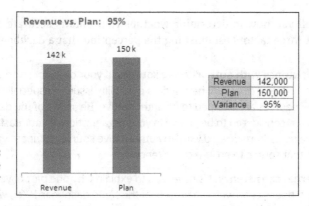

Revenue	142,000
Plan	150,000
Variance	95%

FIGURE 15-1:
Don't use charts for charting's sake.

Is My Dashboard User-Friendly?

TIP

Before you distribute your dashboard, you want to ensure that it's user-friendly. It's not difficult to guess what user-friendly means:

>> **Intuitive:** Your dashboard should be intuitive to someone who has never seen it. Test it out on someone and ask them whether it makes sense. If you have to start explaining what the dashboard says, something's wrong. Does the dashboard need more labels, less complicated charts, a better layout, more data, less data? Get feedback from several users.

>> **Easy to navigate:** If your dashboard is dynamic, allowing for interactivity with macros or pivot tables, make sure that the navigation works well. Does the user have to click in several places to get to their data? Is the number of

drill-downs appropriate? Does it take too long to switch from one view to another? Again, test your dashboard on several users. And be sure to test any interactive dashboard features on several computers other than your own.

» **Prints properly:** Nothing is more annoying than printing a dashboard only to find that the person who created the dashboard didn't take the time to ensure that it prints correctly. Be sure to set the print options on your Excel files so that your dashboards print properly.

Is My Dashboard Accurate?

Nothing kills a dashboard or report faster than the perception that the data isn't accurate.

TIP

I can't tell you how to determine whether your data is accurate. I can, however, highlight three factors establishing the perception that a dashboard is accurate:

» **Consistency with authoritative sources:** If your data doesn't match other reporting sources, you'll have a data credibility issue — especially if those other sources are deemed to be authoritative. Be aware of the data sources that are considered to be gospel in your organization. If your dashboard contains data associated with an authoritative source, compare your data with that source to ensure consistency.

» **Internal consistency:** It's never fun to explain why one part of your dashboard doesn't jibe with other parts of the same dashboard. You want to ensure some level of internal consistency within your dashboard. Be sure that comparable components in different areas of your dashboard are consistent with each other. If there is a reason for inconsistency, clearly notate those reasons. It's amazing how well a simple notation clears up questions about the data.

» **Personal experience:** Have you ever seen someone look at a report and say, "That doesn't look right?" They're using what some people call "gut feel" to evaluate the soundness of the data. None of us looks at numbers in a vacuum. When we look at any analysis, we bring with us years of personal knowledge, interaction, and experience. We subconsciously use these experiences in our evaluation of information. When determining the accuracy of your dashboard, take into consideration organizational "anecdotal knowledge." If possible, show your dashboard to a few content experts in your company.

Index

Symbols

#SPILL! error, 51–52

$ (dollar) symbol, 20

* (asterisk) wildcard, 63

? (question mark) wildcard, 64

@ symbol (implicit intersection operator), 54

~ (tilde) wildcard, 64

+ (plus) operator, 60–61

© (copyright symbol), 173

A

Above Average conditional formatting scenario, 158

accuracy, dashboards, 344

agile release cycle, Microsoft, 2

area charts, 189

Arial font, 128

Array argument

  FILTER function, 58

  SORT function, 55

  SORTBY function, 56

  UNIQUE function, 57

array formulas

  dynamic arrays, 51, 52

  FREQUENCY function, 224–225

  legacy arrays, 51

  limitations of, 321

  spill range, 50

aspect ratio, 145, 336–337

Assign Macro dialog box, 266

asterisk (*) wildcard, 63

at-a-glance views, 11

Average function, 80

axis scaling, sparklines, 148

B

background, limiting use of, 18, 340, 342

bar charts, 194–195

  in-cell, 212

  pie charts vs., 333–334

Below Average conditional formatting scenario, 158

Between conditional formatting scenario, 155

BI (business intelligence), 1

bins, histogram, 221–228

borders

  de-emphasizing, 340, 342

  removing, 178, 328

  tables, 123–126

Bottom 10 % conditional formatting scenario, 158

Bottom 10 Items conditional formatting scenario, 158

bucketing data, 221–228. *See also* histograms

bullet graphs

  adding data to, 239–240

  creating, 236–239

  displaying performance against target, 235–243

  formatting, 241–243

  horizontal, 241–243

  overview, 235

  qualitative bands, 241

business cycles (seasonality), 207

business intelligence (BI), 1

Button control, 263–264, 266

By_array argument, SORTBY function, 56–57

By_col argument
SORT function, 56
UNIQUE function, 57

C

caching
pivot cache, 76
Power Query, 116–117

Calibri font, 128

Camera tool
bullet graphs and, 242
consolidating ranges into one print area, 179–180
creating small charts, 180
finding, 176–177
overview, 177–178
rotating objects, 180

Change Chart Type dialog box, 197–199, 237–238, 244–245

chart junk
borders, 328
data-to-ink ratio, 327
defined, 327
gridlines, 328
label overload, 329
legends, 329
trend lines, 328
unnecessary axis, 329

chart titles, 21, 332, 341

charts
area charts, 189
aspect ratio, 336–337
bar charts, 194–195, 212, 333–334

chart feeders, 216–217, 227, 244

column charts, 189

grouping bottom values, 219

grouping top values, 216–219

in-cell bar charts, 212

line charts, 188

linking to PowerPoint
manually updating links, 313–314
overview, 311–313
turning off automatic updating, 314–316

pie charts, 333–334

primary axis, 200

secondary axis, 200–201

separating, 334–336

statistical charts, 220–223

tables vs., 343

thermometer-style, 234–235

Check Box control
defined, 263–264
overview, 266–267
toggling on and off, 268–270

CHOOSE function
capturing data corresponding to selected region with, 280–281
formulas, 44–45
Index_num argument, 44
overview, 43–44
Value argument, 44

clip art, 18, 327

Col_index_num argument, VLOOKUP function, 35

color, use in formatting
applying to numbers in tables, 135–136
labels, 21
limiting use of, 18
sparklines, 147
tables, 122–123

W

widgets, infographic, 182–183

wildcard characters

  asterisk (*) wildcard, 63

  question mark (?) wildcard, 63

  tilde (~) wildcard, 64

Win/Loss sparklines, 141–142, 149–150

workbooks

  extracting external data from, 111–112

  limiting access to specific worksheet ranges, 307–310

  overview, 303–304

  password-protected, 305–306

  read-only access, 304

  removing workbook-level protection, 306

  sharing

    Excel Web App, 321

    exporting to PDF, 316–318

    linking charts to PowerPoint, 311–316

    to OneDrive, 318–320

  workbook structure, 310–311

worksheets

  adding form controls to, 264–265

  limiting access to worksheet ranges

    applying worksheet protection, 308–309

    Delete Columns action, 309

    Delete Rows action, 309

    Format Cells action, 309

    Format Columns action, 309

    Format Rows action, 309

    Insert Columns action, 309

    Insert Hyperlinks action, 309

    Insert Rows action, 309

    Select Locked Cells action, 309

    Select Unlocked Cells action, 309

    Sort action, 309

    Use AutoFilter action, 309

    Use PivotTable Reports action, 309

X

XLOOKUP function

  asterisk wildcard, 63

  Lookup_array argument, 61–62

  Lookup_value argument, 61

  Match_mode argument, 62–63

  Not_found argument, 61–62

  question mark wildcard, 64

  Return_array argument, 61

  Search_mode argument, 62–63

  tilde wildcard, 64

Y

yearly view, pivot tables, 93–94

Z

zeroes

  hiding, 134

  suppressing, 135

About the Author

Michael Alexander is senior consultant at Slalom Consulting with more than 15 years' experience in data management and reporting. He is the author of more than a dozen books on business analysis and has been named Microsoft Excel MVP for his contributions to the Excel community.

Dedication

To my family.

Author's Acknowledgments

My deepest thanks go to the professionals at John Wiley & Sons, Inc., for all the hours of work put into bringing this book to life. Thanks also to Elizabeth Kuball and Guy Hart-Davis for suggesting numerous improvements to the examples and text in this book.

Publisher's Acknowledgments

Associate Editor: Elizabeth Stilwell

Project Editor: Elizabeth Kuball

Copy Editor: Elizabeth Kuball

Technical Editor: Guy Hart-Davis

Production Editor: Mohammed Zafar Ali

Cover Image: © Photobuay/Getty Images

Leverage the power

Dummies is the global leader in the reference category and one of the most trusted and highly regarded brands in the world. No longer just focused on books, customers now have access to the dummies content they need in the format they want. Together we'll craft a solution that engages your customers, stands out from the competition, and helps you meet your goals.

Advertising & Sponsorships

Connect with an engaged audience on a powerful multimedia site, and position your message alongside expert how-to content. Dummies.com is a one-stop shop for free, online information and know-how curated by a team of experts.

- Targeted ads
- Video
- Email Marketing
- Microsites
- Sweepstakes sponsorship

20 MILLION
PAGE VIEWS
EVERY SINGLE MONTH

15 MILLION
UNIQUE
VISITORS PER MONTH

43%
OF ALL VISITORS
ACCESS THE SITE
VIA THEIR MOBILE DEVICES

700,000 NEWSLETTER
SUBSCRIPTIONS
TO THE INBOXES OF
300,000 UNIQUE INDIVIDUALS
EVERY WEEK

# of dummies

Custom Publishing

Reach a global audience in any language by creating a solution that will differentiate you from competitors, amplify your message, and encourage customers to make a buying decision.

- Apps
- Books
- eBooks
- Video
- Audio
- Webinars

Brand Licensing & Content

Leverage the strength of the world's most popular reference brand to reach new audiences and channels of distribution.

For more information, visit **dummies.com/biz**

PERSONAL ENRICHMENT

Staying Sharp
9781119187790
USA $26.00
CAN $31.99
UK £19.99

Facebook
9781119179030
USA $21.99
CAN $25.99
UK £16.99

Guitar
9781119293354
USA $24.99
CAN $29.99
UK £17.99

Investing
9781119293347
USA $22.99
CAN $27.99
UK £16.99

Beekeeping
9781119310068
USA $22.99
CAN $27.99
UK £16.99

Digital Photography
9781119235606
USA $24.99
CAN $29.99
UK £17.99

Meditation
9781119251163
USA $24.99
CAN $29.99
UK £17.99

Pregnancy
9781119235491
USA $26.99
CAN $31.99
UK £19.99

Samsung Galaxy S7
9781119279952
USA $24.99
CAN $29.99
UK £17.99

iPhone
9781119283133
USA $24.99
CAN $29.99
UK £17.99

Crocheting
9781119287117
USA $24.99
CAN $29.99
UK £16.99

Nutrition
9781119130246
USA $22.99
CAN $27.99
UK £16.99

PROFESSIONAL DEVELOPMENT

Windows 10
9781119311041
USA $24.99
CAN $29.99
UK £17.99

AutoCAD
9781119255796
USA $39.99
CAN $47.99
UK £27.99

Excel 2016
9781119293439
USA $26.99
CAN $31.99
UK £19.99

QuickBooks 2017
9781119281467
USA $26.99
CAN $31.99
UK £19.99

macOS Sierra
9781119280651
USA $29.99
CAN $35.99
UK £21.99

LinkedIn
9781119251132
USA $24.99
CAN $29.99
UK £17.99

Windows 10 All-in-One
9781119310563
USA $34.00
CAN $41.99
UK £24.99

SharePoint 2016
9781119181705
USA $29.99
CAN $35.99
UK £21.99

Fundamental Analysis
9781119263593
USA $26.99
CAN $31.99
UK £19.99

Networking
9781119257769
USA $29.99
CAN $35.99
UK £21.99

Office 2016
9781119293477
USA $26.99
CAN $31.99
UK £19.99

Office 365
9781119265313
USA $24.99
CAN $29.99
UK £17.99

Salesforce.com
9781119239314
USA $29.99
CAN $35.99
UK £21.99

Coding
9781119293323
USA $29.99
CAN $35.99
UK £21.99

Learning Made Easy

ACADEMIC

9781119293576
USA $19.99
CAN $23.99
UK £15.99

9781119293637
USA $19.99
CAN $23.99
UK £15.99

9781119293491
USA $19.99
CAN $23.99
UK £15.99

9781119293460
USA $19.99
CAN $23.99
UK £15.99

9781119293590
USA $19.99
CAN $23.99
UK £15.99

9781119215844
USA $26.99
CAN $31.99
UK £19.99

9781119293378
USA $22.99
CAN $27.99
UK £16.99

9781119293521
USA $19.99
CAN $23.99
UK £15.99

9781119239178
USA $18.99
CAN $22.99
UK £14.99

9781119263883
USA $26.99
CAN $31.99
UK £19.99

Available Everywhere Books Are Sold

dummies.com

dummies®
A Wiley Brand

Small books for big imaginations

GETTING STARTED WITH **Coding**

Get Creative with Code!

Camille McCue, PhD

9781119177173
USA $9.99
CAN $9.99
UK £8.99

MODDING **Minecraft**

Build Your Own Minecraft Mods!

Sarah Guthals, PhD
Stephen Foster, PhD
Lindsey Handley, PhD

9781119177272
USA $9.99
CAN $9.99
UK £8.99

MAKING **YouTube** VIDEOS

Star in Your Own Video!

Nick Willoughby

9781119177241
USA $9.99
CAN $9.99
UK £8.99

DESIGNING **Digital Games**

Create Games with Scratch!

Derek Breen

9781119177210
USA $9.99
CAN $9.99
UK £8.99

GETTING STARTED WITH **Raspberry Pi**

Program Your Raspberry Pi!

Richard Wentk

9781119262657
USA $9.99
CAN $9.99
UK £6.99

EXPERIMENTING WITH **Science**

Think, Test, and Learn!

9781119291336
USA $9.99
CAN $9.99
UK £6.99

CREATING **Digital Animations**

Animate Stories with Scratch!

Derek Breen

9781119233527
USA $9.99
CAN $9.99
UK £6.99

GETTING STARTED WITH **Engineering**

Think Like an Engineer!

Camille McCue, PhD

9781119291220
USA $9.99
CAN $9.99
UK £6.99

WRITING **Computer Code**

Learn the Language of Computers!

Chris Minnick and Eva Holland

9781119177302
USA $9.99
CAN $9.99
UK £8.99

Unleash Their Creativity

dummies.com

dummies
A Wiley Brand